The University of Surrey

A History of
Shaping the Future

The University of Surrey

A History of
Shaping the Future

Jaqueline Mitchell

2011
University of Surrey

British Library Cataloguing in Publication Data.
A record for this book is available from the British Library.

ISBN 978-0-903384-65-0

To purchase a copy, please contact:

University of Surrey
www.surrey.ac.uk
01483 689169

Designed and typeset in Minion Pro by
Strathmore Publishing Services, London EC1
www.strathmorepublishing.co.uk

Origination by Strathmore Publishing and the University of Surrey

Printed and bound in England by Butler Tanner & Dennis

Contents

Chapter 1

Beginnings at Battersea: 1891–1966

Origins and Early Days

The Charter of the University of Surrey was granted in 1966, but the origins of the University truly begin with Battersea Polytechnic Institute, in south-west London, whose foundation stone was laid by the Prince of Wales (later King Edward VII) on 20 July 1891. Two and a half years later, on 8 January 1894, the Polytechnic Institute received its first students. It was a propitious beginning.

HRH The Prince of Wales arrives to conduct the formal opening of Battersea Polytechnic Institute on 24 February 1894. (Westminster/ Kingsway College Archives)

The opening of the Polytechnic Institute was part of the late-Victorian educational expansion and reform, which was itself a response to the recognition that industrial and commercial growth in Britain would demand more technologists and that current educational provision was inadequate to meet this need. (The Polytechnic Institute should not be confused with those later polytechnics established following the 1966 White Paper, *A Plan for the Polytechnics and other Colleges*, which were intended to provide specialist higher education for those destined for industry and commerce; while Battersea and its sister colleges taught technical subjects, their remit was much broader.) The 1870 Education Act had established basic elementary education, but secondary education was patchy, if existent at all. Though a Board of Education and a Science and Art Department (1853) had been established, during the 1870s and 1880s it had become apparent that British education was poor compared with that of other European countries where there were already several 'technical universities'. British government committees, in particular the Royal Commission on Technical Instruction 1882–84, advocated more systematic scientific and technical education.

The situation was particularly acute in London, where the population was expanding rapidly, drawing in thousands of young men and women from the provinces, Ireland and overseas in search of a better, more prosperous life, and where the diverse manufacturing base required a skilled workforce. In 1890 it was estimated that out of London's three quarters of a million people between the ages of 16 and 25, only 2 per cent of the young men and a very small number of women were in education.

Steps were being taken, however. The Technical Instruction Act of 1879 allowed county councils and boroughs to levy a rate for the support of technical and manual instruction. The previous year a Royal Commission had been appointed to investigate the parochial charities of the City of London, whose funds were directed to benefit the local poor, many of whom had now moved out to suburbs such as Battersea. This resulted in the founding of the City Parochial Foundation, which committed most of its funds to polytechnic education in London – Battersea would be one of the beneficiaries. (The City Parochial Foundation remained a major funder of the polytechnics up to 1939, making grants of £2 million to them in all.) In 1887 the South London Polytechnics Committee was formed to set up three polytechnics at Battersea, Southwark (Borough Polytechnic; now South Bank University) and Elephant and Castle (now Goldsmiths College). Philanthropist Quinton Hogg's Regent Street Polytechnic and to a lesser extent the newly opened People's Palace in London's East End (later Queen Mary College), with their blend of technical and recreational elements, provided the model for the new institutions. Nine were established across the metropolis, serving 30,000 students altogether.

The University Charter, granted by HM The Queen in Council, 9 September 1966.

At Battersea, local industrialists such as Henry Tate, the sugar magnate, who contributed £10,000, supported the building fund. The Charity Commissioners agreed to fund half the building cost, and later an annual endowment. Another important source of funds was 'whisky money', the new government duty imposed on beers and spirits, distributed via the newly established Technical Education Board (set up by London County Council with responsibility for technical education across the capital in schools, technical institutes and polytechnics). With this backing and other funds following a public appeal, two and a half acres of land on the defunct Albert

The Grant of Arms for Battersea Polytechnic Institute, awarded in 1932, later also used for Battersea College of Technology. The arms show a book, symbolising learning, and three swords, symbolising the City of London and the three original polytechnics for south London, of which Battersea was one.

Exhibition Palace site was bought and the building of Battersea Polytechnic Institute proceeded quickly.

The first meeting of the Governing Body, under the chairmanship of Henry Tate, took place on 22 October 1891. One of its first tasks was to appoint a Principal. Formerly the Assistant Master in Engineering at Dulwich College, Sidney Wells had then been appointed Senior Lecturer in the Department of Civil and Mechanical Engineering at Yorkshire College, Leeds (which went on to become the University of Leeds). Young (only 27 at the time of his selection for Battersea), self-confident and energetic, he was judged the ideal person to take forward the new Polytechnic Institute, and he took up his post in January 1894 as the first students arrived.

Sidney Wells, first Principal of Battersea Polytechnic Institute 1893–1907. (Westminster/Kingsway College Archives)

A few weeks later, on 24 February 1894, the Prince and Princess of Wales, accompanied by their daughters Princesses Victoria and Maud, conducted the official opening in front of a crowd of enthusiastic spectators. The new Polytechnic Institute on Battersea Park Road, in its imposing buildings complete with statues on the front façade, was designed, in the words of an appeal to local residents for donations, to 'provide a complete Technical and Recreative Institute for the people of Battersea, Clapham, and Wandsworth'. There were administration rooms on the ground floor, class, lecture and music rooms on the first floor, and art schools, laboratories and photography rooms at the top. It aimed to be a 'noble Institution, where the Priceless Treasures of Art, Science, and Literature shall be within reach of all, and where all classes of the people may assemble to enjoy the pleasures of healthy recreation and pure and rational amusement'.

From the first, the Polytechnic Institute fulfilled its ambitious purpose. A total of 115 classes in 64 subjects was offered, from natural sciences, mechanical engineering and building to art, commerce, music and languages. Of the 2406 students enrolled that January, over half were aged between 16 and 25, and over a quarter were women. Most were from the 'poorer and artisan' classes. Fees varied from 10 shillings per session (September to May) for two evenings a week in Science and Trade classes to £4 for a complete session's course in preparation for the London University BSc. A number of scholarships were available for those in need, funded by Battersea Borough Council or local companies.

The east corner of Battersea Polytechnic Institute soon after the opening of the Great Hall (on the right of the photograph) in 1899.

Most of the courses were highly practical, and there were well-equipped laboratories with, for example, special provision for work in the chemistry of paper-making and testing, and for oils, soaps, fats and candles, as well as plumbers' and pattern-makers' shops. Classes were largely at an elementary level, since most students would have had no education beyond that. There were six departments: Mechanical Engineering and Building Trades, Electrical Engineering and Physics, Chemistry, Women's Subjects, Art, and Music. Most of the staff were part-time, some of them being actively employed in their trade; Mr Searle, for instance, who taught a course in plastering, was manager of the Plaster Department of Veronese Ltd.

Classes, of one to two and a half hours, were generally held in the evenings, so as to allow students to come after work, the building staying open until 10 pm six nights a week. There were also special day classes for

'Apprentices and other young Artisans' in geometrical and mechanical drawing and carpentry and joinery. These led to examinations by the Science and Art Department and the City and Guilds Institute. The Polytechnic Institute's first short session saw eight students pass the Intermediate Science Examination of London University. There were 157 exam passes in May, June and July 1894; within ten years, the number had risen to 1047.

The Great Hall and the Tate Organ presented by the sugar magnate Sir Henry Tate, whose son Edwin chaired the Governing Body. (Westminster/Kingsway College Archives)

From the beginning, the Polytechnic Institute attempted to give students a rounded education, and to attend to their general welfare. Cycling, cricket, football, harriers, lawn tennis, rambling, chess, sketching, swimming and debating clubs and societies were opened in the first year, and others were set up as time passed. The two gymnasia were open every evening, and after the Great Hall was built in 1899, Saturday evening entertainments were on offer to both students and the general public. Sir Henry Tate presented an organ to the Polytechnic Institute on its tenth anniversary, and from then on Wednesday recitals were given. It was here too that prizegivings were made.

Discipline was strict. Smoking, dancing and the consumption of alcohol were forbidden, although a blind eye seems to have been turned to the latter in later years, and after the Polytechnic Institute became a College of Advanced Technology in 1957, the ban was lifted altogether. Regular dances were being held by the time the ban on them was lifted in 1932. The most stringent rules regarded contact between the sexes. There were separate common rooms for men and women, as well as a 'large refreshment room, where students and staff can obtain almost anything, from a good square meal to a bath bun, and at reasonable prices'. Although the clubs and societies were mixed, talking to someone of the opposite sex in other circumstances was a major disciplinary offence. A certain decorum was also expected: in 1909 the Principal wrote to the Head of the Domestic Science Department to upbraid a youngish member of staff who had immodestly worn an open-necked blouse! Political and religious societies were not allowed, despite protests from many generations of students.

During the day the building was used by Battersea Polytechnic Secondary School; originally a mixed school, in 1905, for reasons of space, the school split into two, the boys' school remaining in the main Polytechnic Institute and the girls' school moving to Clarence House near Clapham Common. In addition there was a School of Domestic Economy for Girls and a Training School for Domestic Economy. These were highly successful, several boys winning scholarships to Oxford or Cambridge. The Training School was recognised as a Teachers' Training School from October 1895. While this enabled the Principal to employ more full-time teachers, Sidney Wells' ambitions lay in making the Polytechnic Institute a centre for higher education. In 1896/97 the prospectus offered London BSc courses in physics, mathematics, chemistry, botany and biology, and two years later, the Physics Department stated that 'students can be admitted to the laboratories for the purpose of carrying out research or other special work'. By the early 1900s, the Principal and seven other staff had been designated 'recognised teachers' of the University of London, enabling them to teach courses leading to internal London University degrees. This was no mean achievement: for a working man of poor or modest means to gain a degree was an attainment almost beyond comprehension for most, and Battersea was a real pioneer in affording them the means to do so.

By its tenth anniversary the Polytechnic Institute had set in place a good basis for future development, and had already gained some notable successes. It had also established good links with employers, a feature of University of Surrey life which has continued. Some local employers agreed to exempt their apprentices from overtime on class evenings, while Messrs. Simpson & Co. of Pimlico instituted a scheme of year marks for its apprentices, dependent on attendance and performance at classes, and the London and South West Railway Company began sending its Nine Elms apprentices to early morning classes.

Demand for expansion was there almost from the beginning. By 1904 four additional buildings had been completed, and the number of students had risen to almost 5600. Three new workshops had been added in 1895, an engineering lecture room and a drawing office completed in 1901, and a block of three floors for the Domestic Economy School was in use from 1903.

The Polytechnic Institute's first Principal, Sidney Wells, stepped down in

BATTERSEA POLYTECHNIC

DOMESTIC SCIENCE
DEPARTMENT.

HOUSEHOLD COOKERY

RECIPES.

Parts I. and II.

PRICE 1/6.

HUDDERSFIELD:
J. BROADBENT & Co., PRINTERS, LTD., HIGH STREET.   40713

The title page of *Household Cookery Recipes*, issued by the Polytechnic's Domestic Science Department. The first edition was published in 1914. By the time a metric edition was published in 1973, over 400,000 copies had been sold, and the 'Battersea Cookbook', as it was often called, had become a standard textbook in schools and colleges.

1907. He was replaced by Dr Sidney Rawson, previously Director of Education to Worcestershire County Council, but also with experience of industry as a works chemist with Globe Alkali Works in St Helens, Merseyside. A year later Edwin Tate announced his decision to retire from the chairmanship of the Governing Body and to give the Polytechnic Institute a new library which was opened in October 1910.

Consolidation and Progress

The next decades would be ones of consolidation and quiet progress. Some subject transfers between London institutions assisted this process: Battersea gained Engineering, and much later, Metallurgy, from Chelsea Polytechnic – both subjects in which Battersea, and later the University of Surrey, would come to excel. Following the 1902 Education Act and the 1904 London Education Act, the London County Council (LCC) Education Committee took over the work of the Technical Education Board.

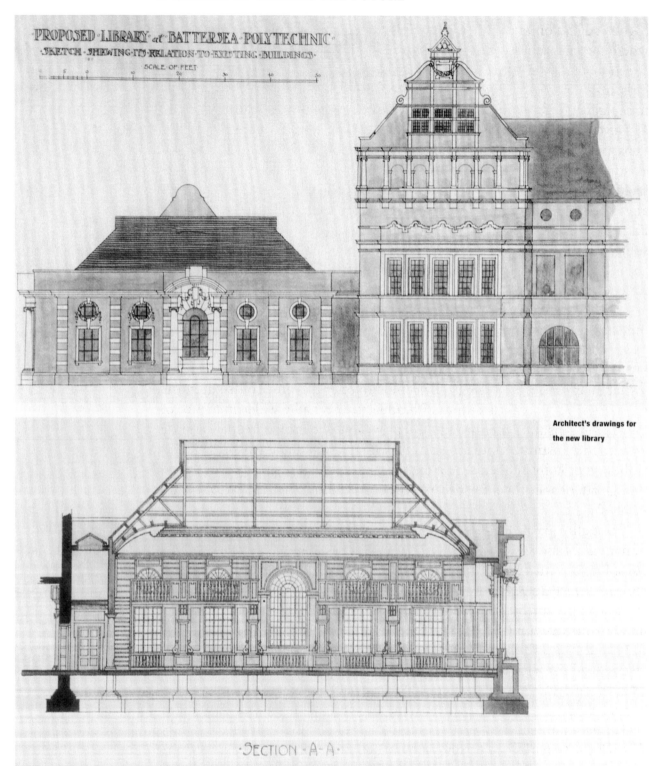

Architect's drawings for the new library

Architect's drawings for the new Library.

For some time there had been doubts about the wisdom of polytechnics continuing to provide secondary education, given the burgeoning numbers of students and competition for time and space between the schools and the higher education evening classes. This was certainly the case at Battersea where the laboratories and workshops were becoming less and less available to school pupils. Finally, the Polytechnic Institute decided to remove first the girls, in 1905, from the Day Science School, and then four years later the boys, to separate premises. The School of Domestic Economy was closed in 1918.

Development and expansion continued, however, with the opening of new departments in Music and Chemical Engineering and the enhancement of existing ones. By 1914 there were 110 students registered for internal degrees, including new courses in mechanical and electrical engineering – more than any other London polytechnic. Courses in chemical engineering began at Battersea in 1909 and for many years it offered the only evening classes in the subject in the UK – making its Department of Chemical Engineering there and subsequently at the University of Surrey the oldest in the country. Full-time undergraduate and postgraduate courses in the subject started after the Second World War. The Polytechnic Institute continued to forge links with industry, establishing a number of advisory committees. The first of these, in 1913, was in connection with the paper trade, and it was followed a year later by a Chemical Engineering Advisory Committee.

Battersea was also the first polytechnic to offer a degree course in music, from 1912. As well as its output of graduates, this had a wider influence on Polytechnic Institute life through the provision of concerts, recitals and the Polytechnic Institute Operatic Society, which gave annual performances of Gilbert and Sullivan operas. The regular entertainment evenings continued, though attendances later fell because of competition from the nearby 'Picture Palaces' at Lavender Hill, Wandsworth and Clapham Junction.

The outbreak of the First World War precipitated a decline in numbers of both staff and students as men went off to fight, and there was a certain curtailing of activities, with some courses dropped or transferred elsewhere. However, the Polytechnic Institute also responded to the times, running training courses for engineers and workers in munitions factories, as well as doing much valuable research on explosives, and manufacturing shells, machine parts and tools. The Domestic Science Department gave special courses on first aid and home nursing, as well as economical cookery. In December 1915, courses for the training of disabled soldiers were begun, and by 1920 over 500 had taken them and been able to return to civilian employment.

The appointment of a new Principal soon after the war ended spearheaded the drive to establish a reputation for high-quality research and teaching, especially in chemistry. This was aided by the fact that the transfer of courses in wartime, originally temporary, was made permanent, with the LCC accepting that Battersea Polytechnic Institute would become 'the centre in South London for day work in engineering up to the standard of the ordinary degree of engineering' and promising to provide up-to-date equipment and accommodation for this purpose.

Dr (later Sir) Robert Pickard was appointed Principal in 1920, replacing Dr Frank Newman, who had led the Polytechnic Institute through the difficult war years. Previously Principal of Blackpool Technical College and a consultant to the cotton and leather industry, Dr Pickard was to focus on the academic side of the Polytechnic Institute's work. His timing was fortuitous, since the previous year the Ministry of Reconstruction had recommended substantial expansion of higher education, and to that end government spending rose exponentially to around £59 million by 1921, though it was later reversed by the 'Geddes Axe'.

One of Dr Pickard's first moves was to recruit Dr Joseph Kenyon, previously his laboratory assistant in the Chemistry Department at Blackpool and co-author with him of research papers, to head the Chemistry Department at Battersea, a role he retained for 30 years. The Royal Society's memoir of Kenyon describes the research school he founded there as 'second to none as a source of fundamental and inspiring ideas'. Both 'superb experimentalist and outstanding tutor', according to colleague Professor Alwyn Davies, within a year of his arrival three of Kenyon's students had started PhD research, and Kenyon himself soon began research projects for industry.

Dr Kenyon's leadership generated some notable successes. As well as awarding 13 PhDs in the five years from 1922, the department produced four Fellows of the Royal Society: Dr Joseph Kenyon himself; Mike Partridge (a student at Battersea in the 1930s), and Professors Martyn Symons and Alwyn Davies (staff members in the early 1920s). Another student of that time was Mark Doughty. First employed as a 15-year-old lab-boy in 1936 and later

Dr Joseph Kenyon.
(Royal Society/© Godfrey Argent Studio)

The young Mark Doughty as a technician in Dr Kenyon's chemistry laboratory at Battersea Polytechnic Institute, c. 1938/39. (Professor Emeritus Mark Doughty)

as Dr Kenyon's personal assistant while he completed his studies at Battersea, he attributes his successful career as research chemist and chemistry teacher to Dr Kenyon's encouragement. 'I am astonished at what those few square feet of bench produced in a lab that was badly cramped, badly serviced and ill equipped,' he says.

The Polytechnic's Chemistry Department was an early centre of academic excellence. In this remarkable photograph, dating from 1956, appear one current Fellow of the Royal Society, Dr Joseph Kenyon (front row, fourth from left); two future FRSs, Alwyn Davies and Martyn Symons (back row, third and fourth from right) and two future Pro-Vice-Chancellors of the University of Surrey, V.S. ('Griff') Griffiths and John Salmon (front row, second and third from right). Dr Kenyon had recently retired as Head of Department, but remained a very active researcher. His successor, Dr F.R. Goss, is on his left in the centre of the picture.

It was not only in chemistry that the Polytechnic Institute gained recognition. In 1922 the Institution of Electrical Engineers accepted the Polytechnic Institute's Diploma in Electrical Engineering as exempting students from its associate membership examination. By the 1920s the number of degrees awarded annually was around 30 or more, whereas it had been fewer than 20 before the war. Dr Pickard's ambition, stated in his 1926/27 report to the Governors, to 'raise the status of the Polytechnic Institute and to consolidate its work as one of the premier technical institutions, not in London, but in the United Kingdom', seems to have been fulfilled. His successor, George O'Riordan, appointed in 1927, who had wide experience of engineering training and teaching, focused on reorganising and strengthening engineering studies at the Polytechnic Institute.

Charles Arcus' bench at Battersea. Dr Arcus studied under Dr Kenyon in the 1930s and later returned to Battersea as a lecturer, moving with the institution to Guildford. (Matthew Arcus and Sue Pounder)

As student numbers climbed, Battersea Polytechnic Institute continued to add to its facilities. Hygiene laboratories were built in 1912, funded by the Drapers' Company, and in December 1929 a three-storey west wing, with two new chemistry laboratories, a large refectory, a needlework room and two classrooms, was opened by The Princess Royal, who became the Polytechnic Institute's patron. One of the most important developments was the opening of the first hostel, mainly for women students, in 1910, at a house in Clapham Common. Student residents came from India, the Netherlands, Canada, Scotland, Ireland and Wales, as well as from more distant parts of England – evidence of the Polytechnic Institute's wide reputation and its internationalism from its early days. By 1920 four more houses in the same block were in use.

Under Dr Pickard, societies and extra-curricular activities also flourished. A sports ground had been rented in Dulwich from 1910, but this became too small for the high level of use and the City Parochial Foundation was persuaded to buy ground at Merton Abbey near Mitcham and to lease it as an athletic ground to Battersea and Chelsea Polytechnics. Opened in 1922, generations of students continued to use it until the move to Guildford. Other activities included a dramatic club, an engineering society and literary and debating societies. By this time there was also an Old Students' Association which, as well as bringing together students of all subjects, funded payment of fees for students in hardship. In 1928, the Principal encouraged the students to combine their Day and Evening Students' Representative Councils (originally set up in 1907) into one official body representative of all students that would also take responsibility for student functions and activities. Later this developed into a Students' Union, its first president being appointed in the early 1930s.

The Polytechnic Institute could not avoid suffering the impact of world events in the 1930s. The Great Depression, precipitated by the Wall Street Crash, saw a temporary cut in teachers' salaries and led to a drop in student numbers. The LCC also decided that some courses should close, most notably practical trade classes in engineering, such as those for fitters, turners, foundry workers, pattern-makers, motor vehicle repairers and electricians. At the same time, with pressure on space, the Art Department, whose output was small, was closed. Having fallen from 4000 in 1920/21 to 3000 in the mid-1920s, student numbers recovered somewhat to around 3000–3200 by the end of the 1930s.

The greatest shadow, of course, was that cast by the coming war, for which the Polytechnic Institute had begun to make preparations. When the Second World War was declared on 3 September 1939, an Air-Raid Wardens' Post was established, as well as the means to deal with gas attacks. There was a sharp fall in student numbers as a result of the war, although they recovered after 1940, spurred by two scholarship schemes to train young engineers. Hugh Jones, a student in 1943–44, remembers his studies being regularly interrupted by sirens and running for cover, and spending a considerable amount of time on air-raid warden duties: 'It was part of normal life; you studied, and you did what was necessary for the war effort.' An evacuation plan for the Domestic Science Training College was put into action at the start of the war and it moved to Shrewsbury, returning to Battersea in 1940 in time to lead the Food Education Campaign. Later, the local 'Londoners' Meal Service', which provided midday meals to the public, was based at the Polytechnic Institute. Evening classes were abandoned during the Blitz, but although the railway hub at Clapham Junction and the marshalling yard at nearby Nine Elms made it a target, the Polytechnic Institute received only three direct hits during the war, and these did little damage.

As with the First World War, the Polytechnic Institute made its own contribution to the war effort. The Engineering Department's workshops were put to use by the Ministry of Supply manufacturing high-precision gauges. Training courses for military personnel were run, mainly in machine tool and fine handwork, while the Chemistry Department trained analytical chemists, and the Electrical Engineering Department anti-aircraft teams and wireless mechanics. There were also Sister Tutors' courses in the Hygiene and Health Department. The playing fields at Merton were turned over to allotments. One remarkable example of cooperation during the war was the organisation of

3000 students from Battersea Polytechnic Institute and Northern Polytechnic, as well as schools, colleges and youth organisations from all over London, to help bring in the harvest in Wiltshire in 1943: about 225,000 tonnes in total. It was the largest scheme of its kind in the country and was repeated in 1944 and 1945.

The Post-war Years

The end of the war brought an influx of returning servicemen and transformed the Polytechnic Institute, revitalising it. Professor John Salmon, who joined the Chemistry Department in 1948 (and subsequently became Head of Department and Pro-Vice-Chancellor), recalls the energy and enthusiasm to learn of these new students and how they 'helped to turn the Polytechnic into a real powerhouse. … There was a real sense of pride in the Polytechnic and in the Department among staff and students. This was coupled with the staff's real enthusiasm for teaching and research.'

As with the end of the First World War, that of the Second brought renewed interest in education. The Education Act of 1944 promoted primary and secondary education, but more significantly in 1945 the Government announced that funding for universities would more than double, from £2,149,000

A group of students on the Polytechnic Institute roof, 1947: Samuel Levin, Mark Doughty, Charles Arcus, Harry Hookway, Dr Joseph Kenyon (Head of Department), Michael Hargreaves, Charles (Ted) Searle, Ian Anderson and Robert Crick. (Matthew Arcus and Sue Pounder)

to £5,900,000. The resulting expansion of higher education was dramatic and extraordinary, and Battersea, where those registered for internal University of London degrees soared from 377 to 505 in a decade, was one of many institutions to benefit.

Social and sports activities received a boost too. Despite continuing rationing, in 1947 the Polytechnic Institute's magazine *Polygon* reported that the Christmas dance, complete with streamers, Christmas tree, band and cabaret, had gone 'with a swing'. There were monthly dances with bands or jazz groups, sometimes going on all night. While the Operatic Society waned in the 1950s, the Dramatic Society was revitalised, staging several performances in the following decades. From 1954 the Polytechnic Institute also staged International Evenings in the Great Hall. Ernest Littauer, a student in 1954–61, who secured his first job at Lockheed through his Battersea research advisor (he stayed at the company for 33 years, becoming Vice-President of

Ernest Littauer's graduation as BSc was overseen by HRH The Queen Mother at the Royal Albert Hall. Most Battersea graduates were enrolled in the University of London and it arranged to have Harrods as the authorised photographer for the graduation ceremony. (Ernest Littauer)

Staff–student cricket match, summer 1948. The staff umpire (back row, far right) was Dr West, the Polytechnic's Principal. H. Arrowsmith (second row, second from left) was the Polytechnic Secretary and Clerk to the Governing Body. Third from the left in the front row is Dr J.H. Elton of the Chemistry Department; he left the Polytechnic to run the Baking Research Association but later returned to the University as Visiting Professor in Biochemistry. (Westminster/Kingsway College Archives)

Research at Lockheed Martin Missiles and Space Company), remembers how 'Representatives of our polyglot population performed national dances and other acts, enabling us to get a feel for the cultures of Africa, India, China, the Middle East, Australasia and Europe.'

The post-war period was the start of a new era in other ways too. With the advent of the motoring student, cars began to be parked on the forecourt of the Polytechnic Institute and in adjacent streets. More parking space was found by uprooting the shrubs in front of the building, but parking would be a perennial problem, both at Battersea and later at Guildford.

The majority of students were still local, however, and staff were conscientious in teaching the young men and women, many of whom would otherwise have limited opportunities for improvement. Tension nevertheless grew between the delivery of elementary diploma and higher-level classes. Several departments now offered postgraduate studies and at least two, Chemistry and Mechanical Engineering, were carrying out significant research.

Dr Ralph West, Principal of Battersea Polytechnic Institute 1947–57, and of Battersea College of Technology 1957–60.

The appointment of Dr Ralph West, previously Head of the Chemistry Department at Northern Polytechnic, as Principal in 1947 heralded rapid change. With the transfer of elementary courses to other institutions, the Polytechnic Institute began to focus solely on degree courses and courses leading to recognition by professional bodies. Day students increased to 900 in the late 1940s, while the number of part-time students fell, not least because of the demanding revised University of London degree courses (part-time degree courses ceased altogether in 1960). 'Sandwich' courses were also introduced, allowing students to spend significant amounts of time in industry or the workplace, a development that made the most of the Polytechnic Institute's continuing strong links with the commercial world and equipped students well for life beyond Battersea. The Polytechnic Institute, Dr West boldly claimed in 1953, was now 'the foremost Technical College in the country for advanced work'.

Accommodation remained a continuing problem, however, particularly since higher-level teaching required more sophisticated facilities. The Polytechnic Institute gradually expanded, taking over a nearby primary school

Professor Lewis Elton, who arrived at Battersea in 1958. In 2007, he was awarded the Learning through Enquiry Centres of Excellence Award for Outstanding Contributions to Enquiry Learning.

immediately after the war, recolonising the Domestic Science Training College's quarters after it separated from the Polytechnic Institute, and opening a new east wing in 1954. This eased the problem, but never really resolved it. Lewis Elton, appointed Head of the Physics Department in 1958, remembers having to locate members of his expanding department in a forgotten old office full of old furniture and in niches at the end of corridors. By 1960, the Polytechnic Institute was operating from five sites in Battersea and Putney, much of it in depressingly poor condition.

Although the Domestic Science Training College, which from 1948 was under direct control of the LCC, eventually separated from the Polytechnic Institute, Battersea continued to offer courses in domestic subjects 'for women', and when Chelsea Polytechnic closed its Domestic Science Department, its staff, students and equipment were all absorbed by Battersea. By 1949 a

A class on reception work in the Hotel and Catering Department's purpose-built reception area in December 1955. The lecturer is Rik Medlik, who had just joined the Polytechnic staff. He went on to become Professor and Head of Department, retiring in 1977, after which he became Professor Emeritus. (Sue Walton)

Training for silver service, *c.*1956. A group of students from the Battersea Polytechnic Institute carry trays up stairs in order to learn the basics of becoming waitresses and waiters. (© Hulton-Deutsch Collection/CORBIS)

higher-level Department of Hotel and Catering Management had emerged, quickly to gain a good reputation within the industry. A silver-service training restaurant, serving *haute cuisine* to visitors and staff, and a flat in which to practise housekeeping skills were later added.

Although immediately following the war the number of international students had fallen, numbers then began to rise again and in 1953 were given a boost by the Polytechnic Institute taking over the Engineering Department of the Polish University College (PUC), its students, some of its staff and its building in Putney. The college had originally been formed by the Polish Government-in-exile in 1942 as the Commission for Higher Education, to train scientists and technologists for post-war reconstruction in Poland. When Poland fell into Soviet hands most students and staff stayed in England and in 1947 the PUC was made responsible for preparing its students (ex-servicemen and those leaving Polish secondary schools in Britain) for external University of London degrees.

This move also enhanced the Polytechnic Institute's standing. Academic standards at the PUC were high and the eight academic staff from the institution included some distinguished scholars, among them Professor Z. Klomensiewicz, who had invented the glass electrode in 1908. Another who made the move from the PUC to Battersea was the mathematician Henryk Zugalski, who had fled to Britain after the invasion of Poland. No one knew it at the time in Battersea, but back in Warsaw he had been one of those involved in breaking Germany's Enigma code: he had devised a new method of breaking the code after the Germans altered their enciphering procedure

Henryk Zugalski, of the Polish University College, who worked on breaking Enigma.

in 1938. The absorption of the PUC was also to have a lasting influence. Although the University of London's curricula were followed for the PUC students, their courses retained the thesis element of the Polish system, a practice integrated into Battersea Polytechnic Institute's own Diploma in Technology in the late 1950s.

College of Technology

A significant move towards becoming a research-focused institution was Battersea becoming a College of Advanced Technology (CAT) in 1956. By the mid-1950s, Britain was uncomfortably aware both that its future prosperity probably depended on having sufficient trained technologists and that it was ill prepared for this compared with other countries. While, according to *The Times* of 1 March 1956, the United States had 136 graduate engineers per million and the Soviet Union 280 per million, Britain had but 57. The Government's response was to announce that it planned to create CATs, institutions that would teach advanced technology to university standard, and to introduce a new qualification, the Diploma in Technology (Dip. Tech.), with degree status and a thesis requirement, but also a practical remit to make students fit for careers in industry.

Battersea Polytechnic Institute seized this opportunity to rebrand and was among the first eight CATs to be established. The official change of name came in June 1957 (the Government later dropped the word 'Advanced' from the title and Battersea never used it in its title). This was more than just a change in nomenclature, however. It signalled a strengthening of research, with teachers involved in research allowed to drop their teaching requirement, the introduction of the post of Reader in order to attract staff with experience in research, and recognition of the College's academic standing. Government funding was available for the improvement of libraries, laboratories and other study facilities, and also for new student residential accommodation. The introduction of the Dip. Tech. was particularly significant for Battersea, since it was able to adopt the new qualification for its already existing diploma courses. Representatives from industry were also invited to join the Governing Body.

The student profile also began to change. Non-advanced courses were, over a period of time, quietly dropped or transferred elsewhere. Further, as students were now free to study outside their own boroughs, the LCC had to charge the same fee to those inside and outside its region, making Battersea more attractive to students from, for instance, nearby Croydon and Wimbledon, who had previously had to pay higher fees. In the early 1960s more than 60 per cent came from outside the LCC area; in 1920 the figure had been only about 5 per cent. By then almost all students were 'students only', a far cry from the institution's early days and even 1926/27, when clerks and those of similar occupation formed the majority.

During the College's last decade at Battersea, research thus played an increasingly important part, with Ralph West, Principal, driving it. When Lewis Elton had arrived as Head of the Physics Department in 1958, research activity had been negligible: the department had won its first research grant and admitted its first research student only the previous year. Ten years later, the number of postgraduate students had shot up to 40 and the department had gained international recognition. As new heads of department were appointed in the late 1950s, research in other disciplines, particularly engineering and metallurgy, where a postgraduate Crystallography course was introduced, also got under steam.

Brian Eyre, one of the first four students to take the new Dip. Tech. in Metallurgy, having first studied for Ordinary and Higher National Certificates (HNC) at Battersea, recalls how they 'were exposed to frontiers of the subjects, for example in common science (Lionel Shrier) and advanced physical metallurgy (Peter Modowink)'. It was this, he says, that pointed him towards becoming directly involved in research himself; now Senior Visiting Fellow in the Materials Department at the University of Oxford, his previous posts include being Chief Executive and Deputy Chairman of the United Kingdom Atomic Energy Authority and Chairman of the Council for the Central Laboratory of the Research Councils.

It was not all science and technology, however. In 1948, the Polytechnic Institute had instigated a 'cultural hour' each week when lectures would be given on subjects outside the technological courses' curricula. Now, conscious of wanting to provide a broad education, the College introduced 'Liberal Studies' (later known as General Studies) for all students, about three hours' per week study outside the main disciplines, including a weekly lecture from an external speaker. It remained on student syllabuses until the 1980s. Other changes also came as a result of Battersea becoming a CAT. Political and religious organisations were allowed, and within a few years, there was a branch of the Christian Union, a Catholic Society and a Church Society. By 1963 there were societies for the Liberals, Socialists and Conservatives, as well as the Campaign for Nuclear Disarmament.

Towards a Modern University

By the early 1960s, Battersea College was assuming the form of a university in many ways, yet was constrained in others. Most of the 1171 full-time under-graduate students for 1960/61 were reading for a degree or a Dip. Tech. and there were over 100 postgraduate students. The majority now came from out-side the LCC area, and two new halls of residence, opened in 1961 and 1966, allowed for growth in the number of students from outside the region. There had also been an extension to the Engineering Block. The buildings that served the Polytechnic Institute's ever-growing community still left much to be desired, however, with classes held in annexes and research facilities gener-ally lacking: 'Overcrowding is very bad indeed', commented the Principal, Ralph West.

There were other difficulties too. Although the proportion was growing, only about 10 per cent of the staff were recognised by the University of London. There remained, too, a problem of perception of the new Dip. Tech.,

Aerial view of Battersea College from the west during the early 1960s.

23

which was often regarded by those outside the institution – parents, employers and potential students – as somewhat inferior to a standard degree, even if in some respects it prepared students for the workplace rather better. The number of degrees awarded remained small – eight Dip. Tech. in 1959, and 12 the following year, even if half of these were Firsts, while in 1960 the total number of degrees was just 174 – and there was a high failure rate, up to 40 per cent of enrolled students failing to gain a degree or diploma at all. The College also had few women, only 16 per cent of the total of 1283 students in 1961. And until 1962, when CATS were funded directly by the Department of Education and Science, the Principal had to obtain approval for many decisions from the LCC.

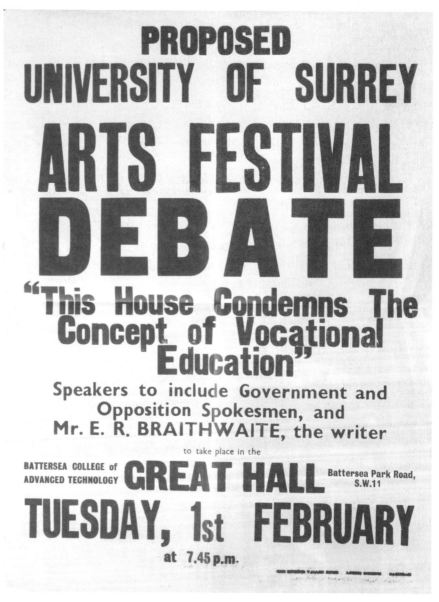

Battersea students enjoyed a lively cultural and social life. The Arts Festival Debate took place in the mid-1960s when the College was looking forward to becoming the University of Surrey.

At the same time, there were broader concerns about education. While the economy was booming, there was an awareness that Britain was threatened by its European competitors, some of whose economies were growing more rapidly, and the Government commissioned the Robbins Committee to look into the provision of higher education and propose improvements. The demography of Britain was also changing. The 1960s heralded the maturity of the 'baby boom' generation that followed the Second World War, a generation that was now heading towards higher education. Young people now also had higher aspirations,

Dr Peter Leggett, Principal of Battersea College from 1960, and the University of Surrey's first Vice-Chancellor.

discarding old class and gender expectations, so that many from families which had not previously been in higher education were starting to consider it. Demand for college and university places was therefore beginning to show signs of rapid increase in the future.

Such was the situation facing Dr D.M.A. Leggett when he took over the reins from Ralph West after his retirement in 1960. Clearly a radical solution was required, and Peter Leggett (as he was always known) was to be the one to provide it. A month after his arrival, Dr Leggett presented a paper on the College's 'future development' to the Governors. The nub of this was that as the number of students studying science and engineering would increase, the College would need to expand. If the number of students was limited to 2000, then a two-and-a-half-acre site for development to the west of the College would be required; if more than this, then a move to a new site would be necessary. He returned to the issue a year later, when he presented the Governors with three options: expansion of the present site by compulsory purchase (unlikely to be obtained, as previous experience had shown); a move to a bigger site in London; or a move to a larger site of at least 100 acres, probably outside London and south of the Thames.

Dr Peter Leggett pressed on colleagues the need to make a decision, but he did not bulldoze the matter through: his method was to seek views on the various proposals from a broad spectrum of staff in discussion groups and through other means, and to disseminate information so as to keep those involved fully informed. His timing was good. The Government was committed to making substantial investment in higher education, and the 'plate glass' universities (Sussex, East Anglia, and so on) were already being planned. When the Robbins Committee reported in 1963, it recommended expansion of higher education (with students increasing to more than double their current rate by 1980/81). CATS were to be upgraded to Technological Universities, awarding their own degrees, with an additional 3000 to 5000 students at each institution. While the technological emphasis would remain, the new universities would have a broader remit to cover the arts and humanities, and research would play an important part in their role.

At Battersea, events had by then begun to move rapidly. On 10 January 1962, the College's Governing Body had agreed to look for a new site and had set up a Development Advisory Committee for this purpose. Various sites were discussed, from Crystal Palace to Stevenage, and from Cornwall to Bracknell and Barnes, but, in the end, on 2 May, the decision went to Guildford. Primary considerations were that the town was near south-west London, close to several research institutes such as the National Physics Laboratory, had a large single site available, and was at least moderately enthusiastic at the prospect of having a university. Having lived in the town for some years before his move to Battersea College, Peter Leggett also had personal links with it and knew many of those who would be instrumental on the town's side in the decision making.

Enjoying the Charter Ball given to mark the grant of the University's Royal Charter. In the centre are Mr and Mrs Sidney Rich. Sidney Rich was Chairman of the Governors at Battersea from 1952 to 1966, and served as the University's first Chairman of Council from 1966 to 1975. (David Varney)

The portico of Battersea Polytechnic Institute emblazoned with its new signage for the 'University of Surrey'.

Lengthy discussions with Surrey County Council and Guildford Borough Council, as well as meetings with local interest associations, followed. Although there was a group of local residents antagonistic to the development, whose rumblings continued for some time to come, the majority were not, and the local newspaper, the *Surrey Advertiser*, was for the project. Influential support also came from, among others, Sir Richard Nugent, the long-serving MP for Guildford, and his wife, Ruth, well-known and popular figures in the town. On 28 February 1964 agreement was reached with the councils on a site for the new university to the north-west of the town. The College then determined on two locations: Stag Hill, just below Guildford Cathedral, for the principal university buildings, and Manor Farm, for playing fields and postgraduate institutions. Land would be acquired from Guildford Borough Council and the cathedral for the former, while the latter involved negotiations with tenant farmers and local housing associations. Eventually the matter was settled, and on 14 May 1964 the Government agreed that it would provide the resources 'as part of the programme for the expansion of higher education', subject to planning permission being obtained.

In the meantime, the College had continued to develop academically. The Departments of Civil and Mechanical Engineering, formerly united, were separated, and the College replaced its first computer, constructed by the Department of Electrical Engineering, with a purchased 'Sirius' digital one. There was also expansion of the arts and social sciences, with the old Liberal Studies courses becoming in 1962/63 a department in its own right, and then being renamed the Department of Humanities and Social Sciences. Many new courses were introduced over the following years and General Studies became part of the department in 1966.

By the end of 1965 initial funding for the University had been agreed, a development plan prepared and planning permission granted. As part of its undertaking to provide £1 million of funds, Surrey County Council stipulated the name of the new university. The Queen was formally petitioned for the grant of a charter and the establishment of the institution, and in August 1966, the University of Surrey Act was passed. The University also received authority to bear arms: the crest showed a stag (of Stag Hill), its hoof resting on the key to education, standing above a shield on which is depicted a checked device symbolising the arms of the Warenne family, former Earls of Surrey and Sussex, with the woolpacks of the Borough of Guildford to either side, and three swords below, representing the three London polytechnics built south of the Thames.

HRH The Duke of Kent unveils the Polytechnic war memorial, which commemorates members of the Polytechnic who gave their lives in the two world wars. It was re-erected and rededicated in Wates House, the staff and postgraduate centre, in 1989.

On 9 September 1966, the Grant of Charter formally established the University of Surrey. It had been a protracted process, but the final step was a seemingly ordinary one. The charter was brought by a messenger, who leapt straight back into the taxi from whence he came after delivering the long, thin parcel to Dr Peter Leggett, who announced its arrival with a loud 'Whoopee!' Battersea College now ceased to exist. In its place, the University of Surrey would rise, taking with it the College's students, its staff and much of its ethos, aspirations and ideals.

Chapter 2

The University of Surrey: 1966–1990

Building the New University

The new name of the University of Surrey had been inscribed on the college portico, but it would be another four years before the transition from Battersea was complete. The move was to take place in three phases. Most of the University would relocate by 1968 or 1969, to substandard-size accommodation. Subsequently full accommodation would be realised, without growth in student numbers. Finally, by 1975, additional buildings would provide for expansion to the planned 3000 students.

A photograph of the construction of the nave of Guildford Cathedral on Stag Hill, 1957, showing the bare fields below, where the University was built. (Photography Department, Guildford School of Art, Jan L. Malecki/Guildford Cathedral)

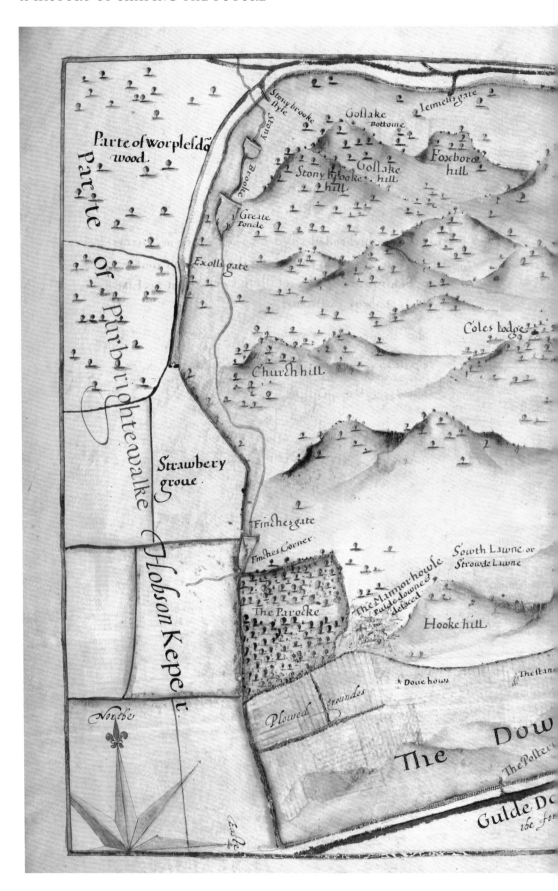

An early survey of Guildford Park carried out by James Norden for King James 1 in 1607, showing Stag Hill. (British Library)

31

Aerial view of Guildford c. 1966, showing Stag Hill just before building work began.

Guildford now prepared itself to receive the University. Opinions about the new arrival remained mixed. It would, it was hoped, be a major employer in the town, bringing a measure of prosperity and, as the *Surrey Advertiser* argued, 'balance the town's rapid commercial growth, help its cultural life to develop and assure its status'. Yet, there were anxieties, not least about the impact on the countryside surrounding what was still a modest market town. Townspeople were also keen that the University should not just be a 'technical establishment' but offer a full panoply of courses. Principal Peter Leggett's support for the arts and humanities, and the fact that he was already, to some extent, known in the community, no doubt helped win people round. Sir George Edwards, the new Pro-Vice-Chancellor, who had close connections with the county and especially the cathedral, was also able to 'reassure people about the character of the University'.

In 1966, construction was ready to begin. Among the tranche of new universities, Surrey would be one of the quickest to rise. During the 1960s the number of universities more than doubled – alongside Surrey in 1966, Loughborough, Aston, Brunel, Bath, Bradford, City University London and Heriot-Watt were all founded. There were 126,445 full-time university students in Great Britain in 1963/64, of whom two thirds came from professional and managerial families; now these numbers were set to soar and the uptake would become far more diverse – by 1980 there were around 300,000 students at 44 universities. Many of these new universities were built from scratch, increasing student numbers as their accommodation grew. Guildford was different: at Battersea, there were near 1800 students ready to move at once, and rapid expansion was planned thereafter.

The decision to build at Stag Hill also brought its own considerations. Rather than build outside the town, the University would be constructed on the edge of it, developing as part of the town, rather than as an adjunct to it. This was important for both the University and the town: the former wanted to retain the ethos of being part of an urban community that it had had at Battersea, while for the latter the planning demanded that the University be constructed as a dynamic part of the town, contributing to it, rather than separate from it.

Sidney Rich, the University's first Chairman of Council, addresses a meeting against a backdrop of plans of the new campus on Stag Hill. George Grenfell Baines, the University's planning consultant, is on his left, Peter Leggett on his right.

It was to George Grenfell Baines of the Building Design Partnership (BDP) that the task of designing a campus linked to town, below, and cathedral, above, fell. In spring 1964, an Estates and Planning Office was established in Guildford, headed by John Cory-Dixon, and it was here that much of the early planning work was done. When construction work began in 1966, the Principal's (later Vice-Chancellor's) Working Party of academics was set up and it met the Estates Office twice a week.

George Grenfell Baines was closely involved from an early stage, helping to define what the November 1964 Planning Report called the 'physical, psychological and intellectual environment' of the University. The development plan envisaged a 'walking university', with parking on the perimeter, and the buildings clustered together like 'a compact hill town … surrounded by trees, with an encircling wall of academic buildings'. It proposed three sectors of activity: a central spine of administration (Senate House), library, Students' Union, restaurants, lecture theatres and so on; academic buildings, including laboratories, and staff offices; and residences. The academic buildings would provide flexible space above with specialist laboratories and workshops below.

The campus takes shape.

Vertical walkways and bridges would link the three zones to facilitate contact between disciplines, and there would be glimpses through and beyond to the distant landscape. Apart from Senate House, no building was to be more than four storeys high, so as not to impede views of the cathedral. Today, much of this original plan is still evident, despite a large and continuing building programme.

Treasury and University Grants Committee (UGC) delays in approving contracts and releasing funds put back the start of building by six months to October 1966, but by 1969 construction was well advanced. By then capital costs were estimated to be £6 million, of which the Government provided half. The remainder came from the local councils and a major fundraising appeal,

Toast List

Grace by the Lord Bishop of Guildford, The Rt. Rev. George Reindorp.

Her Majesty the Queen by H.M. Lieutenant of and in the County of Surrey, the Rt. Hon. the Earl of Munster, P.C., K.B.E.

The University of Surrey by The Lord Nugent of Guildford, P.C.

Reply by the Rt. Hon. Lord Robens of Woldingham, P.C., Chancellor of the University of Surrey and Dr. D. M. A. Leggett, M.A., D.SC., F.R.Ae.S., F.I.M.A., Vice-Chancellor of the University of Surrey.

The Foundation by Sir William Mullens, D.S.O., T.D., D.L., the Treasurer of the University of Surrey.

Public Address and closed circuit TV services generously provided by Philips Industries at cost.

The programme for the fundraising event held at Stoke Park on 10 May 1968.

Aircraft designer and industrialist Sir George Edwards (1908–2003), the University's first Pro-Chancellor, with test pilot Joseph 'Mutt' Summers CBE (right), and behind them a Vickers Viking aircraft converted as a flying test-bed for Rolls-Royce Nene turbojet engines. Two Vikings were converted in this way, becoming the world's first commercial jet aircraft. (Photo by Keystone/Getty Images)

launched in May 1968 with a dinner for 2000 guests in a marquee in Stoke Park organised by Lord and Lady Nugent, which in the end raised £3.75 million.

While building progressed, an Academic Advisory Committee advised on the constitution, governance and structure of the new university. After some discussion, it was decided that, in common with other educational institutions, the University would be run by a Court (drawn from local people and institutions, with limited authority), Council (derived from the Governing Body) and Senate (derived from the Academic Board, but with representatives from the Students' Union).

An early task was to select the University's first high officers, their choice critical as they would be important in raising the profile and standing of the University. The first Chancellor was Lord Robens of Woldingham, Chairman of the National Coal Board, who lived nearby; the first Pro-Chancellor Sir George Edwards, Chairman of the British Aircraft Corporation, whose plant at Weybridge was a major local employer; while Dr Leggett himself was elected Vice-Chancellor. The Heads of Department now became Professors (some had been given the title a few years earlier), although all had to go through a selection panel.

At his installation on 22 October 1966, Lord Robens proclaimed that the University 'represents the technology of the future. Its purpose will be to identify the scientific needs of the second half of the 20th Century, to apply a practical inventiveness and to train young men and women into the new ways of thinking.' Three years earlier, at a Labour Party Conference on the brink of the election, Harold Wilson had sounded a call to arms for more scientists through the expansion of universities, for the alliance of scientific research with industry and for a Britain that would be 'forged in the white heat of the [scientific] revolution'. The University of Surrey, on its modern campus, ready to build on its early research-centred teaching, was to seize the day.

Above: The first high officers of the University, pictured in 1988. Those pictured include Peter Leggett, former Vice-Chancellor (far right), Professor V.S. Griffiths, former Pro-Vice-Chancellor (third from right), Ron Eatwell, former Librarian (far left). Peter Timms, first University Secretary, is thought to be third from left. The others are unknown. (P.J. Southgate)

Right: Surrey's first Vice-Chancellor, Peter Leggett, and (behind him) Lord Robens, the first Chancellor, wearing the University's new academic dress for the first time.

The installation of Lord Robens of Woldingham as the University's inaugural Chancellor, Guildford Civic Hall, 22 October 1966.

Site visit by Lord Robens (centre), the first Chancellor of the University. (*Surrey Advertiser*)

For students, the 1960s was the beginning of a new era in other ways too: in 1966 Barclaycard introduced consumers to the credit card, England won the World Cup, mini-skirts were the popular fashion, the Soviet *Luna 9* made the first unmanned landing on the moon, and John Lennon famously told the world that 'the Beatles were more popular than Jesus'. Nevertheless, while this was a time of, as the Students' Union President of the time David Varney put

The first meeting of University Council: Sidney Rich, Chairman of the Governors, is in the centre of the top table with, to his right, Peter Leggett, Vice-Chancellor, and Peter Timms, University Secretary. John Salmon is fourth from the left, with Lewis Elton behind him in the centre of the back row.

Reminder of Battersea: a lamp standard relocated on the new campus.

it, 'pop, protests, political activism and passions indulged', relations between Surrey students and staff were notably harmonious. This was perhaps helped by the facts that the University made a positive effort to include students directly in decision making, with representation on the Senate and on the committees dealing with buildings and estates, and that the Dean of Students, Mike Clark, was approachable and well liked. Indeed, at the Students' Union annual dinner in 1968, Vice-Chancellor Peter Leggett was cheered and given honorary membership.

There were major academic developments in this period. At the new university students were to be divided roughly equally between science, engineering and human

The prototype Nodus space truss re-erected as the Space Structures Research Centre at the University of Surrey, shown here with the cathedral behind. (Tata Steel Europe UK Ltd; Professor John Chilton).

sciences, so new departments were created for Economics, Sociology, Psychology, Languages and Regional Studies. A Biological Sciences course was also established and Music was boosted by the innovative Tonmeister™ course for students interested in the 'technological aspects of music – sound recording, radio, television and film studio work'.

Emphasis on the subjects' practical application continued. Under the direction of Professor D.R. Chick, Electrical Engineering began to develop expertise in ion implantation, essential in the evolution of microchips, while the Mechanical Engineering Department started to explore biomechanics. The Space Structures Research Centre, which was founded in 1963, played a central role in advancing design techniques in space structures and exploring stress in these three-dimensional forms, the best-known of which perhaps are the London Eye, the Eden Project in Cornwall and Stansted Airport Main Terminal. In 1966 the Centre sponsored the first international conference on space structures.

Until 1970 the University functioned from both Battersea, where C.W. Tonkin, the Pro-Vice-Chancellor, directed the institution, and Guildford, where Professor V.S. 'Griff' Griffiths, 'a wonderful negotiator' who was able to ease the transition process and resolve disputes with a canny charm, effectively ran the building operations. There was, says David Varney, by now a 'yearning to be a university'. The move itself was not without its problems – not the least of which was that when the first ten departments transferred, instead of settling in over the summer of 1968, they were only able to arrive the day before the students that autumn. 'Disaster was avoided by an uncomfortably narrow margin', Peter Leggett remembered, as they found themselves with no heating, only a partial electricity supply, and telephones unconnected. Food had to be served from a marquee, as the restaurants were not ready, and the site was so muddy that the University bought a supply of wellington boots for general use. Further delays lay ahead, but by 1970 the University had fully settled into its own campus at Guildford.

Professor V.S. 'Griff' Griffiths

About 1400 meals a day were served in a hastily erected marquee with a field kitchen attached.

Early Days at Guildford

Although there were the inevitable teething problems, there was no doubt, in the words of David Pollard (later University Director in Engineering Education and Training), that in those first years Guildford 'was an exciting place to be. We were planning new courses, establishing whole new subject areas, and expanding others. We were also dealing with far more students. Whereas there had been 100 first-year students across all four engineering disciplines at Battersea, now each one was admitting nearly that number.'

And these students had rather different expectations from the cohorts of earlier times, even from those of a decade earlier. In 1969 the age of legal majority decreased from 21 to 18; students were no longer 'children', but young adults, vociferous in making their views known – and soon to express their views in the first election (in June 1970) at which teenagers could vote, which Ted Heath, to the surprise of many, and perhaps even his own, won – and independent in taste, their choice of entertainment and dress. There were far more female students than hitherto, too, though they remained in the minority until the mid-1990s, and in principle if not always in practice a strong notion of equality now reigned between the sexes: Germaine Greer's *The Female Eunuch* was published that year, 1970, *Spare Rib*'s first issue came out in 1972, and the Women's Liberation Movement was raising women's political consciousness on both sides of the Atlantic. The new generation of students was eager to exploit the new freedoms.

There was a lively social atmosphere at Surrey, with staff-versus-student football and cricket matches, and an active Students' Union. In 1970, the Union held the first Free Festival (later Free Arts Festival). With collaboration from organisations in and around Guildford, the festival grew, and by 1974 was attracting over 3000 people to events including 'musical items, both classical and pop, art exhibitions, poetry reading, films, folk concerts and theatre groups'. In 1973, the Union established its own radio station.

Some of the University's first cohort of students.

A Surrey University Social Action Group was formed to organise students to do voluntary work in the local community. Initial fears about how the University might impact on town life – mainly related to students' unruly behaviour and noise issues – readily disappeared as Bill Bellerby, a long-term Guildford Borough councillor, recalled: 'People realised that the University would be an asset to the town, which indeed it has proved.'

With the move to Guildford, the University began to extend the strong links with industry that had been such a feature of Battersea life. By 1971/72 the professional placement year was mandatory in 26 of the 37 undergraduate courses and optional in seven others. A Bureau of Industrial Liaison, one of the first in British universities, was established to develop collaborative research and consultancy projects, to increase industry's use of the University's specialist equipment and to organise short courses and workshops. This also provided useful additional income – and it pointed the way towards the far more extensive commercialisation of research that would become such an important element of the University of Surrey in future years. The Managing

The Free Arts Festival, *c.* 1977. (*Surrey Advertiser*)

Directors' Club, drawing on the expertise of local industry and organisations, founded and chaired by Sir George Edwards, also provided an invaluable source of advice and experience in the early years in particular. It was quite active, with membership climbing to over 100 in the 1970s.

Professor Lewis Elton at one of the first art exhibitions in the Physics corridor at Battersea, which he organised.

The hoped-for integration of town and gown also began to take place. The University's Centre for Adult Education (which later became a University department) offered a wide range of activities for 16- to 21-year-olds, including science and arts extension groups for sixth-formers, as well as Workers Educational Association courses for the wider community. In 1974 the Centre took over responsibility for adult education in south-west Surrey, and in 1978 for the whole county. The University also began a programme of in-service education for professional groups, such as teachers, health workers and the rescue services, in particular the fire service, the antecedents of today's continuing professional development courses.

The University also began to make its mark on Guildford's cultural life. Professor Lewis Elton had staged the first exhibitions of art in the Physics Department corridors at Battersea. At Guildford these continued in 'rather better corridors'. Among the artists to exhibit during the first ten years were local artists such as Charles Bone, Brian Dunce, Sir George Pollock, Ronald Smoothey and James Winterbottom, as well as David Hockney. One early outstanding exhibition was of works by the Romanian painter Arnold Daghani, who had escaped from a German forced labour camp in 1943, just before those imprisoned were put to death. In 1997 the University opened the Lewis Elton Gallery with an exhibition of prints by Picasso, *Histoire Naturelle*, since when it has continued to flourish. In its first year on campus, the University also inaugurated the Guildford Festival of the Arts.

Open days and University stands at the Surrey County Show helped not only to foster community links but to keep the public informed about progress on Stag Hill as building continued. By the start of the 1970/71 academic year, five academic buildings, Senate House, Hall, three restaurants, the Lecture Theatre Block, the first part of the Library, two residential courts and 40 acres of sports fields were complete and, in the words of the *Architects' Journal*, the 'campus works efficiently and looks thoroughly established'.

There were significant academic developments in the 1970s too, with the launch of combined courses, the first being Metallurgy with a foreign language, as well as courses in Telecommunications, Toxicology, Science Education and French. A Home Economics Centre was established to house the new multidisciplinary Home Economics course, though the Home Economics Department, as it later became, was closed in 1984. General Studies, an important and unusual part of the Surrey curriculum, continued, taking up about 10 per cent of students' time, and broadening the student experience. There were weekly lectures in the first two terms, after which students selected two courses from a wide range of options outside their degree subjects.

The Lewis Elton Gallery at the University in 2009, with Claire Phillips' exhibition *The Human Face of Death Row* in progress.

A significant appointment in this period was that of the new Professor of Physics in place of Professor Elton, who moved to the new Department of Science Education in 1971. Daphne Jackson spent her entire working life at Battersea and then Surrey, and she was to have a long-lasting influence both on the University and on academic life generally. A pioneering researcher in nuclear physics, and with interests in radiation and environmental protection, Professor Jackson remained the only female Professor of Physics in the country until 1989 and contributed greatly towards raising the University's reputation in the field. As President of the Women's Engineering Society, she also championed women in science and engineering; she was involved in establishing both the Women in Science and Engineering initiative to encourage girls into the disciplines and the Women Returners' Fellowship, designed to aid women with families back into high-grade technological or scientific work.

The continuing growth in student numbers placed increasing demand on central services, causing them to expand dramatically. The Library, for instance, which had 26,185 books in stock in 1963/64, had 111,654 books by

Professor Daphne Jackson OBE (1936–91), appointed Professor of Physics in 1971, receiving an honorary degree from the University of Loughborough in 1990.

Aerial view of the campus, 1970s.

1970/71, with book issues standing at over 84,000. Whereas some of the other new universities had a large local population, the majority at Surrey came from Battersea and were thus far from home and beyond a sensible commute. Providing sufficient accommodation was therefore a major issue. In the early 1970s construction continued apace, adding four academic buildings, the Sports Hall, the Students' Union, Wates House, three residential courts, the Library, the Teaching Block, and maintenance and stores buildings. The new residences at Stag Hill Court incorporated a rethink regarding student accommodation, so that instead of the 56-unit houses of Battersea and Surrey Courts, the new courts, designed by Robert Maguire and Keith Murray, were based on ten-person units, each with their own front door, in order to afford students a greater sense of identity alongside their independence.

However, the early 1970s also brought the first episodes of student unrest at the University. Student protests were widespread in this period, of course, provoked by a variety of causes from poor food to political activism, and reaching their peak with the major demonstrations of 1968, but at Surrey the students had been relatively peaceful. Then, at the end of the spring term in 1973, there was a rent strike in protest at increased residence fees. When the University threatened to sue those who had not paid their fees, the top two floors of Senate House were occupied for six days. Eventually, a compromise was reached: a reduction in the fee increases for 1972/73 and 1973/74. Students were also given representation on the Finance and General Purposes Committee of Council. Two years later, there were further sit-ins, though these were not as widely supported. This time the University did take legal action, and won. At the same time it introduced a regulation barring any student with outstanding debts from being awarded a degree.

A New Vice-Chancellor and a New Culture

By the mid-1970s the University had settled into its new life at Guildford, yet the new Vice-Chancellor, Anthony Kelly, appointed in 1975 on Peter Leggett's retirement, found a certain insecurity about its status around campus. By 1974/75 there were 2646 students, nearly 600 more than in 1970/71, and 900 more than in its transitional year of 1967/68. Though less than originally anticipated, this was no mean feat, and the number of applicants who made Surrey their first choice was growing, despite a national decline in student applications at this time. The graduate employment rate was also something to be proud of: of the 553 students who graduated in

Professor Anthony Kelly, the University's second Vice-Chancellor.

summer 1974, only six remained unemployed by that December. Yet 17.7 per cent of students left the University without any qualification at all, which, although no more than the national average, caused considerable disquiet.

On his arrival at the University of Surrey, Anthony Kelly commented:

> The University did not feel itself as established as it should have been, nor as confident, despite the good work being done in many departments. On the whole the old Polytechnic culture still prevailed, with many staff concentrating purely on teaching, and not being engaged in research.

Peter Beardsley, Academic Registrar for more than 30 years, said that those at Surrey recognised this: 'Many staff had a strong belief in professional and vocational education, and a strong attachment to teaching and to their subjects and departments.'

Professor Kelly's leadership was to bring in an era of change. His brief was to expand research activities and so to enhance the University's status and reputation, and with a background as a distinguished materials scientist – he was elected a Fellow of the Royal Society at only 44 – who continued his own research alongside his other responsibilities, and with good international ties, he was well placed to do so. His previous post had been as Deputy Director of the National Physical Laboratory (NPL), the UK's largest and oldest scientific research establishment. While there, he had been seconded to the Research and Development Department of ICI, where he had studied industrial management. He thus had the interest, contacts and inclination to foster strong links with industry.

Initially some found Professor Kelly daunting, but it soon became obvious that he was driven by a belief in the need to deliver better education in the UK in order for it to compete, and a determination that universities should foster a new spirit of enterprise. Perhaps the most important achievements during his time were the founding of the Surrey Research Park, in 1984, and

Lord Robens, the outgoing Chancellor, Lord Hamilton of Dalzell, Lord Lieutentant of Surrey, Chancellor-elect HRH The Duke of Kent (who was installed in January 1977), and the Vice-Chancellor, Professor Anthony Kelly, at the tenth anniversary dinner on 10 November 1976.

beginning what is now more or less the standard format of courses at Surrey, the four-year degree, with a year out in industry or the professions. Yet he also supported the arts and encouraged a general enhancing of the student experience. One way, unusually, in which the latter was expressed was in making himself available to students for consultation one evening a week.

These were difficult years in which to instigate ambitious plans for expansion, with high inflation and a squeeze on the economy. The Government's economic difficulties led it to reduce the number of funded university places, so that the University Grants Committee (UGC), which had in Professor Kelly's first year in post (1975/76) suggested a one-third increase in student numbers by 1981/82, reduced this in 1977 by 500 to 3500 full-time undergraduates. The UGC also had a stranglehold over university finances, allowing Surrey, as Professor Kelly recalled:

> little room for initiative … There was hardly any freedom to manoeuvre – you had to go to the UGC for everything you wanted to do. In fact the UGC told you what to do, even though they wrapped it up politely in that nice way the English have.

A student in the Electrical Engineering Department, 1970s. (Photograph taken by Thomas A. Wilkie AIBP FRPS)

Consolidation was thus the way forward in Professor Kelly's early years, with resources focused on, as the 1977/78 *Annual Report* put it, 'those things we do very well indeed in scholarship and research'. Though when Professor Kelly arrived at Surrey, research income was, he stated, only just over £300,000, 'a relatively insignificant sum in relation to the University's overall budget', some notable developments were pushed through. The University introduced its first degree course in Nursing Studies and extended the Department of Electronic and Electrical Engineering's ion implantation service to become a national facility. With funding from the University's Tenth Anniversary Appeal, Guildford Borough and Surrey County Councils, it also established a new Institute of Industrial and Environmental Health and Safety (later renamed the Robens Institute in honour of the University's first Chancellor), which was later strengthened by merging with the Wolfson Bioanalytical Centre. Its remit included research, training and public education.

Academic procession emerging from Holy Trinity Church in the High Street, Guildford, on the occasion of the Thanksgiving Service held to mark the University's tenth anniversary.

Student Life and Political Unrest

By late 1975, with completion of the sixth residential court, Guildford Court, the University could accommodate 1887 students on campus, three-quarters of the total. Campus life became busier. By 1975/76 there were 109 student societies, and social and sporting life flourished. There had been a concerted effort to promote physical fitness through provision of a broad range of sports activities, and the students had clearly responded: around two-thirds now took part in regular sports, from dance workshops to football, fitness classes to riding, hockey to cross-country running. Hundreds of students participated in the Sunday afternoon competitions between the courts of residence. By the beginning of the 1980s there were 42 University sports clubs; 29 teams entered the University Athletic Union championships in 1980/81, the women gaining 13th place overall, the men 17th, out of a total of 40.

On the arts side, students took part in workshops in painting and pottery, and there were poetry readings, concerts, lectures, exhibitions and, in 1981, the first Literary Week, which brought celebrated writers and critics to

Guildford. In 1981 the Charter Ball was held again, after a four-year break. The previous year, the Quiet Centre had been opened to provide a contemplative haven for students and staff alike.

This was also a period of political engagement. In the late 1970s the Government found itself facing economic crisis and a 'winter of discontent'. Inflation soared, workers' strikes against pay curbs proliferated – even the gravediggers went on strike against pay freezes – and unemployment rose, to 1.1 million in 1979. In the coming election the Conservatives would run an effective campaign that 'Labour isn't Working'; support for the Government had collapsed, ushering in Thatcherism in its wake.

No one was immune from the impact of the cuts and curbs. In March 1977, students occupied Senate House for two weeks in protest at the Government's sudden and substantial increase in university tuition fees due to take effect that autumn. Most UK students would be unaffected as their fees were paid by local authorities, but those who were self-financing and students from overseas would have to pay the increase. Feelings ran high throughout the country and sit-ins and marches were widespread. At Surrey, the University agreed to help students during the first year of the increase, and the Vice-Chancellor wrote to the Prime Minister to register the University's disquiet at the change. Other political issues were also on the Students' Union agenda in this period of political unrest, unemployment and disarmament among them.

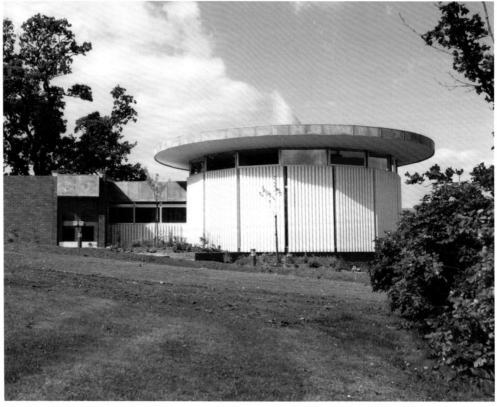

Opposite: Allan Wells, who later joined the School of Engineering, won the 100m title at the Moscow Olympic Games in 1980. This picture shows him just after the start of the second round heats. Taken by Chris Smith, four-time winner of Sports Photographer of the Year, the picture was voted the best black and white sports action picture of the 1980s, and then the best black and white sports action picture of the twentieth century. (Chris Smith)

The Quiet Centre, funded by an anonymous donor and inaugurated in 1980.

Cuts in the 1980s

By the beginning of the 1980s the universities had suffered a series of cuts in central government funding, but worse was to come. The advent of the 'Iron Lady', Mrs Thatcher, had not been welcome. Many in the universities felt she had little sympathy with the academic world, despite the benefit she had herself derived from it. Just as important, the economy was now in its worst slump since the Second World War: unemployment had continued to rise and was now the second highest in Europe, topping the three million mark in January 1982, with one in eight people out of work. In the Conservative Government's first budget in March 1981, public expenditure was cut by £3.5 billion. Cuts in university funding were not long in coming, but the UGC cuts were far deeper and more extensive than anyone had anticipated. 'In 1981 the whole University community was justifiably shocked by a drastic reduction in funding and there were severe staff reductions', stated Leonard Kail, University Secretary 1980–92.

Professor Otto Pick, who created the International Relations Section in the Department of Linguistic and Regional Studies, and who did much to ease the cuts through in the 1980s.

The UGC guidance on the cuts indicated that the annual recurrent grant, the University of Surrey's principal source of funding, was to be cut by 13 per cent for the year 1981/82, and then be cut further to an overall decrease of 25 per cent by 1983/84. Undergraduate numbers would be sliced by 14 per cent to 2470 in the same period, with the burden of the loss in the humanities and social sciences (28 per cent against science and engineering's 8 per cent). The devastation felt was compounded by the fact that the cuts would start to take effect in three months' time.

The anger and distress felt were not only professional but personal. David Pollard, University Director Emeritus of the School of Engineering, recalled how any 'optimism that was still present in the University evaporated', and Vice-Chancellor Professor Anthony Kelly was 'deeply hurt'. There was anger too when it became clear that the UGC had selected the former CATs for the sharpest cuts; indeed Surrey had not even come off the worst of these, Bradford, Aston and Salford each having their grants reduced by 30 per cent in the three years. With their focus on the real world of work, rather than the 'ivory tower' world of academia that Mrs Thatcher so disliked, and with some of the ex-CATS located in areas of high unemployment, many of the new universities and polytechnics felt the savagery of the cuts unjustified. There

54

was also deep resentment that the relatively new arts and social sciences departments were to suffer most, and that there had been no recognition that at Surrey these courses had been developed with the same business and professional focus as its science and engineering courses. Courses at the more 'traditional' universities, often with more theoretical approaches, suffered far less from the cuts, it seemed.

NOT FOR PUBLICATION, BROADCAST, OR USE ON CLUB TAPES BEFORE 1430 HOURS THURSDAY 2 JUL 1981

UNIVERSITY GRANTS COMMITTEE
14 Park Crescent London W1N 4DH
Telephone 01-636 7799 ext

The Vice-Chancellor
University of Surrey
Guildford
SURREY
GU2 5XH

Your reference

Our reference 44/52/021
(Circular Letter 10/81)

Date 1 July 1981

SURREY.

3. The Committee's advice on particular subject areas is as follows:

ARTS

The Committee recommends a significant decrease in student numbers in Arts and Social Studies. It invites the University to consider discontinuing Philosophy.

SCIENCE

The Committee recommends that intakes to Nursing and Nutrition should be maintained at their present levels. It recommends a decrease in the number of students specialising in the Mathematical Sciences and a significant decrease in numbers in Biological Sciences.

4. The Committee would wish to discuss with the University the future provision of Arts-based subjects and of courses in Human Biology.

Yours sincerely,

Edward Parkes

EDWARD PARKES.

The letter from the University Grants Committee 'recommending' cuts in courses and student numbers at the University.

Although Professor Kelly made vehement protests and attempted to persuade the UGC to moderate the cuts, the University was forced to implement them. The unwelcome task of doing so fell largely to Professor Otto Pick, the recently appointed Pro-Vice-Chancellor and Chairman of the Academic Policy Committee, aided by University Secretary Leonard Kail and others, and strongly supported by Council. It was of course an unpleasant experience for everyone, with 289 jobs being lost (though there were no compulsory redundancies), but Professor Pick was well liked, which helped, and his handling of the issue with sensitivity, and the fact that he took care to avoid any unnecessary impact on students and their welfare, enabled an outcome acceptable to most to be obtained.

In the end, three departments were closed, Philosophy, Human Biology and Home Economics. The last of these was the most controversial since the department was held in high esteem and offered the only course of its kind in the UK, but there seemed to be no other way to achieve the cuts required and it was therefore accepted as the least damaging option. Nursing students were allowed to transfer to Biochemistry, in line with the UGC's recommendation

HRH The Duke of Kent opens the Surrey Research Park.

that 'intakes to Nursing and Nutrition should be maintained at their present levels'. General Studies, for so long part of the ethos of the institution, both at Guildford and earlier at Battersea, was dropped as a compulsory element; its replacement, Elective Studies, survived until the 1990s. Thirteen other courses were also stopped, many of them the innovative combined honours courses designed to equip science and technological studies students with an understanding of the languages, societies and economies of the UK's trading partners in Europe, and thereby to fit them more ably for the international workplace.

For the departments left, there was often major restructuring. Metallurgy and Materials Technology, for instance, lost one in four of its teaching staff and one in three of its support staff, necessitating a re-allocation of work. Yet because posts were cut through early retirement and natural wastage, while some staff were able to move jobs within the University, there was remarkably little bitterness. The effect of the cuts in some areas was felt much more in the long term, with loss of much of the budget for new books in the Library and far less money available for equipment, conferences and so on. It was a time of great upset and, as time was to show, sadly and significantly underlying the cuts was a political policy of removing state support for higher education – the effects of which would become more greatly felt in the coming years. Nevertheless, the University managed to come out of the whole experience, as the 1981/82 *Annual Report* stated, able 'to look forward with its corporate spirit intact'.

The Research Park

One perhaps unique way in which the University of Surrey responded to the cuts was to found the Surrey Research Park, thereby giving it the means to generate other, independent, streams of income and reduce its reliance on central funding. As a result, by 2010 less than 25 per cent of the University's income would derive from core funding (in 2008/09, income from the recurrent funding body grant for English universities as a whole was 31.7 per cent of total income); by the end of 1996, the Research Park had contributed over £20 million to University finances and by the end of 2010, £71 million. At the same time, the Research Park's link to the University has given students a direct demonstration of how research can be productive in commercial terms, and collaborations between the University's research teams and Research Park companies have been instructive in showing how the two can feed off each other and work together fruitfully. Establishment of the Research Park, in fact, took the University's ethos of working with industry, which had informed its operation since its earliest days, one step further.

The establishment of the Surrey Research Park has probably been the most important factor in the development of the University from the mid-1980s, not only crucial in putting its finances on a firm footing, but also transforming its academic standing and giving it, in particular, a presence on the international stage. It has also been key in Guildford's development as an economic and technological hub in the south-east.

The notion of a research park had first occurred to the Vice-Chancellor, Professor Anthony Kelly, back in 1977, after he spent much of the summer vacation working in the research laboratories of Atlas Capo, a high-technology company whose labs stood in:

> an attractive park. There were researchers from all over the world, which brought a real international culture to the place. I remember thinking, Guildford is an attractive place too, where people enjoy living, and it has good communications. And we, the University, have land to spare. So why don't we build a university research park?

The Surrey Research Park as it looked when the first tenants arrived in 1985.

The concept of a dedicated research park where industry would carry out research, development and design in collaboration with university academics and researchers was quite a novel one; only Cambridge, with its Science Park, then had a similar operation in the UK. The time was also right. Low-cost computing was coming in, making researchers less confined to working in large companies with huge capital reserves, and putting research and development in the grasp of smaller teams, or even a single researcher.

At the University, too, there was considerable support. In 1977, after Lord Robens' retirement, HRH The Duke of Kent succeeded him as Chancellor. The Duke's interest in promoting British exports chimed well with the University's ambitions and the desire to expand links with industry. The appointment of Sir Monty Finniston, the industrialist, as the second Pro-Chancellor (Sir George Edwards retired in 1979) was also timely. The University also needed to get the town on side, and here too they were lucky. Eric Twyford, Chief Executive of Guildford Borough Council

An aerial view of the Surrey Research Park, 1980s.

(until retirement in 1984) was quick to recognise its potential, as John Humphries, a property lawyer who later became Vice-Chairman of Council and a leading member of the University's Research Park Sub-Committee, explained: '[He] did not take long to be convinced of the potential benefits of the Research Park in terms of bringing additional money and jobs to the town. He also realised that Guildford's future prosperity would depend on high-tech companies.' For the University, the Research Park's role in commercialising new scientific and technological ideas and applications developed by its academics, and the propitiousness of having a nest of technological companies actively involved in such work as its neighbour, would prove to have invaluable long-term benefits. While for the tenant companies themselves, there was the advantage of easy access to the University's research teams and expertise, as well as the growing benefit of sharing a location with other companies in related fields.

Though there was some concern at the Borough Council about the use of hitherto green space at Manor Park for the development, by 1983 outline planning permission had been granted, with a restriction limiting use to 'research, development and design activities, in any science, including social sciences, that is complementary to the activities of the University of Surrey'.

In 1982, Dr Malcolm Parry, previously in an academic post where he taught human physiology and ergonomics, became Director, a role he has retained ever since. It was to him that the task fell of turning the idea into reality. He identified three types of user of the park:

- small start-up and spin-out companies and small specialist parts of larger companies carrying out research, development and design engineering, and science-based companies, including those involved in information and communication technologies
- medium-sized companies and larger research facilities of multi-site companies
- large headquarters and research facilities of high-technology based companies.

Market research revealed that analysis was likely to be largely computer-based, with little need for big laboratories. A Master Plan and Development Manual was therefore adopted for the Park to be developed in three zones, small, medium and large, for companies of different sizes, with different

The BOC staff newspaper *Pennant* announces the beginning of construction of BOC's new Development and Executive Centre at Surrey Research Park in February 1985. (Image courtesy of BOC)

origins, and likely to be working in widely varying technologies. An 'incubator centre', now known as the Surrey Technology Centre, was also planned, where small companies could originate, before moving to larger units.

In 1983 building began. Funding came solely from the University, but for a project of this size it could never be covered by normal development funds. A long leasehold on a small area of the University's land was therefore sold to the Associated Examining Board (now AQA) for £1.23 million to pay for the installation of the initial infrastructure. Trusthouse Forte also leased part of the University's land next to the A3 to construct an hotel. The University then targeted companies in chemical and process engineering, where it had decided Surrey's strengths lay, as potential under-tenants. A focused marketing campaign followed. 'I never doubted that Surrey's buoyant economy, its proximity to London and the two major airports, and the links with the University would prove attractive', said Malcolm Parry. A site was sold to BOC UK Limited for its headquarters and technical centre, now known as the Priestley Centre (after Joseph Priestley, who discovered oxygen). This enabled the University to build a first phase of speculative buildings, called Chancellor Court, all of which were let 'off plan'. The new rental income supported further borrowings and the development of the rest of the Research Park. The University's total investment by 2000, when 85 per cent of the Park was complete, amounted to £32 million – but it was valued at more than £75 million, while income that year exceeded £6 million. In 2011 it was valued at over £100 million and had a rent roll of over £9.5 million.

In 1984 construction of the Surrey Technology Centre (STC) started. It opened in 1985 and the first tenants moved into the building that summer. As each new development was completed, the rental income provided funds for further construction and facilities at the University. The number of companies at the Research Park grew rapidly, from 16 when the STC opened, to 65 in 1989. In 2011, the figure stood at 115, with over 2500 staff. Of these, 21 were graduate companies from the STC.

Perhaps the most important company at the Research Park from the University's point of view, and the one that has brought it greatest renown, is Surrey Satellite Technology Limited (SSTL), a major university spin-out company established in 1985 and specialising in delivering and operating small satellite technology for customers around the world. Since its foundation SSTL has brought enormous benefit to the University. In January 2009, Surrey sold an 85 per cent stake in SSTL, by then, according to the BBC, 'the world's leading manufacturer of small satellites, producing low-cost platforms for Earth observation missions', to EADS Astrium, Europe's largest space company, for a not insignificant sum. Nothing else could perhaps more clearly demonstrate the clear realisation of the Research Park's ambitions. It represented, said Vice-Chancellor Professor Christopher Snowden at the time, 'one of the largest cash spin-outs from any UK university'. (See pp. 117–26 for the story of SSTL.)

Adult Education and the Guildford Institute

While the University was energetically working its way up the academic pole, it was also developing its services in adult education. In 1982 the University became a trustee of the Guildford Institute, afterwards holding its adult education programme in the building (the association would end in 2008). Originally established in 1834 as the Mechanics Institute, by mid-century around 350 people, about 10 per cent of the local population, were attending its popular lectures and the Institute had also built up a substantial library to serve the townspeople. In 1892 the Institute amalgamated with the rival Guildford Working Men's Institution and took over its newly acquired premises in the old Royal Arms Coffee Tavern and Temperance Hotel. An ambitious programme of activities was launched, both social and educational, and by 1903 membership had grown to 1576.

Ironically, it was the Government's move to create separate technical colleges, such as Battersea Polytechnic Institute, that spelled the beginning of the end of the Institute's independence. Classes once held at the Institute moved to the new Technical College in Stoke Park. The advent of a museum, a picture playhouse (1919) and a public library (1942) were other attractions. Membership gradually declined and by the mid-1970s the building was also in poor repair.

The Guildford Institute of the University of Surrey in the High Street, where the University held adult education classes from 1982 to 2000.

The difficulties of the Institute, however, presented the University of Surrey with an opportunity: the central location of the building would be an ideal outpost for the University's Adult Education Department. The University therefore decided to put funds into the building in return for a share in it and its use for its own adult education classes. The Institute would continue its own lectures, visits and talks, as well as being a venue for other town events. In 1982 the Guildford Institute of the University of Surrey was born.

There was some symbiosis: membership of the Institute stabilised at about 500 while some of the many more who came through the doors for classes every week were encouraged to join. The library continued to be a defining part of the Institute's identity, the number of volumes rising to over 80,000 by the mid-1990s. Numerous people attended the University's classes there and thereby came to know about its other activities, particularly in the arts, on campus. However, upkeep of the building proved more expensive than anticipated – the University's funding amounted to an average £30,000-plus per annum – and in 2008 the association came to an end. The Institute has since operated as an independent organisation once again.

On Campus

There were developments on campus too. After a gap of some years because of financial stringency, construction began again in the late 1980s with expansion of student residences at Stag Hill and at Hazel Farm. New academic buildings were opened in 1989. The Performing Arts Technology Studios, which were designed and specified to BBC recording standards, included

An architect's visualisation of the Performing Arts Technology Studios building, opened in March 1988.

recording, control and editing rooms, as well as practice and studio-cum-performance space. Around the same time, the Wolfson Centre for Cytotechnology (named for the Wolfson Foundation, which funded it to the tune of £600,000) opened. 'This was,' said Peter Goldfarb, Emeritus Professor of Molecular Biology and Director of the Centre for Toxicology, 'to provide a focus at Surrey for the new science of biotechnology, particularly the large-scale growth of human, animal and bacterial cells in culture and to develop advanced technologies for the production of novel vaccines and drugs'. Also in the late 1980s, the Students' Union building, which had been struggling

The Principal of Merrist Wood College and the Vice-Chancellor inspect the cascade which was designed and built by the nearby College's horticulture students in 1983.

The Geodesic Dome was presented to the University in 1982 on the occasion of the Space Structures Conference hosted by Professor Zygmunt Makowski, and is based on the original construction by Buckminster Fuller.

against the seams for some years, had an extension added, known as Chancellors Bar. An unusual building of over 12 interlocking levels designed and conceived in the mid-1960s, the Union building is one of the areas that the University has marked as requiring development in the future.

Attention was also given to the landscaping of the grounds. The University had been built on open meadowland, almost treeless, and although shrubs and trees had been planted, these took some time to mature. From the mid-1970s to the mid-1980s, Terry Bennett, Head Groundsman to 1989, and his successor Nigel Hodge, the Horticulture and Landscape Manager, added planting around the campus to soften the landscape and 'create a sequence of attractive and varied identities' around each academic block and residential court. Though restricted by the heavy clay soil, as Nigel Hodge explains, they

A view of the campus grounds in the 1980s, showing the lake and beyond it the Geodesic Dome.

'tried to use as many evergreens and winter-flowering plants as possible to provide colour and visual interest throughout the year'. The bigger spaces around the campus were given focal points of interest, with gently sloping parkland, for instance, from Senate House to the Duke of Kent Building.

The lakes are also an important feature of the University, attracting swans and other wildfowl, as well as being a favoured gathering place for students taking a break from their studies or enjoying a breath of fresh air while eating lunch. Terry's Pond, below Senate House, named in commemoration of Terry Bennett's work over many years, was created from a steep-sided dew pond in the 1970s, and now meanders gracefully down the slope. In 2009 and 2010 both lakes were drained, dredged, repuddled and the landscape enhanced. There are waterfalls, seats and walkways, and in the last decade a number of modern sculptures have been installed.

The campus is remarkable for the number of plant and tree species, with varieties from all over the world, from the common *Salix alba* 'Britzensis' to Gold-tip oriental spruce and Hungarian oak. Some trees have been planted to note special occasions, a royal visit, for instance, or as a memorial, and one or two are ancient, one on the University's boundary being over 100 years old. Some

66

rare trees and plentiful advice came from sylviculturalist Alan Mitchell, who lived at nearby Farnham. Yet, one man's enthusiasm in particular was really responsible for making the campus an arboreal landscape. Gordon Hartman taught biochemistry at the University from 1965 until his retirement in 2001, and with the University's support he started the University Tree Club, which arranged lectures and visits, and Saturday morning planting sessions.

> I thought the grounds had considerable potential for a good collection of trees which everyone, whether staff, student or just passers-by, would enjoy and also learn from. … We developed a structured plan which aimed to provide a wide range of species, concentrating particularly on trees – such as alder, ash and walnut – suited to the London clay of the site. I was always on the look-out for interesting and unusual trees and, when one became available at a nursery, I would try to find an association with one of my colleagues and persuade them to buy it for the University.

The first planting was the eucalyptus grove to the north of Senate House in 1970, commemorating the move of the Biochemistry Department from the College's Falcon Road annexe near Clapham Junction to the new AY building, and commissioned by the Biochemistry staff.

Two of the more unusual tree species on campus are *Taxodium ascendus* 'Nuten', a pond cypress, one of a small group of deciduous conifers, and *Davidii involucata*, also a native of central China, shown here with its well-known 'handkerchief' leaves.

The planting over the years has added immeasurably to the look and feel of the campus and it has also encouraged wildlife. There are 42 nest boxes around the campus and foxes, rabbits, hedgehogs and badgers are all frequent visitors to the grounds and to the Manor Park and Hazel Farm courts of residence. By 2011 there were over 320 tree species (over 1600 trees in all) and 1000 different plant species, and growing. In 2003, Gordon Hartman and Nigel Hodge wrote a short guide to the most notable trees, *Trees at Surrey*, highlighting 100 of the most distinguished specimens. The tours and talks have been continued by Nigel Hodge and his team and are well attended by the University population and local groups.

A Research-focused University

While the despondent air of the University apparent in Professor Anthony Kelly's first years in office had begun to lift by the mid-1980s, it was to be no easy passage. The squeeze on government spending continued, with a knock-on effect on the universities. In 1986/87, for example, Surrey's grant rose by 0.7 per cent, in effect a cut, so that it was operating on a deficit budget. To make matters worse, from the mid-1980s the clampdown on university places was lifted and the number of full-time students at the University increased by around 150 to 200 a year until the early 1990s. Strides had been made, of course, with the establishment of the Research Park and SSTL, but they were in their infancy. It was clear to Professor Kelly that he would have to 'turn the University around, and the funding situation after 1981 meant that I was able in effect to say to the University, your salvation is in your own hands'.

Professor Kelly's vision was to turn the University into a research-led institution. He felt that the University needed to gain recognition and a reputation for high-quality work, so that it would draw in students and staff excited by the advances being made, who would in turn contribute to Surrey's climb up the league table. Situated at Guildford, the University could feel, in the words of Peter Goldfarb, who joined the Biochemistry Department in 1985, like 'something of a quiet backwater'; in order to succeed it needed to punch above its weight.

Professor June Layson pictured with Dr Peter Brinson of the Calouste Gulbenkian Foundation at the launch of the National Resource Centre for Dance.

A typical student room in the 1980s.

When the Research Assessment Exercise (RAE) was introduced in the late 1980s, Professor Kelly was determined to achieve as many 5-ratings as possible. Said Peter Goldfarb:

> He was the main driver in bringing the University into the top league of research universities. … He encouraged the formation of research groups to develop real expertise in a particular area … it helped enormously that he was seen around the campus a great deal, and also that, although Vice-Chancellor, he led by example and kept up his own research.

Research groups were particularly important in encouraging interdisciplinary collaboration and exchange, and have been a key part of the University's growing success. A cross-disciplinary Biotechnology Unit had already been formed before 1981, and in 1982 the Surrey Energy Economics Centre was established. The Physics Department set up the largest Nuclear Theory Group in the UK, while other research groups focused on criminal justice and the sociology of health and illness. This was a pattern that continued; today each of the four faculties has several research centres, and there is a Research and Enterprise Support Department to aid them and facilitate knowledge-transfer activities throughout the University.

Another innovation came in the early 1980s when Surrey became the first university to offer a degree in Dance. For a long time, Music had been the only performing arts discipline to be offered. In 1981 Professor June Layson was appointed Director of Dance and Drama (she later became Professor of Dance) and the following year the National Resource Centre for Dance was established, to provide courses and publications for dance teaching and study

69

Dance became part of the University's academic offering in the 1980s and has continued to be a strong strand of its teaching and research.

and to develop an archive. Dance was taught at both undergraduate and post-graduate level, though because of reduced funding, the first students had to pay substantial fees.

Professor Kelly was also keen to foster international links, including collaboration with other institutions, especially in Europe. Professor Otto Pick, who had been a researcher for US Secretary of State Henry Kissinger, was instrumental in building a strong International Relations Section within the Department of Linguistic and Regional Studies. It offered combined degrees, bringing together language teaching and study of the countries' politics and culture with international relations. In the mid-1980s a Masters degree in European Area Studies was launched covering the politics and economics of the

European Community and of individual Western European countries, as well as, unusually, of Eastern European countries. The courses eventually evolved into European Studies, at undergraduate level, and the Masters in European Area Studies, while Professor Pick, a Czech who had fled his country as a political refugee in 1948, returned to become a Minister in the Czech Government after the end of the Cold War.

The changes at the University benefitted students, of course. Alison Pring, who studied German and French with Urban and Regional Studies (1979–83) recalls that her placements in Lyon, Vienna and Hamburg proved a 'great training for my FCO [Foreign and Commonwealth Office] postings'. Tim Walton (1988–92), now Vice-President of International Hotel Development for Marriott International, was drawn to his course at Surrey not least because of its reputation as a 'world leader in the field of hospitality and tourism studies …[and because the course was] held in high regard throughout the tourism and hospitality industry'.

Gradually the financial situation at the University improved. In 1984/85 the *Annual Report* was able to deliver the good news that five major contracts for research had been won that year. These included the purchase of a new spectrometer for the Department of Materials Science and Engineering's Surface and Interface Reactions Group, enabling it to be designated a regional centre for electron spectroscopy, and a major social research project by the Department of Psychology on the safe management and disposal of radioactive waste. These five amounted to £1.1 million, and there were over 100 smaller grants worth about £2 million. And research income continued to grow: in 1989/90 the University received £10.8 million. By 1985/86 Professor Kelly was able to point out proudly that 'Surrey now receives a lower proportion of its recurrent income from exchequer grants (52.6 per cent) than any other UK university'.

In 1989/90, the University had 4695 students. The figure had almost doubled in 20 years, though recent increases had been modest. The pace of change was about to quicken, however, with universities opening up to a broader social spectrum, and the 1990s would see the student population almost double again. There would also be increased competition, with polytechnics becoming a new tranche of universities. Challenging times lay ahead.

Chapter 3

Towards a New Millennium: the 1990s

A Year of Celebrations

The year 1991 was a significant milestone for the University, being not only the centenary of the foundation of Battersea Polytechnic Institute, but the 25th anniversary of the University of Surrey. The first substantial history of the University was commissioned; Roy Douglas, author of *Surrey: The Rise of a Modern University*, was a noted historian and had taught at Battersea for 35 years. The University had come a long way. Its early years were important in laying the foundation for the University's future, but the 1990s would see Surrey looking forward, not back.

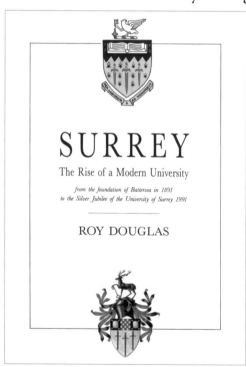

The first thorough history of the University, *Surrey: The Rise of a Modern University*, was published to mark its Silver Jubilee. Its author, Roy Douglas, a noted historian of nineteenth and twentieth-century politics, taught at the University and at Battersea for 35 years.

The beginning of the decade was cause for some celebration. In 1990/91 the number of students tipped over the 5000 mark for the first time, with 3301 undergraduates and 1703 postgraduates. The University also came out number one for graduate employment in *The Sunday Times* survey for 1990: less than 1 per cent of graduates from Surrey were still seeking work six months after graduation. The quality of the University's research also received academic recognition. In the first Research Assessment Exercise, in 1992, the University as a whole received a middle ranking; the Statistics Group achieved the highest ranking possible, two departments – Toxicology and Electrical and Electronic Engineering – were graded 5, and there were 4s for twelve other subjects. Research and contract income was also rising steadily, and in 1990 represented 23.4 per cent of the University's total income – only at Oxford, Cambridge and London was the proportion greater, a remarkable achievement for such a comparatively new university. By 1991 the Research Park was beginning to bring real dividends too, and that year SSTL launched UoSAT-5, its fifth satellite.

Ten years earlier, after the 1981 fees shock, the University had determined on a path that would give it less reliance on the core grant and broaden its activities. The establishment of the Research Park had been one strand of this strategy, and the founding of SSTL another. A third was to make a concerted drive to recruit international students, who from 1981, when government subsidy had been removed, had paid full fees. Recognition of the advances made came in April 1991 when the University gained the Queen's Award for Export Achievement in recognition of its outstanding ability to recruit students from overseas. In 1990/91 the number of overseas students by country of domicile stood at 895, 18 per cent of students

Professor Anthony Kelly (left) and Dr Peter Leggett cut the celebratory cake marking the University's Silver Jubilee and the centenary of the laying of the foundation stone of Battersea Polytechnic Institute in 1991.

(it continued to rise: two years later it reached 1238); in 1981 the figure had been 320. The award was presented by the Chancellor of the University, HRH The Duke of Kent, on behalf of Her Majesty The Queen.

The Queen also made her own visit to mark the centenary and the Silver Jubilee year, 1991/92. She came on a bright, spring day on Friday 20 March 1992 and was given a full tour of the University. Her first stop was at the new Centre for Satellite Engineering, where she switched on a specially designed hologram to inaugurate the new facility. Now known as the Surrey Space Centre, this is an academic centre for the research teams led by Professor Martin Sweeting (now Professor Sir Martin Sweeting) involved in the technical development of the small satellite industry, whose work underpins the commercial activities of SSTL. While there, the Queen received a message from one of the University's satellites and also exchanged messages with President Chiluba of Zambia. At the Great Hall she viewed an exhibition of the University's work. Among the projects that caught her attention were contact lenses for horses (developed by the Department of Chemistry) and natural environmentally friendly antibiotics to protect seeds (School of Biological Sciences). After a lunch hosted by the Chancellor, the Queen attended a Service of Thanksgiving in the cathedral. Her day ended with a walkabout, giving those in the town, as well as staff and students, the opportunity to see her. The day was heralded an all-round success: 'I think Her Majesty thoroughly enjoyed it', said Professor Anthony Kelly, the Vice-Chancellor. This was her first visit to the institution, either at Battersea or Guildford, but it would not be her last.

HM The Queen made her first visit to the campus on 20 March 1992. Here she is seen with the Vice-Chancellor, Professor Anthony Kelly.

Physicist Professor Alf Adams (left), Professor Anthony Kelly (centre) and Dr Gwyn Brown, Dean of International Students, with the flag that marked The Queen's Award for Export Achievement in April 1991. The award recognised the University's overseas earnings from teaching, advanced technology transfer contracts and research programmes, and in particular its success in driving up admissions of students from overseas.

The Surrey Space Centre, a European Centre of Excellence.

A New Vice-Chancellor and a New Political Climate for Higher Education

In 1994, Patrick Dowling was appointed Vice-Chancellor, in succession to Anthony Kelly, who moved to a research position at Churchill College, Cambridge, after 19 years in the post. The University Council had sought to appoint someone of international standing who could guide the institution through what would be difficult years ahead, able to negotiate the increasingly complex relationship between higher education and government, and with the vision to promote the University's expertise in the commercial world beyond. A distinguished structural engineer, Patrick Dowling came from the world-renowned Imperial College, where he had been Head of the Department of Civil Engineering. He also had significant hands-on research expertise in major construction projects such as the Thames Barrier and North Sea oil platforms.

Professor Patrick Dowling, the University's third Vice-Chancellor, who was appointed in succession to Professor Anthony Kelly in 1994.

Professor Dowling would do much to strengthen research at the University, but he arrived at a time when university funding was in decline and was, more than ever before, subject to political sway. This was compounded by the fact that student numbers were rising, and were set to rise even more steeply. The Labour Party target of having 50 per cent of all young people enter higher education by 2010 was first introduced in its 2001 electoral manifesto (in 2003 it was moderated to 'expanding towards 50 per cent'), but a policy to expand the numbers going into higher education was there long before that, with resulting impact.

In the 1980s and 1990s the number of students rose dramatically, while the unit of funding fell, and public expenditure on higher education as a percentage of GDP in real terms remained more or less static (in 1997 it was 0.99 per cent, in 2001 0.96 per cent). Between 1989 and 1997, as the Browne Report (2010) would later reveal, 'universities experienced a drop in funding per student of 36 per cent', with severe restrictions on capital expenditure. During the same period, the number of students in universities increased. In 1992 the number of universities almost doubled when the decision was made to transform the polytechnics (that is, those set up post-1966, rather than old-style institutions such as Battersea) into universities; today there are 115 universities in the UK.

By 1998/99, 39.2 per cent of people aged between 18 and 30 were in higher education and between 1994 and 2000 the number of accepted applicants at universities in the UK rose by 78 per cent. Surrey's student population reflected the national picture. Here, the number of full-time undergraduates went from 3213 in 1989/90 to 5117 in 1999/2000, an increase of 59 per cent

Students model the new corporate identity on the Geodesic Dome.

– the majority of the rise came in the first half of the decade since the Government capped student numbers in 1993, something which had major financial consequences for the universities. Total student numbers at Surrey reached 9132 in 1999/2000, a rise, astonishing even for the times, of 94 per cent in a decade. The real boom had come in the number of postgraduate students, which by 1999/2000 stood at 4015, compared with 1482 ten years earlier, evidence of the drive towards being a research-focused university that Professor Anthony Kelly had begun.

Two other changes in the period were significant. In 1988 the Education Reform Act was passed, which abolished the UGC and replaced it with funding bodies (later, the Higher Education Funding Council for England (HEFCE)) which would deliver monies to universities. Some of this funding would now be dependent on universities achieving certain targets; a portion of it related to the RAE, for instance. The reclassification of the polytechnics, which originally catered for a much broader demographic of student, would also push universities towards the democratisation of entry, or at least towards presenting themselves as doing so. From the perspective of time, we can see that these were first signals towards the re-gearing of twenty-first-century higher education, in which students would become 'customers' and the universities would be expected to produce students in response to the marketplace and the economy.

Such was the difficult financial situation that Professor Dowling confronted in the first years of his vice-chancellorship. The large HEFCE block grant was, said Professor Peter Butterworth, Senior Pro-Vice-Chancellor, 'vital in enabling the University to plan ahead and to establish a distinctive profile', and its fair and equitable distribution was critical. It was to this end that in the early 1990s he had developed the Resource Allocation Method (RAM) and this was fully implemented shortly after Professor Dowling's arrival. The RAM apportioned the HEFCE grant to the Schools, which in turn used it to pay an infrastructure charge for central services, such as the Library and administration. Student tuition fees followed each student to his or her particular School, and specific research grants went to the School concerned. It was a robust mechanism which was flexible enough to absorb the changes necessitated by the advent of tuition fees.

While the Schools were thus to manage their own development

In the 1990s, the University established an acclaimed virtual learning environment in the Surrey European Management School, here being promoted at a student fair.

more intensively, responsibility for the strategy that would drive the University's policy, and in turn that of the Schools, remained with Professor Dowling and Professor Butterworth, as well as Wyn Davies, University Secretary and Registrar. Professor John Turner, the Senior Deputy Vice-Chancellor, was also instrumental in many of the initiatives instigated in this period. They used a central strategic development fund for broader University-wide projects, such as the introduction of a virtual learning environment in the Surrey European Management School.

Soon after arriving at Guildford, Professor Dowling began the process of University-wide consultation and discussion that would lead to an ambitious new *Vision Statement* for Surrey. He later explained the reasoning behind this:

> We needed to work out where we are going as an institution, how we see ourselves, and how we present ourselves to the world outside. In other words, we needed to decide collectively what makes Surrey unique and special, what distinguishes us from other universities.

Developed by the senior executives, in particular Professor John Turner, and launched in 1998, the *Statement* set out the core values that would inform the University's future development. It was based on four principles:

- Working for the world
- Taking the lead in research
- Enriching the value of learning
- Building productive partnerships.

'Our vision is of a University working in partnership with industry and commerce to create an institution of real international standing,' said Professor Dowling. A new corporate identity was also introduced, based on the UniS logo alongside the traditional coat-of-arms.

These were bold and confident moves, but also ones that recognised just how much the culture of higher education was changing. Any hope that the new Labour Government of 1997 would be more sympathetic to the academic world had been quickly dashed. The National Committee of Inquiry into Higher Education, chaired by Sir Ron (later Lord) Dearing, had been commissioned under John Major's Government, but the Dearing Report, published two months after the general election, maintained the Opposition's stance. In its wake, maintenance grants were abolished – though this had not been recommended by the Report, which on the contrary suggested they be enhanced – and replaced by student loans, and from the 1998/99 academic year tuition fees of up to £1000 paid up-front directly by the students themselves (or their parents), rather than local authorities as had been the case hitherto, were introduced. There would also be a further decrease in unit funding, with a cut of 6.5 per cent over the next two years, despite the Dearing Report's observation that such a measure would be damaging.

The impact of the Dearing Report on University life was wide ranging. Not the least of it was a drop in student numbers, put off by the fees. The number of applicants fell by 2.7 per cent in 1998 over the previous year, and by a further 0.8 per cent in 1999, though application numbers were to recover quite quickly. The students most vulnerable to the effect of the fee increase were those from less affluent areas and from families with only modest or low incomes. The Government, however, seemingly unconscious of the contradiction in policy, set up national targets to broaden the uptake of university education. In 1999 about 72 per cent of young people from social group A (professional) were in higher education, in contrast to 13 per cent from social group E (unskilled). The University fully supported the Government initiative, though Professor Dowling felt that it would 'be difficult to meet, especially in Surrey, which has highly atypical educational and socio-economic profiles'. A number of ventures to broaden access were set up, including tutoring and mentoring, as well as a bus to visit pupils in local schools.

The Dearing Report also created a more competitive environment between universities, in which the richer, better endowed universities, as well as those that were stronger either overall or in particular subject areas, were likely to win out in the battle for the best students. Students would also come to be much more shrewd in analysing the benefits which a university education would give

The Biotechnology Bus which took science to local schoolchildren was one of the University's successful initiatives for raising aspirations and promoting wider access to university education. Brian Street, Member of University Council and on the Bus Management Committee, is shown with Anne Riggs from the Department of Educational Studies.

them and, especially with the growth of alternative sources of information on the internet, such as thestudentroom.co.uk, increasingly deft in comparing institutions' pros and cons. It was a challenging environment for all concerned.

Building for the Future

Despite the difficulties, the University made considerable academic progress, and also began extending the campus. 'Hand in hand with our new vision, we are progressing the largest building programme on campus since we came to Guildford in the 1960s,' Professor Dowling stated in the *Vision Statement*, with projected capital expenditure to the end of the century of around £50 million. 'In addition to enhanced academic facilities, with the very latest technology, Surrey students continue to see dramatic improvements in social and recreational facilities.'

During the 1990s universities were important and significant architectural patrons. To accommodate the projected rise in student numbers, many set about extensive building projects, and Surrey was among them. By 2010 the building boom at British universities had grown to around £3 billion. Although capital spending was slashed by the HEFCE in 1995 by over 50 per cent in the following three years, this did not deter what was regarded by many

An aerial shot of the Stag Hill campus as it looked at the end of the 1990s.

as necessary outlay – in fact, in many cases, the new buildings were seen as sources of income, through the increasing commercialisation of university activities and provision of sports and science parks (Loughborough and Tamar (Cornwall) Science Parks, for instance, were both founded in the mid-1990s) and other facilities which served an external as well as internal community. Many universities, including Surrey, were also not as reliant on core funding as they had been in earlier years and so they continued to develop their campuses.

By the 1990s, though the original plan of Stag Hill as a clustered hill town with walkways between its three zones and a variety of pedestrian spaces was pretty well intact, the buildings themselves were beginning to show signs of wear. The growth of the University had put a demand on its structures which was way beyond that anticipated thirty years before, and the University also wanted to give physical shape to its forward-looking ethos and vision at the end of the twentieth century. In 1997 HRH The Duke of Kent opened the Austin Pearce Building (Architects Design Partnership), named in honour of the University's Pro-Chancellor Emeritus, Sir Austin Pearce. The £6.6 million building has four lecture theatres, with the rooms able to be combined into two larger spaces, for both University use and hire for conferences and seminars. This period also saw the refurbishment of the Mullens and other academic buildings.

The new buildings that appeared in the decade leading up to the new millennium attempted to give the University a renewed sense of identity.

The Duke of Kent Building, opened in 2000 by HRH The Duke of Kent, which houses the Faculty of Health and Medical Sciences.

HRH The Duke of Kent unveiled a plaque to mark the opening of the building named after him on
13 March 2000. With him are Professor Rosemary Pope (left) who was the Head of the European Institute
of Health and Medical Sciences (EIHMS) from 2000; Professor Jim Bridges, then Head of the European
Institute of Health and Medical Sciences (second left); and, to the Duke's right, the Vice-Chancellor,
Professor Patrick Dowling. Behind the Duke's shoulder is Sir William Wells, then Vice-Chairman of
the University Council.

Perhaps the most successful – and certainly one of the most celebrated – is
the Duke of Kent Building. Completed in 1999 at a cost of £12 million, it
houses the Faculty of Health and Medical Sciences. Named for HRH The
Duke of Kent, who by then had been Chancellor of the University for over
twenty years, the 7500sq m building was opened by him in March 2000.
Looming above the lake like the prow of a ship, the landmark five-storey
metal-clad building houses two floors of teaching rooms, with a further floor
dedicated to computer rooms, laboratories with dedicated clinical skills teaching areas, an ergonomics research facility, a gait laboratory, and a shape, in-
strumentation and micro-engineering laboratory. Natural light floods the
atrium and the use of timber Glulam beams for the roof structure creates a
stunning open-plan area on the top floor, where at the tip of the prow a staff
common room commands wonderful views of the surrounding area.

It has, wrote *Building Design* at the time, 'become a new landmark, visible
from the town centre, the railway and the A3. Its shiny, corseted silhouette is
fashionably sexy …' Standing on the edge of the campus on the pedestrian
route between town, university and cathedral, the Duke of Kent Building links
the three and acts as a gateway to the campus. Designed by architects Nicholas
Grimshaw & Partners, the building won the Concrete Society Award in
2000 as one of the top 100 buildings in the world and, locally, the Guildford
Heritage Award and the Guildford Society Award.

The portrait of Professor Daphne Jackson by Jane Allison, which was commissioned to hang inside the Advanced Technology Institute.

Construction also began on two other innovative buildings that were to open in the early years of the new century. The landmark £10 million Advanced Technology Institute (ATI), designed like the Duke of Kent Building by Christopher Nash of Nicholas Grimshaw & Partners, was opened by Lord Sainsbury of Turville, Minister for Science and Innovation, in October 2002. Research activity in the Advanced Technology Institute spans the fields of solid-state electronics, optoelectronics and photonics, ion beam technology, theoretical and computational modelling and collaborative research in biosensors, food science and so on, to stimulate cross-disciplinary research at the cutting edge of the development of high technology. The facilities include a state-of-the-art laboratory and clean rooms, optical and specialist laboratory workshops, offices and meeting rooms. The University's low-energy approach is evident in the use of natural ventilation for the cellular space and mixed mode ventilation for the open plan research area. A further £4.5 million investment in May 2003

The award-winning School of Management Building, which was opened by Dr Kim Howells MP in 2003.

provided equipment for nanoelectronics research and high performance computing. The building is also known as the Daphne Jackson Building, after the woman who served as Dean of the Faculty of Science for some years (see Chapter 2), and her portrait hangs inside.

The new Advanced Technology Institute, also known as the Daphne Jackson Building after Professor Daphne Jackson, who taught physics for many years.

85

The Surrey European Management School was founded in 1989 and within three years was offering MBA programmes. In 1992 the School opened its first overseas centres, offering MBAs by distance learning in Singapore and Hong Kong. This form of delivery, innovative for the time, was very successful and expanded rapidly over the next five years, so that by the late 1990s the School was operating in ten centres around the world. By then it was also offering an MSc in Management and Masters degrees in specialist areas of business such as marketing and business management.

The second building to be constructed in the late 1990s was the School of Management Building, which was opened by Dr Kim Howells MP, Minister for Higher Education, in 2003. The previous year the School of Management had been formed to bring the Surrey European Management School, by then the largest centre of graduate students on campus, together with two other units, the School of Management Studies for the Service Sector and the Management Development division of the School of Education. The new School building, completed at a cost of £14 million and designed by Caroline Buckingham of HLM Architects, draws the eye with its gold buff bricks on the two upper storeys, strip windows and blue-grey curtain walling for the stair towers. Zinc cladding picks out key features such as the stair tower flanks. A large lecture room seats up to 418 people and there are also seven seminar rooms and computer laboratories. In front of the building is a large open piazza area with seating and a fountain, making it an attractive meeting place for the whole University community.

The Lakeside Restaurant's Head Chef and Manager John Walter with Hospitality students in the restaurant's kitchen.

The building ably demonstrates the University's commitment to sustainability and energy efficiency. The central atrium has triple-glazed windows with integral blinds, and lighting levels are controlled by a sensor on the roof. The building is cooled at night by an absorption chiller utilising waste heat from the University's combined heat and power plant. It has won two awards, a Heritage Award from Guildford Borough Council for Environmental Sustainability and Guildford Society's 2004 Award for Best New Building.

Housed within the building is the Lakeside Restaurant which, as well as being a fundamental part of the School's Hospitality Management programmes, operates as a professional, fully functioning business. It offers lunchtime *à la carte* fine dining, as well as excellent value themed *table d'hote*, such as the medieval and Mexican menus in February and March 2011, prepared by the students. Managed by Head Chef John Walter, the restaurant uses local ingredients wherever possible, and the wine list features Denbies Estate on Surrey's North Downs alongside bottles from as far afield as Lebanon. Lakeside also provides the venue for an increasing number of functions, from wedding breakfasts and birthday celebrations to corporate events. In 2010 John Walter also took a turn on Farnham Food Festival's Cookery Demonstration Trailer, providing culinary tips to enthusiastic local cooks. The University has developed a high reputation for its food, and in 2010 received a Gold award in Surrey County Council's Eat Out Eat Well scheme, which aims to encourage healthy eating. Hilary Harris, the Functions Coordinator at Lakeside, is enthusiastic about the campaign. 'I think it's about increasing public awareness,' she said. 'The award shows a commitment that we have got our customers' best interests at heart. We are not trying to do the "big brother" thing – it's all to do with providing choice.'

Millennium House, nicknamed 'The Train', one of the new residential courts built during the 1990s.

The 1990s also saw expansion of student accommodation. Funding constraints had limited building of campus residences in the 1970s and 1980s and when University Court opened in 1989, it was the first on-campus accommodation to be opened since 1975. Other new student residences soon followed, with the University adding a further 1000 places in nine separate developments between 1989 and 2002; by the end of the period, over half of the University's students who wanted it could be accommodated. Among the new residences were Twyford Court, opened in 1994, and Brickfield Court and Bellerby Court, on the outskirts of the Manor Park campus, five years later. Between them they provide 340 rooms, with a further 50 shared flats at Twyford. Perhaps the most noticeable residential court under construction during the 1990s, however, was Millennium House, known affectionately as 'The Train', and designed by Nicholas Grimshaw & Partners to be in sympathy with the Duke of Kent Building. Completed in 2000 at a cost of £4.5 million, it contains 34 flats of six rooms each.

Local, National and International Links

Professor Dowling is 'arrested' by the Surrey Constabulary to raise money for charity.

When he arrived at Guildford to take up the vice-chancellorship, one of the things Professor Dowling set himself to do was to strengthen the ties with the town; he wanted to make the University of Surrey 'part and parcel of the fabric of Guildford life'. Although the University had been welcomed warmly by Guildford in the late 1960s, by the time Professor Dowling arrived thirty years later, the sense of common purpose had more or less dissipated, though the institution had certainly contributed to local life. There was, as David Watts, Chief Executive of Guildford Borough Council 1984–2002, explained, 'a feeling in the town that the University was up there on the hill, rather remote and self-contained and divorced from the life of the town'.

During the 1990s the University set about strengthening its external bonds. Ties with the cathedral and Guildford's theatres were increased and the University supported the town's (sadly unsuccessful) bids for city status. The University also became more involved in town charity and arts events, such as the annual Book Festival and the Music Festival (see Chapter 5). All this helped to bring town and gown closer together

GUILDFORD 91
international
M U S I C   F E S T I V A L

Patron: Sir Georg Solti KBE

2-17 March 1991

Presented by Guildford Borough Council and the University of
Surrey Music Department and Arts Committee

FREE
OFFICIAL PROGRAMME

so that by the beginning of the twenty-first century, according to David Watts, relationships were 'very cordial and close, and have become increasingly so during the last few years'.

The University also forged strong links with local schools and colleges. In 1991 it founded, with Goldalming and Farnham Colleges, the Surrey Higher Education Compact. John Hobrough, then Dean of Students and Director of the Educational Liaison Centre (ELC), explained that the University 'realised we needed to create "progression routes" to university – in other words, to ease the path for students with the aptitude to study for a degree but who would not succeed in getting to university by the conventional route', and so a number of different routes were created for disadvantaged young people. The initiative expanded rapidly, with 26 other further education colleges in Surrey and the surrounding area, 35 schools and six other higher education institutions joining it.

Top: The programme for the first Guildford Music Festival, 1991.
Left: 'Did the earth move for you?' Tigger and the Vice-Chancellor lead the 'Giant Jump', designed to explain the science of seismology to schoolchildren.

Students benefitted from a range of outreach activities, such as residential taster conferences, and there were also staff development days which brought together teachers from higher and further education and from schools to share expertise. Every student involved in the scheme was guaranteed an interview, with special entry level targets being agreed where appropriate. In the first year just two students from the seven sixth-form colleges in Surrey enrolled; ten years later 11 per cent of the intake came from the Compact scheme.

This was a substantial achievement, and it meant that the University and the other institutions involved were well placed when the Government introduced the drive to widen participation in university in the late 1990s (see above, pp. 76–78). The Compact community, joined by the University of Reading and Kingston University, bid successfully for funding to develop a Regional Accord partnership. This was designed to build and improve the routes into higher education on a regional basis, through shared best practice and strategic planning. Through the scheme many hundreds of students were able to gain higher education places that might otherwise have been beyond them. Following the 2004 Schwartz Report into Fair Admissions to Higher Education, however, the Regional Compact Accord ceased to operate collectively. Several years later the University of Surrey developed a new scheme, In2Surrey, which again allows the use of contextual information in the admissions process. Set in train in 2009, the first students from the newly defined target schools and colleges are expected to apply in 2012.

A University psychology student mentoring a sixth form student from Kings College, Guildford.

Alongside Compact, the University also began some imaginative mentoring and tutoring schemes for local school and college children. These proved so popular and resilient that, despite the ongoing funding and secondary curricula changes, by 2010 the University's ELC was training and facilitating around 250 students as mentors or tutors across nearly 60 schools and colleges. An associated scheme, Schools Without Walls, for sixth-form volunteers in local (mostly primary) schools, was by then operating satellite schemes in the Woking, Farnborough and Aldershot areas. The schemes are an important part of student volunteering. The students are carefully monitored and receive accreditation for their participation, so that it is something they can add to their CVs, but as John Hobrough, Director of ELC in the 1990s, explained, 'most of them find the experience rewarding in its own right and find that it extends their whole outlook on life'.

In the 1990s Guildford was rapidly transforming itself into an economic, commercial and cultural hub for Surrey and its surrounding counties. In 1995 the Government Office for the South East in Guildford (GOSE; the regional government) and, more significantly, the South East England Development Agency (SEEDA; the regional development agency) established their headquarters in the town. This had the effect of making Guildford the regional capital in government and administrative terms, encouraging a range of national and regional initiatives to promote economic growth. It also led to more concrete rewards for the University. As part of its collaborative research and development programme, in 2006 SEEDA awarded a £215,000 grant towards the installation and set-up of a nanogrowth machine at the Advanced Technology Institute. The seed funding encouraged almost £1 million of private sector investment and Surrey NanoSystems, a spin-out joint venture with thin film tool manufacturer CEVP, was later set up to commercialise the technology. The Labour Government's establishment of regional offices and agencies was, however, to be overturned by the Coalition Government in 2010, which abolished both GOSE (in 2010) and SEEDA (scheduled for closure in 2012).

It was also during this period that the University began to make a more focused effort to attract foreign students and to forge international links. Encouraging a diverse cultural background among its students had been part of the University's ethos going back to Battersea days, and when the number

Campus life in the 1990s: as a result of a concerted drive to increase overseas students, their numbers increased dramatically during the period.

91

of foreign students fell sharply in the early 1980s, following the increase in fees, Surrey decided to be proactive in their recruitment. This was not solely because of the financial incentive. While the payment of full fees by such students was to be important in filling the University's coffers, there were other reasons for increasing their attendance, as Gwyn Brown, Dean of International Students 1986–2006, noted:

> The University really felt the lack of overseas students – it simply became a less diverse, and therefore less interesting, place – and we started to appreciate the positive contribution overseas students made both culturally and academically. In addition we realised how much Surrey had to offer students from overseas, who generally view the decision to travel abroad to study as an investment in their future career. Our vocationally focused courses would therefore have enormous appeal to such students.

Taking the attitude that the academics themselves were best placed to promote the University abroad, Vice-Chancellor Anthony Kelly had created the post of Dean of International Students – well ahead of most universities – and in 1991 he established an International Office both to promote Surrey abroad and to manage the welfare of students once they were at Guildford. The increase was slow at first, but by 2001 there were 2111 foreign students, 815 from the EU and the rest from elsewhere, with the great majority of non-EU students coming from the Far East; the total number of full-time undergraduates in 2000/01 was 5285. The increase in the number of foreign students gave the campus, as Fiona Wareham, President of the Students' Union 2000/01, commented, a welcome 'multicultural atmosphere' which added:

> enormously to student life. Just coming to university and learning to live and work with other people teaches you a lot. Here you are also having to get along with people from every part of the world, and this makes the whole experience much richer.

Surrey academics also began to travel abroad regularly, on recruitment missions to feeder institutions, to give lectures and to explore joint research projects, sometimes working with the British Council and similar bodies responsible for promoting British interests in higher education abroad. This was successful in establishing several small exchange schemes for students with universities in the United States and Europe, as well as Singapore and Melbourne. In common with other universities, Surrey also began to create links with similar institutions at an academic level, sharing expertise and co-operating on research projects. The Technical Universities of Prague and Warsaw were rewarding contacts for the Department of Electronic Engineering, and links across several disciplines, including medical science and toxicology, IT and nutrition, have been established with institutions in Finland and the Baltic states. The Guildford Consortium, a non-profit-making group of educational institutions and some twenty small and medium businesses, was formed in 1990 to build education and training capacity in Russia and Eastern Europe. Among its projects have been setting up a small business advice centre and updating the curricula for business studies at Nizhny Novgorod Federal Commercial Institute of Higher Education.

The Federal University and Associated Institutions

At home, the senior management team was keen to formalise the University's links with other universities. In 1994, the University, along with 19 other institutions, founded the 1994 Group, which brings together internationally renowned, research-intensive universities in order to promote their common interests, act as a vehicle for responding to key policy issues and share best methods and practice. The University of Surrey has also benefitted from the networking facility which it affords and the advantage of being able to be recognised and to lobby as part of a research-intensive group.

There was also a move at this time to expand the Guildford 'family', through creating a federal university and associations with like-minded institutions.

The creation of the Federal University of Surrey: senior academics and administrative staff from the University and Roehampton Institute sign the Instrument of Accreditation in 1991. This permitted the Institute to approve taught courses for University of Surrey degrees. Back row, from left: James Strawson, Deputy University Secretary (later University Secretary); Professor Peter Butterworth, Senior Pro-Vice-Chancellor; Professor Alan Crocker, Department of Physics; Gill Redford, Principal of Froebel College, Roehampton; Dr Peter Weston of Roehampton Institute. Front row, from left: unknown; Professor Anthony Kelly, Vice-Chancellor; Professor Stephen Holt, Rector of Roehampton Institute; Peter Beardsley, Academic Registrar of the University.

This would, the Vice-Chancellor felt, increase 'the capacity and strength of each individual institution'. On 1 January 2000 the University of Surrey and Roehampton Institute became a federal university, the latter becoming the University of Surrey Roehampton. Neither a merger nor a takeover of one institute by the other, this was more an agreement to work together in their common interests. The move was the result of two years' deliberations, but their association went back much further.

In early 1980 the University had held preliminary discussions with some London institutions which eventually led to it validating courses elsewhere. The first of these was at Roehampton Institute of Higher Education. Later a similar set-up was established with St Mary's College, Strawberry Hill, and there were smaller-scale links with others. The thought was that these fellow educational establishments, with their focus mainly on arts subjects, would balance Surrey's technological and science bias. In 1980 Surrey began to validate courses at Roehampton, and later it gradually took over delegated responsibility to award its own degrees. Then, in 1998, as a result of their continuing relationship, the two institutions began to explore the possibility of federation.

Federation was marked by a formal ceremony and a service at Westminster Abbey, with an historic Act of Dedication written especially for the event. Professor Patrick Dowling commented at the time: 'The extension of the University of Surrey's Royal Charter, giving us the power to federate with other institutions, is a unique development in UK higher education. Federation will add value to our activities by enabling us to work in partnership with each other. I look forward to the development of many joint ventures involving, where appropriate, other institutions associated with the University of Surrey.'

The alliance offered, on the one hand, for the University of Surrey, a London presence, and access to Roehampton's core arts subjects, while Roehampton benefitted from the link with the University of Surrey's strengths in science and engineering. The collaboration was, however, to prove short-lived. Though some joint courses were developed, most notably one in Local History, in August 2004 Roehampton became a university in its own right.

The University of Surrey also created links with other institutions, however. It validated courses at and subsequently accredited St Mary's University College and Wimbledon School of Art, and also validated courses at the following institutions: North East Surrey College of Technology (Nescot), Guildford College of Further and Higher Education, St John's Seminary, Farnborough College of Technology (it gained accredited status in 2002) and the Southern Theological Education and Training Scheme (STETS). These associations meant that Surrey and the institutions involved could offer a full panoply of courses in the region, complementing each other in offering teaching and expertise in areas outside those of the individual institutions. The University of Surrey also added to its art collection by purchasing pieces from

Wimbledon School of Art, something that has continued under succeeding Vice-Chancellors. The twenty-first century would, however, see Surrey broadening its offering to offer arts courses of its own.

Trapeze Artist by Natalie Staniforth, a sculptor who trained at Wimbledon School of Art, one of the University's accredited institutions during the 1990s. The piece was bought for the University collection by Pat Grayburn, Arts Administrator, and is on display in the Austin Pearce Building.

Campus Life

While the new residences made the biggest difference to student life during the 1990s, there were other changes too. The number of foreign students increased, as noted, giving the campus a cosmopolitan air, and there were dramatic increases too in the number of postgraduate students, particularly those on taught courses, reflecting the demand for higher level qualifications in an increasingly global and competitive employment market. Students following a part-time option were also more evident, their numbers rising from 820 in 1989/90 to 2584 in 1999/2000.

The atmosphere among the students changed too. Gone was the radicalism of the early 1980s, with students much less likely to be politically motivated. Partly, reflected Adam Jakeway, President of the Students' Union 2000/01, this was because of the necessity in the years preceding the millennium for students to pay fees:

> It impacts on every aspect of student life, and certainly affects the effort students put into working for their degree. A lot more students have to work part-time to survive financially. This in turn affects their willingness to participate in student life.

Nevertheless, the Students' Union remained active, running six bars and food outlets, and up to four club nights per week, as well as sponsoring over 60 societies. Alongside 'WORK, and lots of it', Peter Kench (student 1994–2001) remembers regular 100-mile-long 'road racing, like the Tour de France, but round the Surrey lanes dodging horse-boxes instead!'

Students outside Chancellors Bar, 1990s.

A typical student room, 1990s. By then, personal computers were becoming common and individual rooms had their own telephones.

Perhaps the most impactful way in which student life changed during the period was in the use of personal computers, whose spread became a global phenomenon. For universities, first academics and then students, it was the growth of the internet following the development of the world wide web by physicist Tim Berners-Lee in 1989 that was most significant. Today, in an age when smartphones allow us all to have the world at our fingertips, it is hard to imagine how cumbersome the first computers were and how much effort was involved in communication. The first web browser and the first dial-up availability arrived in 1993, while the advent of the various Windows operating systems (the first was launched in 1985) made using computers much easier. The two together brought an explosion of computer use, both inside academia and outside it.

At Surrey, the first computers arrived in the mid-1980s. The computer lab was originally located in the Library and there were three stand-alone personal computers (PCs). During the 1990s the number of computers in the lab grew slowly from around twenty to fifty by 1997, when the move of IT to the Austin Pearce Building precipitated major change. By the end of the 1990s there were 200 computers in computer labs with open access (that is, 24-hour-use availability), and over 1000 other PCs around the campus in central computer labs and in the Faculties. Dial-up network access was by then available in the residences. The difference it made to student life was considerable.

The growth of PCs since 1990 has been dramatic, but it is outshone by the growth of internet usage, echoing the general adoption of digital communication, particularly among the technically aware students attracted to Surrey.

Internet use generally grew enormously during the decade – from 9 per cent of British households in 1998 to 52 per cent of households in 2004, and 73 per cent of households in 2011, with 60 per cent of adults accessing the internet on a daily basis – and the University's use reflects this. In 2004, the University established its own residential network (its ISP), with 50Mb bandwidth. This grew, first to 200Mb in 2007, then to 300Mb a year later, to 600Mb in 2009, and more recently to 1Gb: a twentyfold increase in just over six years. Internet access for the total campus is now at 3Gb capacity, allowing researchers to access live data from their desktops on campus.

By 2005, there was some wireless access available in some of the University's communal areas, its restaurants, common rooms and coffee rooms; now all the main buildings have wireless access. For the later generations of students, a laptop and, increasingly, a smartphone have became an essential part of their life, as vital to them as a toothbrush, as they are constantly online. There are now 30,000 computer ports on campus, 4000 of which are in the residences, and over 400 wireless hotspots, meaning students can connect up from most of the campus. Typically, around 1500 users will be connected to the internet simultaneously through a wireless link during the day.

In the early 1990s conventional phones were largely in use. Today Voice over Internet Protocol (VoIP) phones are provided in the residences and all new buildings, enabling students to make free calls and reducing overall costs. Academic delivery now makes heavy use of a virtual learning environment, which first became available in 2004, allowing lecturers to provide online notes, resources, discussions and assignments related to teaching modules. This is used by students working on campus, at home or increasingly by students taking Surrey programmes all over the world, particularly in China. The strong technological component of the University's academic programme and its international stature means it attracts students and staff with high expectations of information technology. This continues to push the development of the services provided both on campus and increasingly to a mobile worldwide user base. The IT team, led by Director Roger Stickland, relishes the challenge that advances in technology and rising expectations of users bring.

Strengthening Research

In the late 1990s the University increasingly focused on raising its research profile. Although a great deal had been achieved in the past decade, not least with the establishment of the Research Park (see Chapter 4), the senior management team felt that, as Vice-Chancellor Patrick Dowling said, 'much remained to be done'. The University wanted both to 'achieve real excellence consistently across every area of the University's work' and to get as much public recognition as possible 'for the University as a whole and for individuals within it'.

One way of achieving this was to attract really good young scholars to the University, and in Professor Dowling's first year the Investing in Excellence scheme was established to bring exceptional young lecturers and scientists to Surrey. In all twenty new posts were created, largely paid for by the Foundation Fund (which at that time allocated the majority of income derived from the Research Park). Three Foundation Fund professors were also appointed, with low teaching and administrative loads so that they could focus on research. Twenty-one further Foundation lectureships were supported three years later, in January 1998.

Another initiative was the Surrey Scholars Scheme, launched with a flourish at St James's Palace in March 1997. Underlining the University's desire to collaborate with industry, each scholar in the scheme was sponsored by a particular company or organisation and worked on a key problem in his or her area of activity. In its first five years, the scheme attracted over £1 million of sponsorship from blue-chip companies including Corus, Fina and Petrofina, National Grid, Philips, Unilever and Vodafone, as well as organisations such as Guildford Borough Council and the Lattice Foundation. While it had some notable successes, with the connections students forged giving them a foothold in companies for whom they later worked, the scheme failed to create the new links anticipated and it later petered out. Today, a range of performance-related scholarships are available, as well as bursaries for those from less well-off families.

The launch of the Surrey Scholars Scheme at St James's Palace, London. HRH The Duke of Kent, the University Chancellor, sits in front. Behind him, left to right: Douglas Robertson (University Council); Professor Patrick Dowling, Vice-Chancellor, Sir George Edwards, Pro-Chancellor Emeritus; unknown; Sir Diarmuid Downs (University Council).

Guildford Borough Council sponsored a Surrey Scholar in Environmental Sustainability to conduct research on transport, air pollution and health in the local area. This was Dr Birgitta Gatersleben, based in the Department of Psychology. An experienced researcher from the Netherlands, she specialised in environmental attitudes and behaviour. She is shown here with David Watts, Chief Executive of Guildford Borough Council (left) and the Deputy Mayor of Guildford Borough Council, Councillor Tony Phillips.

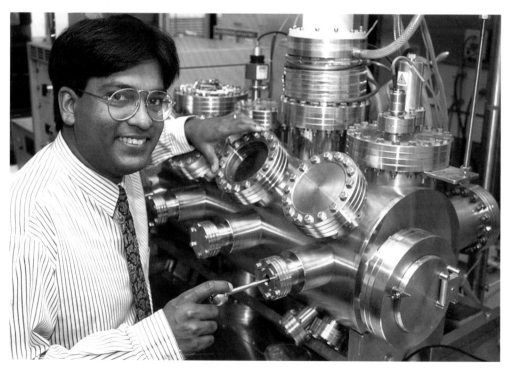

Professor Ravi Silva, possibly the youngest ever Professor of Electronic Engineering in the UK, joined Surrey in 1995. In 2007, he was runner-up for the *Times Higher Education* Young Scientist of the Year. He was elected a Fellow of the Royal Society of Arts in 2007 and a Fellow of the Royal Academy of Engineering in 2008.

The University also made great strides in further developing expertise in particular fields, establishing a number of research centres. In the early 1990s Anthony Kelly had identified four growth areas: satellite engineering, the environment, health sciences and management (see Chapter 4 for more details of research projects). In October 1992 the multidisciplinary Centre for Environmental Strategy (CES) opened, headed by Professor Roland Clift, previously Head of the Department of Chemical and Process Engineering (in 2008 Professor Matthew Leach, past Chair of Council of the British Institute of Energy Economics, took over the position from Chris France who had succeeded Roland Clift in 2005 after many years as his long-standing deputy). This new venture brought together those from a range of disciplines, from engineering through natural and social sciences to economics and philosophy, to find answers to environmental and sustainable development problems, including the design and management of sustainable technologies, systems and infrastructures, and to develop policy and industry-relevant responses to long-term environmental and social issues.

The following year, on 3 December 1993, the Environmental Flow Research Centre was opened by HRH The Duke of Kent, with Professor Ian Castro as its Founder-Director (in 2001, when Professor Castro moved to the University of Southampton,

A student in the Faculty of Engineering works on particulate and multiphase flow metering.

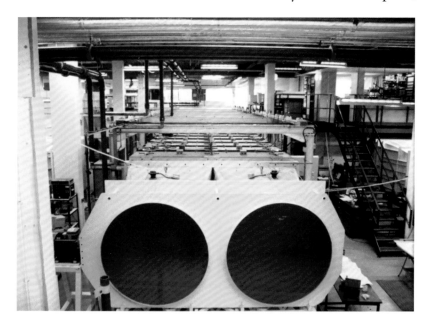

Environmental Flow Research Centre facilities include a fully computer-controlled wind tunnel donated by National Power plc, equipped with comprehensive inlet flow and surface heating and cooling systems for generating neutral, stable and unstable boundary layers and neutral and stable free flows.

Professor Alan Robins succeeded him as Director, a role he continues to hold). The Centre's two large research facilities, the 20-metre wind tunnel and the 12-metre-long towing tank, both donated by National Power, make it a nationally unique resource for studying fluid flow and pollutant dispersion in the Earth's atmosphere, as well as wind power. Also opened in the early 1990s, the Centre for Environmental Health Engineering (now part of the Division of Civil, Chemical and Environmental Engineering) explores the entire water cycle, with projects ranging from water resources surveillance, modelling and management; water treatment, supply and regulation; wastewater treatment, disposal and safe re-use; to pollution control and waste management.

Medical course provision has a long history at Surrey, and the Department of Nursing was one of the first university departments in Britain to run undergraduate degree courses for nurses and midwives. In 1995, the European Institute of Health and Medical Sciences (from 2007, the Division of Health and Social Care of the Faculty of Health and Medical Sciences), headed by Professor Jim Bridges, was established, breaking new ground in providing education and health training for health and medical professionals, and uniting the University's Department of Nursing and Midwifery with three health care colleges formerly part of the NHS. Two years later, elements of the Robens School for Public and Environmental Health joined it, and in the same year courses in chiropractice were introduced. By the turn of the century, the Institute had grown into one of the largest Schools in the University, training over 1000 full-time undergraduate nurses and midwives and 1500 health care professionals in a range of continuing professional development courses.

Those studying midwifery practise their skills in the unit's simulation suite before going out into midwifery practice at one of the local NHS Trust hospitals. Here students monitor a young baby.

The Digital World Research Centre aims to develop user-centred digital media technology. Here, researchers in India were supporting digital storytelling on Nokia phones, to aid the sharing of audiovisual information by communities with limited literacy. Professor David Frohlich and local ethnographer Maxine Frank demonstrate the Story Bank repository to three schoolboys on the balcony of the village ICT centre.

Research focused on five broad themes: older people; mental health; communities, organisations and health; education and health care; and the clinical aspects of care. Practice Development Units, which provided forums for discussion of evidence-based practice and education and identified practice-related issues in need of review, and Clinical Academic Units, which disseminated best practice in relation to the care of patients, provided the essential links between research and clinical practice. At around the same time, and in similar vein, a Centre for Neurosciences was formed, bringing together expertise in fundamental and applied neuroscience, and working closely with clinical neuroscientists in regional hospitals and with pharmaceutical companies.

During the 1990s the Department of Psychology became the largest UK provider of postgraduate psychology training, offering courses to meet the needs of the NHS, the police, the prison service and business. Its research on colour perception showed that, contrary to widespread belief, people from different language groups see colours differently. The Digital World Research Centre, opened in 1998 and the first UK centre of its kind, is a collaboration between social scientists and engineers dedicated to researching how people interact with digital technology. 'Our research findings will have a real impact on future technological innovation and business strategies,' said Dr Richard Harper, the Centre's first Director. The Centre also puts considerable emphasis on developing and forging links with business and industry. Among other centres that opened in the late 1990s were the Centre for Vision, Speech and Signal Processing, under Director Professor Josef Kittler, and the Centre for Research on Ageing and Gender which was set up under the directorship of Professor Sara Arber and Dr Kate Davidson (the latter retired from the Department of Sociology in 2009). The Uni**S** Materials Institute, which was set up by Professors John Watts, John Hay and Peter McDonald (from 2002 this was called the Surrey Materials Institute), united the University's materials-related activities from a variety of disciplines, for research on interface science and engineering, surface phenomena and materials functionality, with applications in such areas as health care, crime and security, and smart materials. First headed by Peter McDonald, John Watts took over as Director in 2004.

One of the most innovatory centres established at this time was perhaps the Institute of Sound Recording, headed by David Fisher. Founded in 1998, it has since developed an international reputation in psychoacoustic engineering and research into the human perception of sound. Home to the world-famous Tonmeister™ undergraduate degree course in Music and Sound Recording, it has also completed several successful projects in collaboration with industry, with companies ranging from Bang & Olufsen to BBC Research and Development, the Institut für Rundfunktechnik and Sony BPE.

By the end of the decade, the Research Park had also become a significant part of the University of Surrey. Among noteworthy collaborations between Research Park tenants and the University in the 1990s were those of BOC Gases and process and chemical engineering specialists at the University which resulted in new food freezing techniques for the food processing industry,

A student practises his skills in the Institute of Sound Recording.

and AGROL's collaboration with the School of Biological Sciences in the development of superbugs to turn agricultural waste into ethanol. Income from the Research Park was now increasingly significant: during the 1990s £26 million was handed to the University, approximately half of which was used to fund building projects, and half academic ones such as the Digital World Research Centre (mentioned above) and new lectureships.

Recognition and Awards

The growing depth and breadth of the University's research bore fruit in the Research Assessment Exercise (RAE) for 1996, which revealed a marked improvement over the previous one. Electrical and Electronic Engineering's rating rose from 5 to the new top rating of 5*, placing it among the top departments in the country. Toxicology retained its 5 rating and Sociology

Professor Alf Adams (right), who was made a Fellow of the Royal Society in recognition of his ground-breaking discovery of the strained quantum well laser, now at the heart of digital technology worldwide. This photograph was taken in 2004 when he was awarded a 'Proof of Concept' by the University's Research and Enterprise Department. Head of Enterprise, Anthony Woolhouse (left), presented the prize.

moved up from a 4 (in 1992) to 5 to join it. There were now 12 departments with a 4 ranking. In all, 22 per cent of the University's research-active staff were now in departments rated 5 or 5*, signifying 'world-class' research standard. By the time of the next RAE, in 2001, Surrey was making its mark among the top-rated research academic institutions. Three research groups achieved the 5* rating: Electronic Engineering (which included Computing), Subjects Allied to Medicine (the research activities of the School of Biomedical and Life Sciences, the Postgraduate Medical School, the Human Psychopharmacology Unit and the European Institute of Health and Medical Sciences) and Sociology. A further seven subjects achieved a 5 rating. This meant that a remarkable 60 per cent of the University's research-active staff now worked in areas ranked 'world-class'.

Such results were, naturally, a source of pride throughout the University, and satisfaction that its strategy to achieve research excellence was not only working, but being recognised externally. The response of Professor Bill Gelletly (Head of the Department of Physics 1993–97; Head of the School of Physics and Chemistry, 1997–2002) was typical:

> It is very pleasing that the RAE Panel has recognised the high quality of the research of our mainly young staff. Their work is imbued not only with the true spirit of intellectual enquiry but with an entrepreneurial spirit as well, in tune with the ethos of UniS. This is the platform on which Surrey's Physics Department will go from strength to strength and contribute not only to our understanding of the world around us but to improvements in the quality of life of all our fellow citizens.

Money of course follows success, and so research grants and funding became much easier to acquire in the years that followed, but the achievements of the University were also now being recognised on an individual basis. Honours from learned societies gathered pace. In 1996, to the heartfelt acclaim of his colleagues at Surrey, Professor Alf Adams (now Distinguished Professor of Physics) was made a Fellow of the Royal Society, perhaps the most eminent and certainly the oldest scientific academy in the world. His election was in honour of his discovery of the strained quantum well laser which is now at the heart of most technologies that require the transfer of digital information, such as CDs and DVDs, as well as powering the internet, memory devices and printers. About one billion are made each year, representing a market of around $10 billion annually, making it almost certainly the Surrey invention with the greatest commercial impact.

This was the first Fellowship of the Royal Society (FRS) to be awarded to the University, although Joseph Kenyon, Head of Chemistry at Battersea (see p. 12) had been a recipient of it almost 60 years earlier. Vice-Chancellor Patrick Dowling was elected FRS at the same time. Today, there are four Fellows of the Royal Society, 21 Fellows of the Royal Academy of Engineering, one Fellow of the British Academy and six Fellows of the Academy of Social Sciences. This means it has one of the highest number of academicians for a university of its size and age, a remarkable achievement. The calibre of the University's staff was also recognised in the appointment of a number of staff to advisory panels for the government and NGOs. In the mid-1990s, for instance, five Surrey staff members (Professors Roland Clift, Barry Evans, Nigel Gilbert, Michael Kelly and Martin Sweeting) served on panels for the Government's Technology Foresight Programme, which aimed to help the business community, scientists and engineers to cooperate in exploiting emerging markets and new technologies, while Professor Jim Bridges, then Head of the European Institute of Health and Medical Sciences, was one of 16 scientists on the European Commission's Scientific Steering Committee.

The decade had begun with an award from The Queen, and it was to end with not one, but two. During the 1990s the Surrey Space Centre and its commercial development arm, SSTL, under Professor Martin Sweeting, had continued to develop microsatellites and to work on a wide range of subsystems for other satellite missions, and the development of a smaller nanosatellite and larger minisatellite. In 1997 SSTL was selected as the only non-US supplier to NASA's Rapid Spacecraft Acquisition Programme. During the past seven years its microsatellites had been used on ten low Earth orbit missions, and a further five missions were scheduled to be launched in 1998/99. It was in recognition of this work, its excellence in teaching and

The University was awarded The Queen's Anniversary Prize for Higher and Further Education in 1997.

research work in satellite engineering and communications (which also honoured the University's Centre for Communication Systems Research) that in 1997 it was awarded The Queen's Anniversary Prize for Higher and Further Education. The following year, SSTL was awarded The Queen's Award for Technological Achievement for the development of low-cost lightweight satellites.

HM The Queen visited the campus for the second time on 4 December 1998 when she presented Professor Martin Sweeting of the Surrey Space Centre with The Queen's Award for Technological Achievement. With her are Franco Ongaro from the European Space Agency (left) and Mark Allery from SSTL.

The Queen herself presented the second award when she visited the University of Surrey on 4 December 1998, accompanied by HRH The Duke of Edinburgh. In accepting it, Professor Martin Sweeting, Director of the Surrey Space Centre, remarked on the Centre being 'a unique environment where the synergy of both academic excellence and commercial enterprise applied to small satellites has achieved remarkable results in pioneering affordable access to, and the exploitation of, space'.

On this, her second visit to the University, The Queen toured an exhibition of Surrey's work in the Austin Pearce Building and met University high-fliers, among them the four medal winners at the Kuala Lumpur Commonwealth Games held three months earlier. At the Surrey Space Centre's newly extended building the visitors donned clean room coats to enter the assembly, integration and test facilities. Here they saw three satellites under construction, PICOSat, a microsatellite for the US Air Force, UoSAT-12, a 350kg University of Surrey experimental minisatellite, and TiungSat, a microsatellite built for Malaysia through a technology transfer programme. The Duke of Edinburgh also inaugurated the Surrey Space Club, an international forum for the sharing of research and ideas, which is also intended to act as a spur to international collaboration on research projects, and even cooperation in the joint launching of constellations of satellites.

The University had come a long way. Looking back in 2002, Vice-Chancellor Patrick Dowling felt that 'Our own research profile has been transformed over the past decade, as the 2001 Research Assessment Exercise demonstrated. Now 89 per cent of our research is rated as of either international or national significance.' The University's income from research

University of Surrey alumnus Ross Brewer is the four times British Men's Artistic Gymnastics Champion 2003–2006 and also competed for England at three Commonwealth Games, winning two team Gold medals – the first in 1998 in Kuala Lumpur and second in 2002 in Manchester – and one team Bronze in Melbourne. He was one of the University athletes who met the Queen on her visit in 1998. (Ross Brewer)

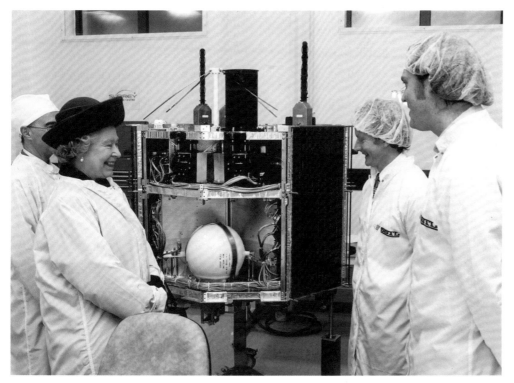

Wearing sterile clothing, HM The Queen visited the clean room in the Surrey Space Centre on her second visit to the campus.

grants and contracts had also doubled in the 1990s, bringing it towards the top of the research league, alongside such luminaries as Oxford, Cambridge and the London School of Economics. Surrey now needed to 'reinforce and extend our international reputation for leading-edge research', but the University would give equal attention to applied research, developing and commercialising products in association with partner companies. 'We stand ready,' Professor Dowling said, 'to meet the challenges of the next century as an institution that understands the real world.'

Chapter 4

Research, Enterprise and Innovation

When Vice-Chancellor Christopher Snowden joined the University in 2005, one of the things that he determined to focus on was research, which he saw as fundamental to its role:

> The University is a research-led institution pursuing learning, scholarship and research with the aim of advancing and disseminating knowledge. We are committed to working closely with our students, business, government and civil society to transition knowledge to the benefit of humanity.

Since the millennium, and especially in the years since his appointment, the University has become increasingly research-led. There has been a drive to recruit world-class researchers in key areas. In Strategy 2007–2017, Professor Snowden highlighted 'Increase in the quality and volume of research' as one of the key strategic challenges for the University; while Surrey's research record had 'traditionally been strong', its challenge now was 'to attain a rate of growth in research income which will support the quality and volume of research to which we aspire'.

The need to grow research also reflected changes in government policy. The 2002 government report *Investing in Innovation*, following that year's Spending Review, promised a 'substantial and dedicated stream of capital for universities, worth £500 million per year by 2004–05, to develop their science research infrastructure and to allow them to plan their future with certainty'. The research councils were to benefit from an additional £120 million from 2005–06 and there was to be 'an additional £50 million per year by 2005–06 to support collaborative research and development on key emerging and pervasive technologies such as nanotechnology'. The Government planned to expand the Higher Education Innovation Fund (HEIF) and, in response to the Roberts Review of the supply of people with science, technology, engineering and mathematics skills, the PhD stipend for research council-funded students would be increased by 25 per cent.

The following year, Charles Clarke, Secretary of State for Education and Skills, outlined the Government's vision in *The Future of Higher Education*: 'We see a higher education sector which meets the needs of the economy in terms of trained people, research and technology transfer.' The Government would increase spending on research and support the establishment of twenty Knowledge Exchanges. A new Arts and Humanities Research Council was to be set up. There were downsides: a larger proportion of the core grant would be dependent on performance ratings, and in future universities would need to look to endowments and other means for a higher proportion of their income.

For the University of Surrey, knowledge transfer and commercialisation of research is key. Vice-Chancellor Patrick Dowling saw Guildford as the 'hub of a world-class region with a significant concentration of knowledge-based

NUGENT ROAD

10	Kobe Steel Europe Ltd
20	Policy Master plc
20	Signal Computing Ltd
20	Caradon Plastics Ltd

Roads on the Research Park are named after eminent scientists and technologists, and Surrey personalities. Here Lord Nugent (1907–94), the long-serving MP for Guildford who was such a support to the University in its early days, stands by the sign that bears his name.

companies and research', and at the end of 2000 Uni**S**ventures was set up to cover the University's spin-off activities. In 2001/02 its intellectual property rights section's licensing income increased to £105,000, with the University holding 31 revenue-generating patents. The University's Business Skills Unit (funded by the HEFCE's Higher Education Reach Out to Business and Community scheme) provided an interface between business and industry, identifying business needs and then finding ways in which the University could fulfil them through courses delivered off-campus, distance learning packages and consultancy. A business hatchery helped budding entrepreneurs bring their ideas to market. Uni**S**direct also had venture capital to provide seed funding for spin-out enterprises.

Uni**S**direct became Research and Enterprise Support (RES) in 2006. The key difference is in bringing together the various support functions, 'with one common goal which is to maximise the value to the University and impact of our research in both societal and commercial terms,' says Keith Robson, its Director. It has been an effective change: Hospitality and Food Management, one of the stars of Faculty enterprise, has attracted healthy research grants and contracts for a number of government and industry bodies including the Department of Trade and Industry, the World Tourism Organization, the Food Standards Agency and the International Travel Catering Association.

The University of Surrey's growing research activities and the increasing level of both its research grants and contracts and income from knowledge transfer and spin-out companies has, despite the recent recession, been an

The Rt Hon. David Willetts MP, Universities and Science Minister, at the SETsquared 10th anniversary conference 'Changing Worlds', 13 October 2010. (SetSquared Partnership)

undoubted success story of the past ten years. In 2009, the University was one of 12 institutions to be awarded a £3.85 million Knowledge Transfer Account by the Engineering and Physical Sciences Research Council (EPSRC), and it was also granted two of the fifty Doctoral Training Centres (worth £12 million, and supporting 12 students each) by the EPSRC to run for five years from 2009 (Micro and Nanomaterials and Technologies, and Sustainability for Engineering and Energy Systems). These are, says Professor Matt Leach of the Centre for Environmental Strategy, 'major investments by the research councils in PhD level training here, and engage us directly with many leading companies, which is very valuable, and reinforces the University's claim to be "number one for jobs"'.

In a virtuous circle, with research grants and income from contracts with commercial enterprises rising, and thereby the quantity and quality of research increasing, the University has also seen a rise in its RAE-related grant. This has made it less reliant on government cash, something of particular value in today's stringent economic climate. The Research Park has to date passed £71 million to the University and the sale of SSTL released over £35 million. Much of this can be seen in concrete form in the new buildings that have risen around the campus, but it is also evident in investment in research, new academic posts and support of new ventures.

Hot Topic speakers at the FHMS Festival of Research, 2009. Left to right: Malcolm von Shantz (Sleep and Chronobiology Research Theme), Andrzej Kierzek (Systems Biology Research Theme), Anne Arber (Health Care Practice Research Theme), Katrina Charles (Public and Environmental Health Research Theme), Nick Plant (Pharmacology and Toxicology Research Theme), Guy Simpson (Cancer Research Theme), Graham Stewart (Infectious Diseases Research Theme) and Johnjoe McFadden (Materials and Nanoscience Research Theme).

The organisation into four Faculties in 2007 was intended to promote a more coordinated approach to research and enable the University to make strategic bids to major funding bodies. The 'Incubator Centre', the Surrey Technology Centre, has also been instrumental in enabling innovative small businesses to make the transition from research to commercialisation. In 2001, the SETsquared Partnership was established by the University of Surrey and the Universities of Bath, Bristol and Southampton; Exeter joined in 2011. The Partnership, whose 7000-plus academics collectively receive nearly 9 per cent of the UK research budget, makes joint bids for funding and maintains and promotes close links with industry, both nationally and internationally, through research collaboration and consultancy. It specialises in the commercialisation and transfer of the universities' research and technologies, and through their business incubation and acceleration centres provides support for new businesses. To date, the top five spin-out companies from the Partnership have created a combined market capitalisation of over £230 million, the Partnership has raised over £225 million of follow-on funding for ventures in difficult markets and it currently supports around 200 high-tech start-up companies through its business acceleration centres.

In October 2010, Professor Snowden reported that the University's research income had grown over 35 per cent in the past two years and that in the recent *Times Higher Education* World League Tables, Surrey was a contender in the top 100 in all categories except 'Citations'. The latter, an 'Achilles heel', is something, says Professor Snowden, to which the University needs to give some attention:

> We must also address the quality of our research publications and recognise that it is essential to publish in specific highly ranked journals to attract citations on our papers. Doing this consistently from now on and over the next three years could raise the University into the Top 100 in the World League Table and position us to perform well in the Research Excellence Framework [the successor to RAE].

In the 2008 RAE, 88 per cent of the University of Surrey's research was rated as 'world class' or of 'international' grade. The RAE was different from previous ones, with graded quality profiles rather than one fixed point, and gradings ranging from 4* ('Quality that is world-leading in terms of originality, significance and rigour') to 1* ('Quality that is recognised nationally in terms of originality, significance and rigour'). This meant that *Times Higher Education* used a grade point average to rank institutions. Surrey was equal 35th, with 16 per cent of its staff ranked as 4*, 39 per cent as 3*, 34 per cent as 2* and 11 per cent as 1*. Four areas of research activity were ranked in the top ten – Allied Health Professions and Studies (joint 3rd), Electrical and Electronic Engineering (2nd), General Engineering and Mineral and Mining Engineering (9th) and Sociology (6th) – and nine areas in the top twenty.

Even in its Battersea days, the University was involved in research, but while important, it was but a small part of its activities. Today, research is integral to the ethos and strategy of Surrey. While the University is justly proud of the early achievements of the Surrey Space Centre and advances in technology, it conducts research across all four Faculties. Students benefit from this through their involvement, and also because it enables them to 'engage with "big" issues directly'. Commercialisation and publication of University research also brings its fruits to a wider audience. The Faculty of Health and Medical Sciences, for instance, has been holding an annual one-day Festival of Research since 2008. This aims to showcase the multidisciplinary work of the Faculty through presentations (usually around a particular theme) and to encourage the work of junior researchers (through the Hot Topic and student/PostDoc presentations), as well as to bring everyone in the Faculty together so as to foster collaboration.

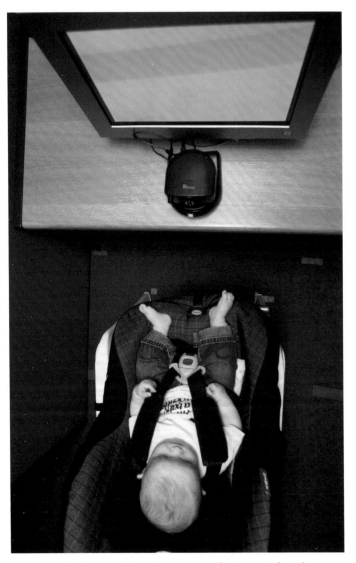

A baby being put through its paces at the Surrey Baby Lab.

Among the general populace, there is sometimes an impression that academic research is done in 'ivory towers' unrelated to the real world. But, as this chapter shows, groundbreaking research at Surrey can directly affect our day-to-day lives. Developments in nanotechnology may help to fight gun crime; investigators of baby development have discovered that babies of four months can already distinguish and show preference for different colours; a single vaccine against meningitis and a urine test for prostate cancer are in development; images transmitted from small-satellite technology are helping relief workers in disaster areas; the Institute of Sound Recording's research into the reception and perception of sound may influence auditoria design; management research has revealed the unique behavioural patterns of international businesses; and water and sanitation research has led to the production of a low-cost, portable drinking water testing-kit for use in aid work. The University's research increasingly reflects the preoccupations of the modern world. 'Though universities often define themselves in terms of their tradition and strengths in research and teaching,' says Professor Snowden, 'they are unusual among cultural institutions in having a responsibility explicitly to the future … they are uniquely well placed to meet what can seem like insuperable global challenges.'

The Satellite Revolution and SSTL

If one person can be said to have spurred the University of Surrey's – and indeed the UK's – undoubted success in satellite technology, that person is Martin Sweeting, now Professor Sir Martin Sweeting FRS. He first came to Surrey as an undergraduate back in 1970. During his final year he began to track American and Russian weather satellites and OSCAR amateur radio satellites, and then, while studying for his PhD, he and a group of other enthusiasts built a satellite. It was, as he recalled in *The Engineer* in 2010:

> considered a pretty harebrained project … but, to everyone's amazement, it worked. … We used the new micro-electronics technology out of consumer products. Because we were just starting out, we had no preconceived ideas and so our satellite was much cheaper, lighter and quicker to make – whilst also extremely sophisticated.

It was an extraordinary achievement, and perhaps just as extraordinary is the fact that he persuaded NASA to piggyback it (free) on one of its rocket-launchers. From such beginnings, Surrey Satellite Technology Ltd (SSTL) – the spin-out company set up by the University in 1985 and since 2008 part of EADS Astrium – pioneered 'commercial off-the-shelf' satellite technology in the

Sir Martin Sweeting (right) receives the Faraday Medal, the Institution of Engineering and Technology's most prestigious award, for his outstanding contribution to the advancement of satellite technology, 1 December 2009. (Institution of Engineering and Technology)

1970s and developed into one of the world's leading companies in the design, manufacture, launch and operation of small satellites. By the end of 2010 it had 34 satellites in space. Its work has been underpinned by academic research carried out by the Surrey Space Centre, which continues to research the many varied aspects of satellite design, control and applications. In 2003 SSTL received the World Technology Network Award for Space and the Queen's Award for Enterprise.

For a smallish, new university, such a large role in space technology development was not, however, an obvious route to take. Back in 1957, when Russia launched the world's first artificial satellite, *Sputnik I*, the capital sums involved in such projects were so large and the technology so complex that no one envisaged that any but the major nations would be able to afford to join the 'space race'. For a long time, this was the case. Though Prime Minister Harold Macmillan announced a British space research programme two years after *Sputnik I*, the results were slow in coming – the first all-British satellite, Ariel 3, was launched in 1967, and it was only in 1975 that the European Space Agency (ESA) was established – and the focus generally remained on space science and telecommunications missions.

It was the emergence of integrated circuits and elementary microprocessors that convinced Martin Sweeting that small, yet sophisticated, satellites could be developed at a fraction of the cost, using 'commercial parts rather than the highly expensive space-qualified parts'. The environment in which the

The first mission control centre, with Martin Sweeting on the right. (SSTL)

satellite would be operated was a demanding one, and so, said Professor Sweeting, they 'tested every component of the satellite in a specially designed chamber that replicated the space environment'. It took the team three years to produce UoSAT-1, launched in 1981 for a total cost of £220,000; it stayed in operation for eight years. Three years later NASA offered Martin Sweeting a second launch – but with only six months' notice! UoSAT-2 was launched in 1984; the first satellite to provide modern digital store-and-forward (that is, email) communications, it is still transmitting signals in orbit today.

Initially, the aim was to produce a satellite for use in the amateur and educational field, but the successful launch of the two small satellites demonstrated their potential and the ability of a small university team to bring satellites to launch in a short period of time – now generally about two years – and on a relatively modest budget, and the effective use to which the satellites could be put. The University set up Surrey Satellite Technology Limited (SSTL) in 1985 as a spin-out company to take advantage of growing commercial demand for small-scale satellites and associated technology. In 1991 SSTL launched its first satellite for a commercial customer.

UoSAT-1, the University's first satellite, launched in 1981. (SSTL)

The early days of the University's satellite programme. (SSTL)

UoSAT-OSCAR II logo. (SSTL)

The satellites in the company's early days focused mostly on digital communications. Within ten years SSTL had launched eight satellites up to 300kg for various international governments and businesses. The company developed a modular design using commercial off-the-shelf technologies (COTS) for the microsatellite platform, which involved stacking a series of identical module boxes to form a body on which solar panels and various instruments could be mounted. Each module houses various microsatellite subsystems. Payloads are housed either in similar modules or on top of the platform alongside antennas and sensors. Alongside its 'commercial' satellites, the company developed similar modular military microsatellites. The first one produced was for the CERISE mission, designed and built for the French MoD for a 700km low Earth orbit and launched by the European rocket *Ariane* in July 1995. Since then others have been launched, including PICOSat for the US Air Force, launched in 1999.

SSTL launched its first minisatellite in 1999, UoSAT-12, and its first nanosatellite in 2000, SNAP-1. Typically, a small satellite weighs between 500 and 1000kg, a minisatellite 150 to 300kg, a microsatellite between 50 and 100kg, and a nanosatellite up to 10kg. SSTL's first nanosatellite was an experimental mission to demonstrate its potential. On board was a four-camera machine vision system, GPS navigation and a butane propulsion system for manoeuvring in orbit. Part of the anticipated use was as micro-inspectors aboard larger spacecraft, a concept then taken up by the USA. The Surrey Space Centre began looking at very small satellites such as PalmSat and the PCB-Sat, a biscuit-sized satellite based on a single circuit board.

Alongside the satellites themselves, SSTL provides ancillary services. In the 1980s the company developed a compact mission control ground station, based on PCs, to monitor the satellites in orbit. This interacts autonomously with the satellite in orbit; if attention is needed, the controller is automatically bleeped to take a more active role. Today, the Mission Control Centre at the Research Park controls the operation of four satellites and oversees the management of several customer satellites in orbit. The company has built and supplied ten ground stations around the world.

From the outset the company also offered satellite know-how technology transfer and training programmes for emerging space nations. Typically, scientists and engineers spend about 18 months at Guildford, becoming involved in the entire life cycle of a satellite from mission analysis through design and build to launch and orbital operations. Over 100 engineers from 14 countries have been trained at SSTL under such programmes, with around 25 undertaking postgraduate degrees – and a number have since gone on to form the foundation of their national space agencies.

Above: The S80/T microsatellite built for the French Space Agency. (SSTL)

Microsatellites are built by stacking a series of identical module boxes to form a body on which solar panels and various instruments can be mounted, with different payloads depending on the satellite's purpose. (SSTL)

Today, SSTL operates from four sites, including the new Kepler Building, an additional 3700sq m technical facility with clean rooms, laboratories and testing facilities, which became operational in May 2011. Satellite manufacturing was moved there from the Surrey Space Centre at Stag Hill, and other elements of production transferred from Tycho House. Built to high environmental standards that include natural ventilation and a sustainable drainage system, attention has been paid to legacy use, with the design allowing for infill floors in the future.

In 2008 SSTL set up a US subsidiary, Surrey Satellite Technology LLC, with offices in Denver, Colorado. At the end of that year, EADS Astrium NV bought a 99 per cent shareholding in SSTL from the University of Surrey, providing it with funds for future growth. The 'landmark sale', Professor Sir Martin Sweeting told the BBC at the time, brought together the two major players in British space. 'Within the UK, we can have a coordinated approach to space, covering both large satellites and small satellites. This makes us a key international player.' Alongside the sale itself, a £5 million R&D programme was signed between the two companies. A high-level steering board consisting of members of EADS Astrium Executive, the University Executive and academics from the Surrey Space Centre ensures that the EADS Astrium and University strategies remain closely aligned.

Surrey Space Centre and SSTL's greatest impact in recent years has perhaps been in observing Earth from space. The Disaster Monitoring Constellation, a Surrey-led collaboration initiated in 2000, currently between the UK,

An artist's impression of the new Kepler Building, opened in spring 2011. The striking new three-storey building is clad in silver-coloured insulated panels on three sides, with the front glazed with vertical blue glass fins. (SSTL)

Nigeria, Algeria, China and Spain, consists of five small satellites and ground-stations; two further satellites, NigeriaSat-2 and NX, are due to be launched in 2011. While each nation owns and operates their satellite independently – Brazil's National Institute for Space Research, for example, has employed its satellite to provide data for deforestation since 2005 – at times of natural or man-made disaster, the seven cooperate to provide observation images from any point on the globe to aid relief teams on the ground. Recent disasters in which the constellation played an important role include the Asian tsunami (2004), Hurricane Katrina (2005), the UK floods (2007), the Sichuan earthquake (2008) and the Christchurch, New Zealand earthquake (2011).

32m GSD image from NigeriaSat-1 satellite of the New Orleans, Gulf of Mexico after Hurricane Katrina, 2005. (NASRDA)

Its most recent development is a collaboration between the Surrey Space Centre and SSTL to send the first 'smartphone' into space. STRaND-1 (Surrey Training, Research and Nanosatellite Demonstrator) is being launched into orbit around the Earth in 2011. It has been developed to demonstrate the advanced capabilities of a satellite built quickly using advanced COTS components. Says lead researcher Dr Chris Bridges:

> Smartphones pack lots of components – such as sensors, video cameras, GPS systems and Wi-Fi radios – that are technologically advanced but a fraction of the size, weight and cost of components used in existing satellite systems. If a smartphone can be proved to work in space, it opens up lots of new technologies for space to a multitude of people and companies who usually can't afford it. It's a real game-changer for the industry.

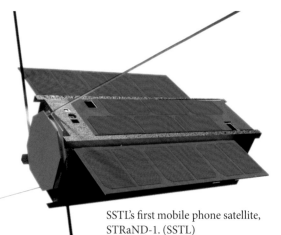

SSTL's first mobile phone satellite, STRaND-1. (SSTL)

Another ambitious programme is SSTL's involvement in European Student Moon Orbiter (ESMO). SSTL is managing the ESA programme which will place a spacecraft in lunar orbit to map the Moon's surface, acquire images and other scientific data. Each spacecraft sub-system, payload and ground segment is being designed, built and operated by a group of students from one of 19 universities based in ESA member and co-operating states. SSTL has also been selected by ESA to supply 14 navigation payloads for the development phase of Europe's global satellite navigation system, the company's largest contract to date. Teamed with OHB System of Bremen, Germany, SSTL will provide the instruments that will form the heart of the navigation system. SSTL also did the pioneering work as prime contractor for the GIOVE-A navigation test minisatellite. On 12 January 2006, GIOVE-A broadcast the first signal from space and on 2 May 2007 it successfully transmitted the first European navigation message from space. Former Surrey Space Centre student Dr Andreas Mogensen has also been selected as one of ESA's next intake of astronauts. One of just six successful applicants from an initial list of over 8,000, he is expected to undertake missions to the International Space Station, the Moon and beyond.

Research collaboration with EADs Astrium has also proved fruitful. The University and EADS Astrium are making joint bids for multi-million euro R&D programmes to support the expanding commercial opportunities for space and this is already contributing significantly to the work being carried out at Surrey. R&D collaboration has extended across the use of novel

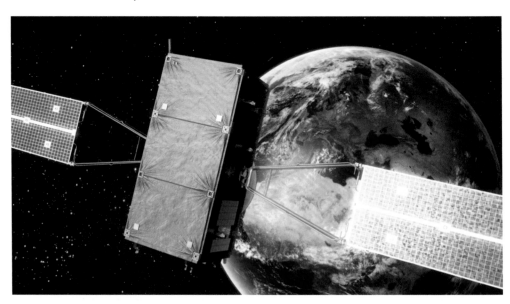

European navigation system satellite against Earth. (OHB-System-AG)

124

lightweight materials, nanotechnology coatings, electronics and communication systems. One of the most exciting and innovative joint projects is the development of new designs for ultra-lightweight and highly efficient electric space thrusters. These are intended for use with solar 'brake' sails that can be deployed to allow satellites to de-orbit and so reduce the growing amount of space debris. In 2010, scientists at the Surrey Space Centre announced that they had devised a 3kg nanosatellite fitted with a CubeSail. A 5sq m deployable sail is now being developed to fit a 10 x 10 x 30cm nanosatellite, which will be used in a demonstration mission launched in late 2011. 'Following successful in-orbit demonstration, the proposed de-orbit system will be offered as a standard de-orbit system for low Earth orbit missions for satellites with a mass of less than 500kg at a very low cost,' said Dr Vaios Lappas, lead researcher on the project.

The CubeSail, developed by SSTL and EADS Astrium as a cost-effective means of clearing debris from space, was revealed in March 2010.

As well as exciting technical developments, the University has collaborated closely with EADS Astrium UK on the UK National Space Strategy. The UK space sector has welcomed £10 million of government investment through the creation of the National Space Technology Programme. Surrey was able to win funding to set up the International Space Innovation Centre Surrey (ISIC Surrey) on the Surrey Research Park. This will support young businesses engaged directly in space technology or in associated downstream services such as environmental satellite data analysis, GPS services and new electronic communication services. The Centre will work in partnership with the International Space Innovation Centre at Harwell, Oxfordshire (ISIC Harwell) – both Centres were officially launched in May 2011 by David Willetts MP – with the University of Surrey taking up membership of the ISIC board. 'These collaborations bode well for the future of the UK space industry,' said Keith Robson, the University's Director of RES, 'with the opportunity to replicate the success that SSTL has achieved ... [in] the next generation of innovative new companies.'

Advanced Technology and Engineering

The University has been a strong player in engineering, electronics and technology since its foundation. The Advanced Technology Institute (ATI) brings together researchers in optoelectronics, photonics, ion beam technology, solid-state electronics, and theoretical and computational modelling. Originally headed by Professor Michael Kearney, who joined Surrey the year it opened, 2002, the Institute's Director is now Professor Ravi Silva, Head of the Nanotechnology Centre (Michael Kearney moved to become Dean of the Faculty of Engineering and Physical Sciences in 2007, a position from which he stood down in 2011). 'ATI provides an excellent environment in which to operate,' said Professor Ortwin Hess, head of the Computation Quantum Electronics Group (to 2010; he is now a Visiting Professor), housed in ATI, 'by linking our theoretical work with the experiments of other groups. The opportunities for exciting breakthroughs are huge.'

The University's work in ion beam applications and optoelectronics has a world-class reputation, recognised by The Queen's Anniversary Award in 2002 (see Chapter 5). Since then, the Ion Beam Centre has moved from silicon chips to working on such diverse projects as developing and testing new cancer treatments (see below), early warning systems for volcanoes and even authenticating Da Vinci paintings. In optoelectronics, new generation devices are being developed all the time, with current emphasis on blue light emitters and surface-emitting lasers, very high-speed modulation of light signals and attempts to get silicon to emit light efficiently.

Surrey was a pioneer in silicon photonics and the work of the Silicon Photonics Group, headed by Professor Graham Reed, led to the establishment of the first silicon photonics company, Bookham Technology, by one of Professor Reed's PhD students, Dr Andrew Rickman OBE (now Chairman of the Rockley Group). The field has evolved in recent years to look at larger and more complex circuits, with applications such as optical interconnects and fibre for the internet. In a significant recent move the Photonics Group used 'a high-intensity pulse from a laser to put an electron into two states at once, a so-called quantum superposition state', a step towards applications such as an affordable quantum computer – which would be able to perform operations on data much more quickly than a standard computer. 'This is a real breakthrough for modern electronics and has huge potential,' said Professor Ben Murdin, at the time Associate Dean of Research in the Faculty of Engineering and Physical Sciences.

Nanotechnology deals with the science and technology associated with dimensions in the range 0.1nm to 100nm, so advances in the field promise more for less: smaller, cheaper, lighter and faster devices with greater functionality, using less material

Surrey PhD student Andrew Rickman, later awarded the OBE for his work and now Chair of the Rockley Group, founded the first silicon photonics company in the UK. (Rockley Group)

Surrey NanoSystems won the 2007 Start-up and University Collaboration Award. Shown here receiving the award are, left to right, Andrea Mica, Director, Ben Jensen, CTO, Gerry Thurgood, CEO, and Professor Ravi Silva, Director. (Surrey NanoSystems)

and consuming less energy. The Nanotechnology Centre (NTC) has pioneered research into low temperature-grown carbon nanotubes (CNT), their functionality and applications. CNTs are rolled up sheets of honeycomb-structured carbon atoms that are typically one ten-thousandth the width of a human hair. The single or multi-walled CNT structures have amazing electronic properties with conductivity better than any other known single element including copper, thermal conductivity better than diamond, and extraordinary mechanical strength surpassing that of high tensile steel.

The NTC's work has enabled it to produce CNTs with biological materials more easily. It has also patented a method to fabricate bespoke devices using 3D manipulation of nanomaterials, with applications such as pocket-size electronic maps, robotic skin sensors and rollable TVs. Most recently, ATI announced that researchers had discovered a way to grow high-quality CNTs over large areas at substrate temperatures below 350°C – thus making the technology compatible with CMOS (a technology for constructing integrated circuits) – which would retain the properties of those obtained at higher

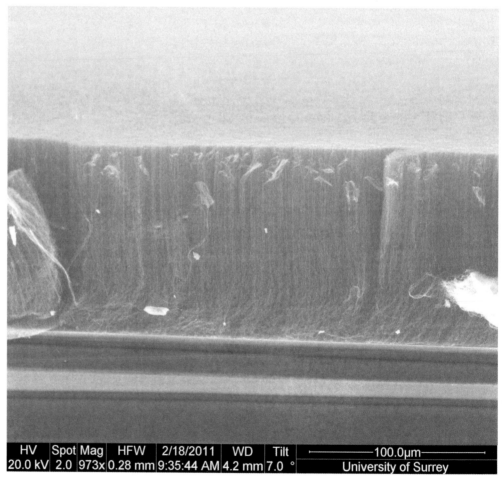

| HV | Spot | Mag | HFW | 2/18/2011 | WD | Tilt | 100.0μm |
| 20.0 kV | 2.0 | 973x | 0.28 mm | 9:35:44 AM | 4.2 mm | 7.0 ° | University of Surrey |

The extraordinary conductivity and other properties of the low temperature-grown carbon nanotubes – shown here at great magnification – developed by the Nanotechnology Centre, mean that it has potential to be used for a host of electronic and biomedical applications.

temperatures. As a result, many potential applications of CNTs – ranging from interconnectors for integrated circuits, solar cell electrodes, supercapacitors, electrodes for batteries and fuel cells to nanocomposite materials for high strength components in body armour, aircraft wings, vehicle chassis and stealth materials – could become feasible and affordable. Professor Ravi Silva, ATI Director, is 'confident that nanotechnology will play a major part in solving many of the world's future technological challenges'. He adds that a spin-out company, Surrey NanoSystems, is now in talks with major semiconductor manufacturers to transfer this technology to the wider market.

In May 2005 the NTC signed a deal with the National Physical Laboratory (NPL) in Teddington for a visiting NPL Strategic Research Fellow to work jointly between Surrey and NPL in order to exploit new and future technological advances in the area of CNT probes and their application in metrological research. This enabled use of the state-of-the-art nanofabrication facilities at ATI and collaboration between Surrey's researchers and the Quantum Metrology Group at NPL. Originally signed for three years, the joint research project was extended in 2008. The following year the NPL and Surrey signed a £10 million deal, supported by a £3.85 million Knowledge Transfer Account from the EPSRC, and other funding from industrial partners and the University, to collaborate more widely on research.

Their research focuses on three areas: communications and signal processing, including advances in mobile communications and internet connectivity; next-generation materials and characterisation, with applications in

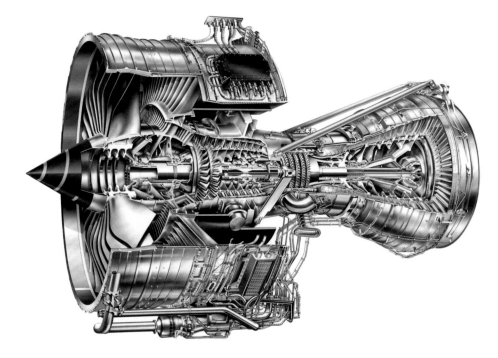

Cutaway view of the Roll-Royce Trent 900 engine, developed by the Thermo-Fluid Systems University Technology Centre, which powers the Airbus A380.

automotive, aerospace and space and satellite engineering; and nanotechnology and photonics. The work is leading to both the development of new standards of measurement, such as that of quantised electrical current conduction, and the creation of new or improved devices for carrying out existing measurements. An example of the latter is the new family of ultra low-noise superconducting quantum interference devices (SQUID) for measuring magnetic fields.

Another of the University's continual strengths has been in engineering, in which it has pioneered a number of new developments over the years. The Thermo-Fluid Systems University Technology Centre (TFS UTC), part of the Division of Mechanical, Medical and Aerospace Engineering, was established in 2003 by Professor John Chew, with support from Rolls-Royce. Fuel makes up around 25 per cent of an airline's operating costs and so pressure is on to improve aircraft performance that reduces fuel consumption, with consequent environmental benefits. TFS UTC develops and uses advanced computational modelling for improvement of turbomachinery internal fluid and thermal systems for aeroengine and power generation applications. Modern subsonic aircraft typically use high-bypass turbofan engines to give high speed and greater fuel efficiency. Academics at the Centre have worked with Rolls-Royce on the development of its Trent aircraft engines used on large civil aircraft such as the Airbus A380. For example, they linked computational modelling of flow around critical components such as turbine discs to computer modelling of the components themselves, predicting disc temperatures, stresses and deflections through a flight cycle, for estimation of component life and engine performance. The Centre is involved in a number of national and international research collaborations. Recent and current research includes interfacing CFD (computational fluid dynamics) with automatic design methods, multiphysics fluid/structure interaction problems such as component thermal analysis and brush seal modelling, multiphase flow, fluidic devices, exploitation of massively parallel computing, numerical solution methods and large eddy simulation of turbulent flow.

Recently, the Division of Mechanical, Medical and Aerospace Engineering has also supported a student project, conducted as part of student coursework, to construct a Formula 1 racing car. Run by the Institution of Mechanical Engineers (IMechE), the object of the competition is to research, design and build a low-cost, single-seater racing car and then test it on the track at Silverstone, Northamptonshire in a series of events. Competition is fierce, with entrants from over 30 countries. In 2010, over 2000 students attended the 13th Formula Student competition from 23 countries. Technical University Munich was crowned the Class 1 Overall Winner, with Surrey, in only their second year of full competition and despite reliability issues hampering their on-track performance, coming 43rd out of 76 entries. This gave the team good reason to expect significantly better results in the future.

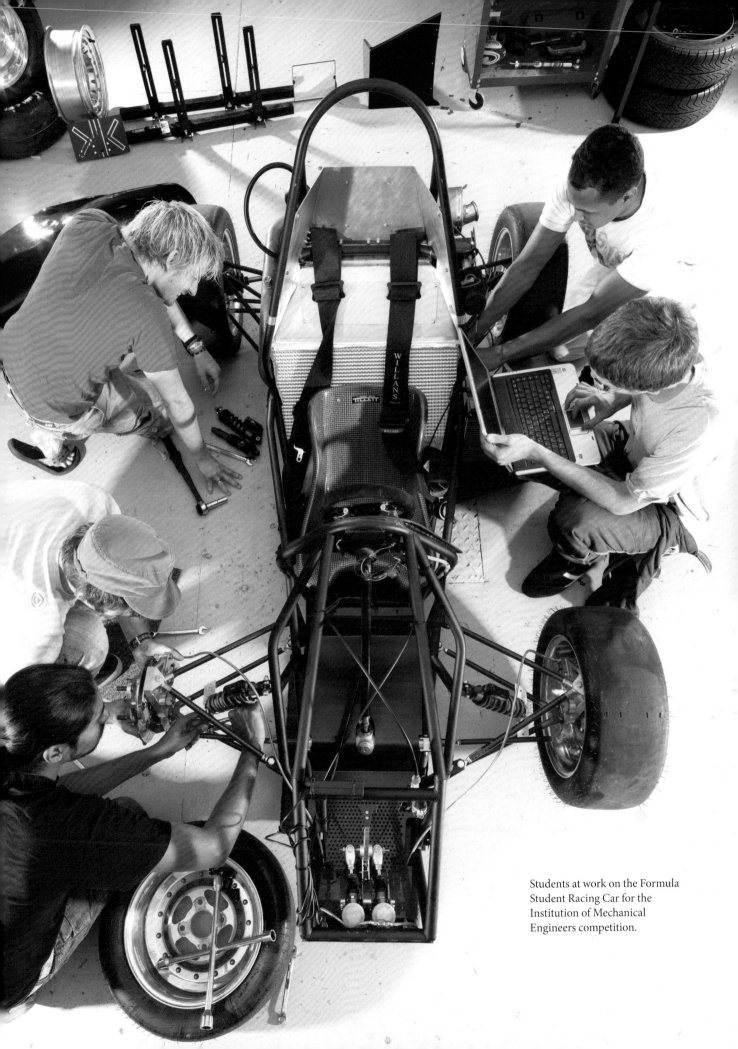

Students at work on the Formula
Student Racing Car for the
Institution of Mechanical
Engineers competition.

A key focus of the Centre for Communication Systems Research's mobile to satellite communications team has been the EU-wide research project ANASTASIA, which was set up in response to the foreseen growth in air traffic and demand for new and/or improved communication and navigation systems. Beginning in 2005, the project was coordinated by Thales Avionics in France, and combined expertise from 29 partners from large industrials, SMEs, universities and research centres from 12 countries. Surrey's role was to devise improved aircraft satellite communication systems.

University researchers are also involved in the relatively new technology of biometrics, with applications in security, authentication and personal identity recognition. Headed by Professor Josef Kittler, the Biometrics Research Laboratory's activities include 2D and 3D face recognition, voice-based speaker recognition and multimodal biometric fusion. The unique feature of some of the solutions developed at the B-Lab is their small footprint, which allows the biometric algorithms to run on a smart card. In 2001 a spin-out company, OmniPerception, was formed by Professor Kittler to capitalise on new facial recognition technology that could withstand the effects of reflective light as well as other computer vision capabilities.

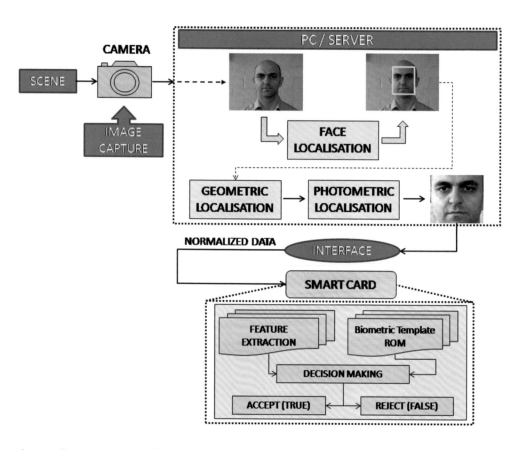

The overall system diagram of the smart card face recognition system developed at the Centre for Vision, Speech and Signal Processing. It was transferred to OmniPerception Ltd, one of the University spin-out companies, in 2004.

Cancer and other Medical Research

A particular focus of the Faculty of Health and Human Sciences has been cancer research, which has been investigated in various disciplines. Nanobiotechnology is a multidisciplinary field exploring the potential of nanostructures for biomedical applications, which, as Professor Ravi Silva, Director of ATI comments, 'promises to develop revolutionary new treatments for diseases like cancer, diabetes or coronary heart disease'. In cancer therapy, research is being conducted into use of nanotubes both directly as near-infra-red heating devices for hyperthermia and indirectly as transporter systems for anti-cancer drugs.

In 2011, researchers at Surrey, part of a large EC-funded project (the CARBIO Marie Curie Research Network) to develop CNTs for biomedical application, reported that they were near to being able to use miniscule capsules 10,000 times smaller than a human hair as drug delivery devices to target cancer-causing agents within human cells. The CNTs are able to deliver payloads such as anti-cancer drugs precisely to tumours, and then be expelled without causing stress to healthy cells. Johnjoe McFadden, Professor of Molecular Genetics and lead scientist for the research programme, said, 'This research shows that CNTs do not accumulate inside living cells so they can be used to deliver drugs or genes without causing any permanent harm.

The Clinical Simulation Suite, opened in 2010 in the Duke of Kent Building, gives students the opportunity to practise the skills necessary to meet the challenges that health care professionals in the NHS face every day.

Although much still needs to be done, this is an essential step to developing CNTs as revolutionary therapeutic agents.'

Another collaboration, in 2007, funded by the Wolfson Foundation, was between the Gray Cancer Institute and the Ion Beam Centre (IBC) to build the world's first vertical-scanning focused nanobeam for use in analysing how radiotherapy affects living cells. It has applications in cancer treatment, as well as exposure to radiation. Tumours vary in their sensitivity to radiation, with some displaying hyper-sensitivity to low doses and others proving resistant. Data from the nanobeam is being used to simulate a virtual tumour *in silico*, which clinicians can then test with different strengths of ion radiation therapy to see what is most effective.

The nanobeam at Surrey is capable of irradiating individual cells in culture, or regions within cells, with precisely counted ions (from protons to calcium ions). This is coupled to a state-of-the-art microscopy imaging platform, developed by the Vojnovic lab (University of Oxford), to offer cell-tracking, white light and fluorescence imaging, and environmental controls for the assessment of radiation response. The vertical orientation of the beam line allows the cell dish to be placed horizontally and irradiated from below, so that cells can be kept in their culture medium and chemotherapeutic agents added before, during or after irradiation to study the combined effects of ion irradiation and chemotherapy. One of the strengths of the research is that the team at the IBC works closely with clinicians in neuro-oncology and neuro-surgery, thus ensuring that the research is clinically relevant and will translate well from bench to bedside.

Monitoring the accelerator and the end-station of the Wolfson vertical-scanning focused nanobeam which is used to irradiate living cells in culture so as to develop better treatments for cancer.

The vertical-scanning focused nanobeam at the Ion Beam Centre in use. It is invaluable in the examination and treatment of tumours.

Virotherapy is another method of cancer treatment in which the University's researchers have been involved. Here the aim is for genetically altered viruses to attack cancer cells, as Hardev Pandha, Professor of Urological Oncology, explains:

> They are human viruses that infect and replicate in cancer cells, destroying these harmful cells and leaving normal cells largely unaffected. Like all viruses, oncolytic viruses seek to penetrate a host cell and 'trick' it into replicating more of the virus until, ultimately, it bursts.

In collaboration with the Royal Marsden Hospital, the team is now evaluating the effectiveness of intravenously administered reovirus as a therapeutic strategy, and in particular how to subdue the body's immune response to it so that it can work.

In March 2011, the University announced a major breakthrough following a three-year research project, with the development of a new, more reliable urine test for the early detection of prostate cancer, which kills over 10,000 men in the UK every year. This has shown that a protein called Engrailed-2 (EN2) – important in the development of the human embryo but whose production, like many similar 'early life' proteins, is 'switched off' at birth – is made by prostate cancers and secreted into urine, where it can be easily detected using the new test. The fruit of collaboration with the Prostate Project charity, the test is simple and quick to administer, offering the potential not only for faster testing in GP surgeries – which could mean lives saved – but also huge savings. It is hoped the test will be in use within 18 months.

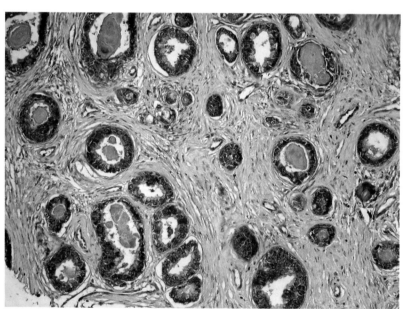

Microscopic view of prostate cancer cells. Prostate cancer is a killer of thousands in the UK each year, and the new test developed by the Urological Oncology team at Surrey's Postgraduate Medical School, which can detect cancer cells in urine, could prove a real breakthrough in tackling the disease.

'In this study [of 288 patients],' said Professor Hardev Pandha, the Prostate Project Chair of Urological Oncology at Surrey's Postgraduate Medical School, 'we showed that the new test was twice as good at finding prostate cancer as the standard PSA test'; and more reliable, since EN2 was not detected in men with non-cancer disorders such as prostatitis, which can cause a high PSA result. With the current EN2 test, men provide a urine sample which their doctor sends to a lab. Professor Pandha said the testing method could, in the near future, be made into an even simpler 'desktop' test that family doctors could perform in their surgeries. The next step is to conduct several large studies in the UK and the USA.

For Sara Faithfull, Professor of Cancer Nursing Practice, researching and aiding the large number of cancer survivors in the UK and helping patients with the side effects and after effects of treatment are as important as more radical interventions. Her research has involved examining these aspects of clinical care, in collaboration with cancer centres in southern England and with groups such as the National Cancer Survivorship Group. For those with long-term needs, self-management by internet and smartphone applications may be the way forward in the future.

Medical research at the University is not, of course, limited to cancer. Johnjoe McFadden, Professor of Molecular Genetics, and Dr Graham Stewart have been researching possible weaknesses in the TB bacillus. There are nine million new cases of tuberculosis each year, but at present vaccination is in-effective and the emergence of 'drug-resistant' strains has made treatment, which takes six months, increasingly problematic. The research team used an *in silico* model of the TB bacillus – the first such model to be built – to test its behaviour, and in particular to look at its unusual dormant phase in which it is very resistant to antibiotics.

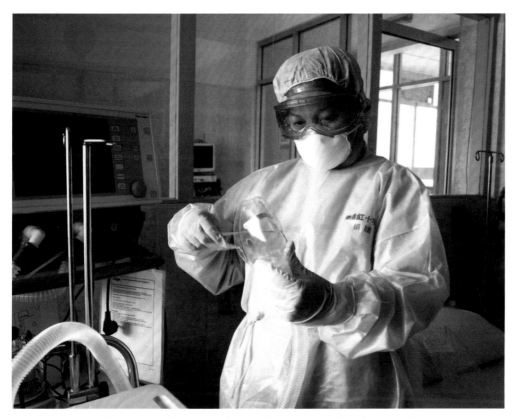

A nurse prepares isolation rooms for suspected cases of bird or swine flu at the Sarjito hospital in Yogyakarta, Indonesia, on 1 May 2009. The World Health Organization had issued a phase five swine influenza virus pandemic warning following the outbreak, with positive reports of the virus spreading to the US, UK and Europe. (Photo by Ulet Ifansasti/Getty Images)

Professor Lisa Roberts, Head of the Division of Microbial Sciences, is leading a research effort in zoonotic diseases. Cross-species infections, such as H5N1 bird flu and SARS, have cost tens of billions of dollars to contain and, because of the prevalence of modern travel, they are becoming more widespread and more frequent. New zoonoses have emerged in the last decade, Professor Roberts explains: 'Our research is focused on understanding how zoonotic pathogens emerge and cause infection in animal and human hosts.' Computer modelling of micro-organisms, as has been done with TB, will, she hopes, enable fast production of drugs and vaccines.

In another piece of advanced research, Professor Susan Lanham-New, Head of the Division of Nutritional Sciences, is working with D3TEX Ltd in developing an innovative textile-based solution and application to combat Vitamin D deficiency in veiled Muslim women. This approach allows sunlight transmission to the skin without flesh being seen and could aid many Muslim women in the Middle East suffering from Vitamin D deficiency as a result of veiling due to religious and cultural customs. With an estimated 9.8 million veiled women in Saudi Arabia alone, the potential market is vast.

Society and Behavioural Issues

The past ten years have seen widespread changes in Britain and the research of some University departments seeks to address problems facing society today and to develop strategies on issues in public debate. Many of these require multidisciplinary approaches. The Digital World Research Centre, established in 1998, aims to develop user-centred innovation in digital media technology and to apply this technology for social benefit through various forms of inclusive research and design. Early work concentrated on understanding the social impact of new technologies such as mobile phones, e-books and the internet. Current work is focused on understanding new forms of media production and consumption, and developing ways of supporting them with novel media genres, formats, devices and services. Professor David Frohlich, for instance, is working with colleagues from the Universities of Cape Town, Swansea and Glasgow on a study investigating how social media sharing systems could benefit people in developing communities with low levels of literacy. A recent apolitical strand is Big Society Research, a network of academics, government and communities looking at existing academic evidence for or against the 'big society'.

The impact of low levels of sleep and sleep problems associated with shift-working, ageing and psychological change have become hot topics in recent years, as the detrimental effects, in higher accident rates, for instance, have become more widely appreciated. The Surrey Sleep Research Centre, headed by Professor Derk-Jan Dijk, was founded in 2003. Internationally recognised, it brings together researchers in sociology and psychology with those with scientific expertise in sleep research. Located in the Surrey Clinical Research Centre, facilities include a 12-bed ward and 12 individual sleep laboratories.

Research into shift work and circadian rhythms are important aspects of the Centre's activity. Research into the effect of different light environments on workers on the British Antarctic Survey ships and the influence of genes showed correlation between the different lengths of the so-called 'clock' gene, Period 3, and whether individuals were at their best in the mornings ('larks') or in the evenings ('owls'). 'It is tempting to speculate that one day some people might choose their lifestyle according to their clock genes,' comments Professor Jo Arendt, a senior member of the sleep research team. Research teams led by Professor Derk-Jan Dijk at Surrey and Pierre Maquet MD at the University of Liege also showed for the first time how genetic differences in brain activity are associated with cognitive performance and fatigue. The findings explain why there are differences in the ability to compensate for lack of sleep, with implications for selection of shift-workers and developing counter-measures for those at risk.

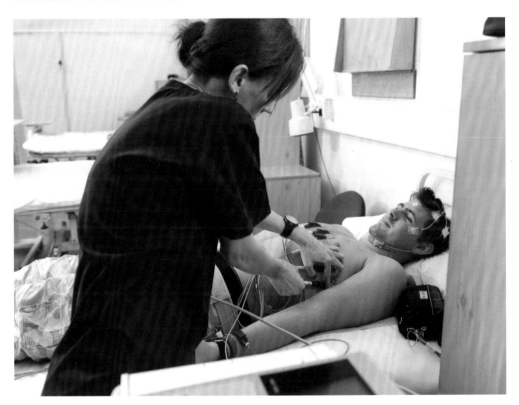

An individual being fitted with equipment to monitor his sleep patterns in the Surrey Sleep Research Centre.

The ageing demography of the UK is one of the great challenges facing us today, with impact on almost every corner of life. Professor Debra Skene's research has been directed towards understanding and treating biological rhythm disorders as experienced by blind people, shift-workers, long-distance air travellers and the elderly. Her team's findings have led to the optimisation of treatments using the hormone melatonin and light to reset the human biological clock. This showed the importance of short wavelength blue light in controlling the human biological clock, and that elderly people are less sensitive to it. The work has important implications for the design of lighting in homes for older people.

Staff watching monitors in the sleep laboratory at the Surrey Sleep Research Centre.

The Centre for Research into the Older Workforce was formed in 2003 with, says its Director, Dr Stephen McNair, 'the remit to investigate how the older labour market works and how society can make better use of the talents and potential of people over fifty'. Early investigations showed that many people would like to remain working part-time after retirement age, a finding with increasing relevance with the age of pensionable retirement being deferred. The survey also showed that high qualifications were a key determinant in obtaining positive career moves post-fifty, with the unqualified being squeezed out of the labour market. Complementary research by the Centre for Research on Ageing and Gender has investigated the social effects of ageing, attitudes to retirement, the social networks of older men and clinical decision making with regard to older patients.

The Surrey Baby Lab was set up in 2000 to investigate how babies and toddlers see colour and to increase understanding of how infants and toddlers develop and interact with the world. Studies have looked at a variety of issues, including whether infants can categorise colours and colour preferences, and how children learn colour words. A special eye-tracking camera allows researchers to record babies' and toddlers' eye movements and the Lab also has equipment that can measure brain activity in response to colour. Initial results show that babies can categorise colours as early as four months old. 'It's a myth that newborn babies are colour-blind,' says Dr Anna Franklin. 'They can see colour, but it does develop greatly over the first few months.' The Lab is now looking at whether babies are drawn more to colours that are commonly liked by adults.

Barely a week goes by without some food, diet or health issue hitting the headlines, from genetically modified foods to increasing obesity and functional foods. The University's Food, Consumer Behaviour and Health Research Centre (FCBHRC), led by Professor Richard Shepherd and Dr Monique Raats, is a cross-disciplinary group integrating understanding of consumer behaviour and choice of foods with research from the biological sciences so as to address these crucial issues. In light of the growing prevalence of diet-related diseases, governments are increasingly concerned to help consumers make healthy, informed food choices and labelling is included in the World Health Organization's global strategy. The FCBHRC is involved in an ongoing programme of research dealing with various aspects of food labelling. A team from FCBHRC led by Dr Raats advised on the design of the UK government's programme of research to evaluate the impact of front-of-pack (FOP) nutrition signpost labelling schemes on purchasing behaviour and consumer knowledge. This work concluded that although levels of comprehension are generally high for all FOP labels, the co-existence of a range of FOP label formats in the marketplace causes difficulties for shoppers.

FCBHRC is also contributing to the EU-funded Food Labelling to Advance Better Education for Life (FLABEL) research project. The most comprehensive study on the topic in Europe, it aims to understand how nutrition information on food labels affects consumers' dietary choices and shopping behaviour. In the first phase of the study, Dr Raats and Research Fellow Charo Hodgkins worked with the team looking at food labels in three different types of store and in five product categories across the 27 countries of the EU and Turkey, more than 37,000 products in all. The most widespread format for information was found to be back-of-pack tabular or linear listing of nutrition content, with FOP most commonly used to give recommended daily allowances. FLABEL is also investigating attention, reading, liking, understanding and use by consumers of different nutrition labelling formats.

Together with researchers from the University of Southampton, Brunel University and Allergy Action Anaphylaxis Campaign, and led by Dr Julie Barnett, FCBHRC investigated how adults with peanut and nut allergies made decisions when purchasing food, with particular attention to food labelling. Research Fellows Jo Leftwich and Kate Muncer used three research techniques, an accompanied shop, a semi-structured interview and a product choice reasoning task, to do this. They found that, as well as ingredients lists and allergy advice boxes, images and product names not intended by manufacturers as allergen risk assessment aids, and external factors such as trust of the producer, informed buyers' choices.

Researchers at the University are also concerned with crime deterrence. In 2010, trials of a high-speed baggage-scanning system developed by Dr Edward Morton while he was at the University of Surrey began at Manchester Airport. A revolutionary CT scanner with no moving parts, it is faster and more reliable than previous scanners. The system was patented by the University and incorporated into spin-out company CXR, run by Dr Morton (the company is now part of OSI Systems).

The high-speed baggage-scanning system developed by Dr Edward Morton, which uses a revolutionary CT scanner with no moving parts. (Rapiscan)

The University's Department of Computing, together with researchers at the University of Birmingham, are working on a secure system of voting technology that would count votes electronically. The problem with current electronic voting systems is that there is no way for the voter to be sure that their vote has been counted. The new system under investigation would mean voters would still put a cross in the box but then the paper would be processed electronically.

The Centre for Research in Social Simulation (CRESS), headed by Professor Nigel Gilbert, is a multidisciplinary centre bringing together the social sciences, software engineering and agent-based computing to promote and support the use of social simulation in research in the human sciences. The NEW TIES project is growing an artificial society using computer programming that develops agents – or adaptive, artificial beings – that have independent behaviours. The project is the first of its kind to develop a large-scale and highly complex computer-based society and it aims to evolve an artificial society capable of exploring and understanding its environment through cooperation, adaptation and interaction. The project's results may have larger implications for information technologies design, evolutionary computing systems, artificial intelligence and linguistics.

Sustainability and the Environment

Most now recognise that global climate change represents one of the biggest threats to the stability of life on earth. The Kyoto Protocol of 1997 set national greenhouse gas reduction targets for industrialised countries and the Climate Change Act (2008) set an aim of reducing UK greenhouse gas emissions by at least 34 per cent by 2020 and 80 per cent by 2050 (against a 1990 baseline). This requires us to rethink the way in which we convert and use energy, and the University's involvement in this is twofold: on the one hand, its research aims to provide solutions; on the other, it has put in place a sustainability strategy on its own campus. In 2000, the University of Surrey appointed Tim Jackson as Professor of Sustainable Development, the first

Surrey's Professor Tim Jackson, the UK's first Professor of Sustainable Development.

Chair related to sustainable development in the UK. An early advocate of the necessity of following a new sustainable economic model, he believes that unless we ditch the growth of consumerism on which many companies are predicated and adopt wholesale systemic change, we are headed for disaster. 'If we are going to be able to create a new economic vision, companies will need to rethink every aspect of their operations,' he told *The Guardian* in December 2010. 'We need to create a clear roadmap to getting to this new territory', with openness about environmental limits, changes in the economic model and 'a shift in the underlying sense of what the good life means'.

Professor Jackson is Director of RESOLVE, an Economic and Social Research Council (ESRC) Research Group on Lifestyles, Values and Environment. The multidisciplinary group, which draws together the Centre for Environmental Research, the Environmental Psychology Research Group, the Surrey Energy Economics Centre and the Department of Sociology, focuses on understanding the links between people's lives, values and the environment and what drives behavioural changes. Its main work has been to look at a number of research themes: carbon mapping and carbon trading; the psychology of energy behaviours; sociological aspects of lifestyles and lifestyle change; projection of carbon lifestyle scenarios to 2030; and the role of government policy in sustainability.

Central to the University's research has been the Centre for Environmental Strategy (CES), which takes a multidisciplinary approach to finding practical solutions to environmental sustainability and new approaches to sustainable development. It focuses on three areas in particular: devising tools, systems and techniques for sustainability, including water resource management, transport planning and transition to a low carbon society; social research on sustainability, including research in behavioural change, fair trading and the social impact on communities of climate change, such as flooding; and the implications of sustainability on policy, strategy and governance at a national and international level. One important methodology developed is life cycle assessment, which seeks to analyse the entire life cycle of a product or service, or its supply chain. Now a cornerstone of European environmental policy, it has become an important tool in, for instance, evaluating waste management and production methods. Researchers are also analysing the effect of wind turbines, using wind tunnel simulation so as to study the full range of atmospheric conditions. The aim is to develop improved methods of design for the next generation of turbines.

There are currently three important strategic University-wide initiatives at CES, all of which bring interested researchers together in networks to share research, exchange ideas and, as Professor Matt Leach, Director of CES, acknowledges, 'ideally to generate larger, often collaborative research bids'. The first of these, the Energy Network (EN), chaired by Matt Leach and Lester Hunt, Professor of Energy Economics, draws together researchers from all four Faculties of the University and from RES. It has monthly seminars with invited speakers, with topics including, for example, 'Energy Efficiency in the Water Cycle' by Malcolm Brant of Black & Veatch. It is developing increasingly strong links with industry, and has created specialist MSc and PhD programmes, such as the MSc in Renewable Energy Engineering. As well as research into, for example, low energy systems and improved materials, the EN collaborates on funding applications; it has won 86 grants worth over £16 million in the past three years. The Food Security Network and Surrey Water Innovation Research and Learning (SWIRL) similarly bring together academics involved in their fields.

Water research has been conducted across the University for over thirty years, and the emphasis given to water and sanitation research led to Surrey being given World Health Organization Collaborating Centre status for the protection of water quality and human health. A notable outcome of the research, led by Professor Barry Lloyd and Dr Steve Pedley, was the invention of the DelAgua low-cost, portable drinking water testing kit. This is now used in over 130 countries and by more than 300 organisations, including UNICEF, Oxfam, WHO and Water Aid, to monitor water quality, particularly in areas struck by disaster.

The DelAgua low-cost, portable drinking water testing kit developed by Professor Barry Lloyd, Dr Steve Pedley and their team, shown here being demonstrated by an Oxfam field worker. (DelAgua)

In a time of water shortage, fresh water from underground aquifers will become increasingly important and the issue of who owns and controls these pertinent. It is this that has become one focus of research for the School of Law's Environmental Regulatory Research Group (ERRG). It has been conducting research into the Guarani Aquifer System which lies beneath Paraguay, Brazil, Uruguay and Argentina. The issues are complex and, alongside collaborative investigation by the countries into the science of the aquifer, agreement needed to be reached on sovereignty. In 2010 ERRG held a conference bringing together 43 experts in international law, hydro-geology and international relations to discuss current policy, and this led to the establishment of the Surrey Centre on Transboundary Aquifers Governance. 'It plugs a crucial gap,' said Francesco Sindico, then Deputy Director of ERRG. 'Our vision is that in five years' time, or maybe less, any government or interested organisation that wants to know how best practice is developing will identify us as the primary source where they can access this expertise.' Working primarily on aquifers in Europe, the Americas and southern Africa, the University's links with the University of São Paulo will be exploited.

One recent practical project undertaken by a SWIRL researcher, Dr 'Shafey' Ahmed, was to train Egyptians to modify cellulosic material from rice straw for use as a disinfectant in water filters. This could also help to resolve the problem of pollution from burning straw after harvest. Conducted in collaboration with the University of Zagazig, north-east of Cairo, which lies at the centre of one of the largest rice-producing areas in Egypt, the project involved six villages with poor water facilities, where systems were installed and training given. The villagers are understandably keen to improve the quality of water supplied from underground pipes, and use of domestic purification units would reduce contamination and make a real difference to their lives.

Professor Adel Sharif, Chair in Process Innovation, is investigating low-cost desalination, water treatment and osmosis applications. By 2025 it is estimated that up to two thirds of the world's population will be in water-stressed environments. The Centre for Osmosis Research and Applications was set up in 2003 to address this problem and the treatment and disposal of wastewater. Adel Sharif and researcher Abdulsalam Al-Mayahi developed manipulated osmosis technology (MOT), a breakthrough technique with applications in desalination plants and in water treatment for cooling towers and renewable power generation through hydro-osmotic power.

A training session for villagers on the water purification system developed by Dr 'Shafey' Ahmed in collaboration with the University of Zagazig, Egypt. (Dr 'Shafey' Ahmed)

MOT is a more environmentally friendly form of desalination with lower energy use and costs, thus making it more affordable for poorer parts of the world. Professor Sharif explains: 'If you take these three components, sun, sea and salt, you have all the necessary ingredients, because the salt itself can be turned into an energy source to help fuel the purification process and even provide a new revenue stream.' Following successful production of a pilot desalination plant on campus, a spin-out company, Surrey Aqua Technology Ltd, was formed in 2006. The company was later incorporated into Modern Water, a start-up which raised funds for the new venture and was then floated on the AIM for £70 million less than a year later. The company's MOT is now being used in desalination plants in Gibraltar and Oman. 'I want to give the world the equivalent of the Microsoft of desalination,' comments Professor Sharif. He was given the Royal Society Brian Mercer Award for Innovation in 2005, and was named winner of the inaugural Academic Enterprise Awards in 2008.

Cutting-edge research is also being carried out at the Advanced Technology Institute (ATI), working closely with EADS Astrium to develop green sustainable energy solutions using space technology. It has recently been

The manipulated osmosis technology desalination plant at Al Khaluf, Oman. (Modern Water plc)

awarded a major EPSRC Knowledge Transfer Account to enable it to exploit the research. The research project aims to use infrared lasers to capture solar energy directly from space and transmit the energy via a satellite system to Earth. Professor Stephen Sweeney, the project leader, comments:

> Exploiting the power of the sun directly from space provides a clean, constantly available source of energy that may be used anywhere on demand – a solar tap. … The challenge for us is to develop the technology to maximise the conversion of infrared laser light into electricity.

Plans include a demonstration solar power mission in orbit.

The Faculty of Health and Medical Sciences is also contributing to the development of renewable resources and clean energy generation. It is involved in the EU-funded ForestSpecs project, coordinated by the University of Helsinki, which is investigating the uses of bark, peat and wood waste products to act as green alternatives to petrochemical-based processes and materials, not only in high value-added products, such as pharmaceuticals, fungicides and plant protection agents, but also in technical products such as adhesives, coating, surfactants and chelating agents. At Surrey, Professor Dulcie Mulholland and PhD student Dorota Nawrot have been developing and optimising microwave-assisted extraction techniques that are much faster and require fewer solvents than conventional extraction techniques. Professor Robert Slade and Dr John Varcoe's group are looking at novel clean energy generation and storage technologies and new ideas for the utilisation of CO_2 as a chemical feedstock. Technologies include hydrogen fuel cells and high power supercapacitors. In partnership with Dr Alfred Thumser and Dr Claudio

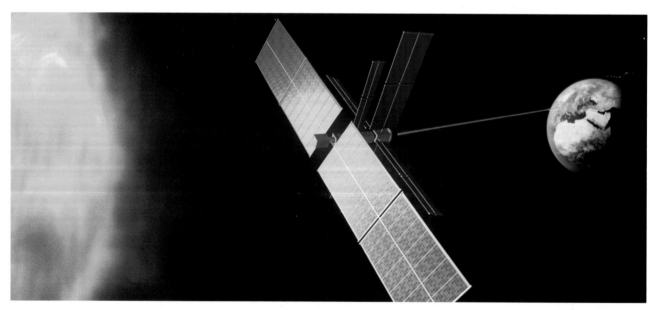

Power transmission by laser is being studied as part of ATI's solar energy project. Shown here is a large satellite that can collect solar energy and redirect it towards the ground using laser beams and special mirrors. (©Astrium/2010)

Avignone-Rossa's research teams, they are also developing microbial fuel cells and electrochemical devices for wastewater treatment and desalination.

The University also puts into practice a sustainability policy. For over twenty years, up until 2000, the University had an Energy Committee and it was the driver behind investment in a 1MW Combined Heat and Power (CHP) plant within the main boiler house in 2001. In 1998 the University established a Sustainability Group, with cross-University representation, to steer its response and strategy, and to ensure engagement with the issues by all. This group took over the monitoring and improvement of energy management from the Energy Committee. Today, Surrey tackles sustainability not only through waste management and resource efficiency, but through procurement and encouraging biodiversity on campus. New buildings are built with low-energy systems and recycling is done wherever possible. Renewable energy supply, through solar power, ground source heat pumps and wind power, is being sought. The University CHP unit has driven down energy use by 10 per cent and saved 1500 tonnes of CO_2 per annum. The horticultural and land-scaping unit operates a 100 per cent recycling system across the 900 acres and has invested in an all-green waste composting facility. There is a Fairtrade Fortnight in March each year and both Guildford and the University of Surrey have been awarded Fairtrade status.

The hard work has resulted in some deserved recognition. In April 2008 the Students' Union won the Silver Standard award at the Sound Environmental Awards. This recognised the Students' Union and the Estates and Facilities Department's 'hard work in this area ... done to make reducing our environmental impact a part of the everyday ethos at Surrey', said Natalie Forrester, Vice-President for Welfare of the Students' Union at the time. The Manor Park development achieved a Building Research Establishment Environmental Assessment Method (BREEAM) rating of 'Excellent'. In 2008, the Estates and Facilities Department won a Green Gown Award for refurbishing and extending the life of its 1960s buildings through careful planning and long-term life cycle analysis, and reducing carbon by 2500 tonnes per annum.

As a result of the steep increase in students and growth of the campus since 1990, emissions at Surrey have grown from 164,000 tonnes of carbon to 240,000 tonnes per annum, though academic-related emissions dropped by some 14.7 per cent in the period. The HEFCE target for reduction in emissions is 34 per cent by 2020 (from a 2006 baseline). This is, says John Davis, University Sustainability and Environmental Manager, 'significant and would mean the University reducing energy use and emissions by 54 per cent from current [2010] levels. There has been nothing like this before.' From August 2010 energy use in all buildings on campus has been metered every half an hour, so as to encourage awareness of use and reduction. A 10 per cent cut in energy consumption at Stag Hill, achievable through small actions of individuals, would reduce utility costs by £600,000 and carbon emissions by 2590 tonnes.

Surrey Research Park

Since its foundation in 1984 (see Chapter 2 for its early history) the Surrey Research Park has grown substantially. Occupancy rates have remained high, generally over 95 per cent, despite the economic dips of the 1990s, and even in the recession from 2008 have been steady. The Surrey Technology Centre, which has always been an important part of the Park and was the first building on the site to be completed, helps innovative start-up businesses. Its long-term success has resulted in two extensions, the most recent of which was completed in 2000. The Centre is also known as the Anthony Kelly Development in honour of the Vice-Chancellor who in 1981 was responsible for the original idea of the Research Park.

Today, around 2700 staff work at the Research Park and it is home to over 140 companies. Significant cooperation between tenants and the University has been and continues to be productive. An early success was Cleansorb, which developed an environmentally friendly technique for repairing oil wells damaged by drilling that uses enzymes to create vinegar in the borehole; previously large quantities of dangerous and environmentally harmful hydrochloric acid were used. It signed its first licence for Arcasolve™ with a

An aerial view of the Surrey Research Park. The Park is now home to 140 companies.

The official naming of Surrey's 'Incubator Centre', the Surrey Technology Centre, and its new extension in 2001 by HRH The Duke of Kent. The building was named the Anthony Kelly Development in recognition of the University's second Vice-Chancellor who took the initiative to establish the Research Park in the early 1980s.

global well service company in 2001 and the product is now used by independent, state and major international operating companies in the USA, Europe, the Middle East, Africa and Asia.

Another high achieving company is Multiple SMART Award winner Disperse Technologies, which won a contract from the EPSRC to apply its novel Thin Film Encapsulation technology to packaging and printing. Today the product is licensed for uses ranging from improved surface coatings for pills and other oral medicines, allowing for more controlled delivery of active ingredients, to deodorants, car fresheners, pesticides and printing inks.

The collaborative nature of the Research Park and synergies between businesses encourages established companies to move to the Park, and the majority of companies are established ones. There are significant clusters in information communications technology, mobile phone technology, software, biomedicine and biotechnology. The Research Park has also been an important part of the story of the growth of the computer games business in Guildford, with some of the world's leading companies involved. Bullfrog, an early computer games publisher, grew substantially while on the Park and, though now located elsewhere, was bought by Electronic Arts. Microsoft Games Studio bought the Park's Lionhead Studios – established by one of the founders of Bullfrog – which in 2001 published one of the most acclaimed games in the sector, Black & White. The Canon Europe Research Centre developed new products that sprung from technical assistance provided by several University groups, ranging from Materials Science and Engineering to Music. Among these was a new graphics package, Render Ware, that was commercialised through Canon's spin-out subsidiary, Criterion Software. One of the most significant companies on the site is Detica, which moved there in 1986 and grew from just thirty staff to in excess of 1200. Now part of BAE Systems, it is today a world leader in many pioneering technologies including internet protocol security.

Dr Alexandre Pechev

Most recently, Dr Alexandre Pechev of the Surrey Space Centre used the prize money from a Royal Academy of Engineering award for his revolutionary new approach to computer game and film animation to found the company IKinema. This uses a system called kinematics to produce lifelike, fluid movement that automatically takes into account the effects of gravity, balance and other forces that affect a character. This makes movement much more realistic. The company has already secured high-profile clients including 20th Century Fox and Escape Studios.

IKinema animation, developed by Surrey Space Centre researcher Dr Alexandre Pechev.

English Literature and the Arts

'Performance lends itself to globality,' says Professor Rachel Fensham, now Director of Research in the Department of Dance, Film and Theatre. Research in the performing arts has strengthened in recent years, with particular emphasis on collaborative performing arts and cross-cultural exchange – one project, for instance, looks at the cultural heritage of dance in Java. As Surrey was the first university to offer a degree in Dance, the subject has always commanded attention both within the University and beyond. The AHRC Research Centre for Cross-Cultural Music and Dance Performance, inaugurated on 1 September 2002, was a collaboration between the University and the Department of Music at the School of Oriental and African Studies, London and the School of Arts at the University of Surrey Roehampton. Directed by Professor Janet Lansdale, Surrey focused on two projects: new directions in South Asian dance and post-colonial identity construction, and transformations in African music and dance performance. The latter recorded and documented the Dzigbordi community dance-drumming group (*habobo*), an important rural Ewe music tradition, and in particular the ceremony which attended the passing of Mishiso Tagborlo.

In 2007, the Department of Dance Studies and the Department of Music and Sound Recording at the University of Surrey launched a symposium and speaker series, Popular Dance and Music Matters, which culminated in an anthology that drew on research developed through these events. Building on this intellectual momentum, a similar collaborative research initiative between scholars and practitioners, Pop Moves, is now under way. Surrey Documentary Group's research is concerned with issues to do with documentation and documentary film that extend beyond film to other modes of documentation in social and scientific arenas.

The University also has a strong reputation in Music. One of the first universities to run courses in jazz, percussion and conducting, and to include a film music option, the University also offered one of the first PhDs in composition and later introduced the possibility of achieving a PhD by choreography or by performance. One headline-grabbing project of the past decade was the development of the Fluid Piano™ by inventor, musician and composer Geoff Smith. Described by *The Guardian* as 'The musical equivalent of splitting the atom' and 'one of the most culturally significant developments in the history of music in the last 300 years', the first public performance was given on 28 November 2009. The piano enables musicians to alter each note individually and separately by precise microtonal intervals per note, before or during performance. This liberates the instrument from the restrictions of 'Western' tuning to make the Fluid Piano™ the first 'multicultural' acoustic piano. The University of Surrey was the educational partner for the Fluid Piano™ project and the first works for the instrument were commissioned by

Surrey's Department of Music and Sound Recording. 'As soon as I heard the news that Fluid Tuning on each note of the piano might be a possibility,' said one of the performers on its debut evening, composer and pianist Matthew Bourne, 'I immediately wanted to know more. After years of patience and tenacity by inventor Geoff Smith, a new prototype instrument now exists.'

Geoff Smith on the innovatory Fluid Piano™. (Rafael Lewandowski, Eureka Media, Poland)

The University is particularly strong in its provision of teaching and research on popular music and film, with former students sometimes winning major awards. Tonmeister™ graduate James Bellamy worked as music editor with Dario Marianelli to create the score for the 2007 film *Atonement*, which won both an Oscar and a Golden Globe for Best Original Score and was nominated for a BAFTA in 2008. Professor of Popular Music Alan Moore's research focuses not only on what the music consists of, but also how the music actually sounds. He has developed a theory of rock authenticity which switches the focus from whether a particular piece of music is conceived authentically towards asking who it authenticates and on what grounds, and he has analysed songs and song lyrics in detail.

Unusually, the Department looks at all stages of sound, from its inception through composition, performance, analysis, recording, reproduction and consumer reception. It is thought that only a handful of concert halls can do full justice to the complete spectrum of musical works. Architects rely on only a limited range of acoustic measurements to test auditory reception. It is to tackle this that the Institute of Sound Recording, with support from Bang &

Olufsen, is developing an 'artificial listener'. This should be capable of advising designers of auditoria and manufacturers of sound systems not only on the quality of the listening experience but also on how they can make improvements. The new system, says Dr Tim Brookes, 'will simulate the way in which a person perceives sound' and its spatial attributes – whether a sound seems near or far, narrow or enveloping. As important, the system is able to be programmed with the performance of existing concert halls, thus allowing comparisons. In theory, a 'virtual' concert hall could be devised, with the 'perfect' listening sound. While the final system is some years away, the initial results are encouraging and already leading to applications in audio systems and hearing aids.

The objectives of the new Department of English, which opened in 2008, include not only research, building up archival sources and symposia, but also collaborations with other institutions. Soon after its foundation, the Department formed links with Watts Gallery (the memorial museum of Victorian artist G.F. Watts) in nearby Compton. In 2012, to accompany the Gallery's major exhibition *Dickens and Art* marking the Dickens centenary, the Department of English will be mounting an international interdisciplinary conference, 'Dickens and the Visual Imagination', with the Paul Mellon Centre, London and Watts Gallery. Reflecting its strong interests in women's writing and the 'long nineteenth century', the Department is also hoping to secure funds to conduct doctoral

Mrs G.F. Watts (Mary Seton Fraser Tyler), 1887, oil on canvas, by George Frederic Watts (1817–1904). She was an important artist in her own right. (© Trustees of Watts Gallery, Compton, Surrey, UK/ The Bridgeman Art Library)

research on the Watts Gallery archive, which includes an important collection of diaries and papers relating to the artist's wife, Mary Seton Watts, an artist, a significant figure in the Arts and Crafts movement and her husband's biographer.

Associated with the new Department is the long-established Surrey Morphology Group (SMG), headed by Professor Greville Corbett FBA. It specialises in linguistic morphology (the study of word structure and associated grammatical information) and investigates the diversity in the possible types of structure found in the world's languages. One of its pioneering functions is making data freely available over the web, both providing databases of challenging phenomena and also contributing to the large-scale *World Atlas of Language Structures* (Oxford University Press), coordinated by the Max Planck Institute, Leipzig. Milestone studies have been made of grammatical gender, number and grammatical ambiguity. The Group has also worked on endangered languages, resulting in publications such as the *Archi Dictionary*. Created in 1992, SMG currently comprises an international team of research staff and doctoral students from the USA, Germany, Malta and Russia, as well as the UK, and has formal research links with Professor Nicholas Evans (Australian National University) and Professor Gregory Stump (University of Kentucky).

The Centre for Translation Studies, established nearly thirty years ago, has an international reputation for its innovative postgraduate teaching curriculum and its research in translation, audio description and interpreting. A recent study has explored the quality of videoconference interpreting in criminal proceedings with a view to developing training modules for legal practitioners and interpreters who are communicating in different locations. The rise of migration and multilingualism throughout the world requires professional translators and interpreters to master an ever broadening range of communication scenarios and skills and to be effective in business, legal, medical and many other settings. Teaching such skills is difficult to achieve with traditional teaching methods. Another project aiming to educate interpreters together with their clients in business and public service settings thus creates an adaptive 3D virtual environment that supports the acquisition and application of skills required by interpreters and those who work with them.

Archives and Learning

As well as the University's own extensive archive, Surrey has two specialist collections. The E.H. Shepard Archive contains illustrations and other material by Ernest Shepard, who famously illustrated *Winnie the Pooh*. It was brought to the University in 1974 by the artist himself, who lived in Guildford for over fifty years. In 1998, the collection was moved into its own space. Alongside the illustrations are manuscripts, the author's 53 handwritten diaries, over 3000 letters, his school exercise books, over 400 drawings from *Punch*, 300 pencil sketches and 250 pen and ink drawings and memorabilia.

The first major exhibition of the material, *The Man who Drew Pooh*, was held at Dulwich Picture Gallery in south London, in 2000; a book was also published on the collection. Altogether 19,000 visitors came to view Shepard's works. Since then over twenty exhibitions have been staged, including shows at Rotterdam in the Netherlands, Winnipeg in Canada and a tour of seven cities in Japan. In late 2007, following discussions with the E.H. Shepard Trust and members of the Shepard family, funding was raised to catalogue the material

E.H. Shepard seated at a desk full of drawing materials, probably taken at his studio at Woodmancote, Lodsworth, West Sussex, where he lived from 1955 to his death in 1976. (E.H. Shepard Archive, EHS/F/10/19)

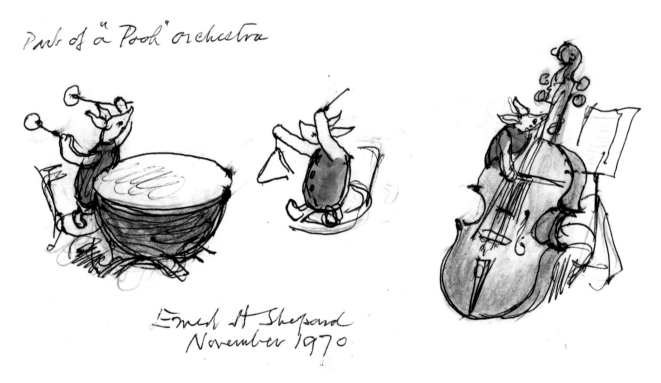

Part of a 'Pooh' orchestra, a biro and watercolour sketch of Piglet playing various instruments, drawn by Ernest Shepard in November 1970. (E.H. Shepard Archive, University of Surrey, EHS/G/6/2; copyright ©1970 The Estate of E.H. Shepard, by permission of Curtis Brown)

and make the catalogue available online, a project completed in 2009. The success of the project was celebrated with an event held with Shepard's grand-daughter in October 2010, which also helped to raise the profile of the collection.

The second specialist collection is the National Resource Centre for Dance (NRCD). The NRCD was founded in 1982 and it acquired its first permanent archivist in 2008. It aims to provide courses for teachers of dance and publications for dance teaching and study, and to house and build upon an existing archive of dance materials. Among the archive's papers, photographs, scrapbooks, set designs and ephemera are a number of special collections, including those of Rudolf Laban, the leading movement theorist of the twentieth century, which focuses on his unpublished writings but also contains thousands of drawings and 800 photographs; the Natural Movement archive of Madge Atkinson; and the work of a number of dance companies, including Kokuma Dance Theatre, London City Ballet and the touring company Extemporary Dance Theatre (1975–91).

Two major cataloguing projects have been undertaken in recent years. Dance Data On-Line, 2002–05, funded by the Arts and Humanities Research Council, put much of the Centre's material online. A more recent project, Pioneer Women, carried out in collaboration with the University's Dance, Film and Theatre Department and Middlesex University's Professor Alexandra Carter, focused on four women dance artists working during the early to mid twentieth century. As well as cataloguing, study days, an exhibition and a book

Nancy Sherwood, modern dance pioneer Ruby Ginner's leading demonstrator, in Hyde Park, 1933. The picture is one of the National Resource Centre for Dance's collection of dance images. (From the Pauline Grant photograph album, Bice Bellairs Collection, NRCD, BB/F/1)

were produced. A major current initiative is Performing the Archive, a range of creative, curatorial and critical projects that examine relationships between the body, memory, social history and archival practices. One of these, a collaboration between the Universities of Surrey and Coventry, is a pioneering project to develop a web-based platform for dance resources in the UK. The Digital Dance Archives will employ innovative search technology to enable the user to find resources not only by text search but also by visual similarity.

Chapter 5

The Twenty-first Century

'The Rising Star of Higher Education'

The beginning of the new millennium saw the University of Surrey facing the future with confidence. The excellence of its research was recognised in the 2001 RAE results (for details, see pp. 105–6). As a result, the research-related element of the HEFCE's allocation of core funding grew to £14.2 million for 2002/03, an increase of 21.5 per cent on the previous year. Research income from grants and contracts had doubled in a decade to almost £20 million in 2000/01. The University was less reliant than ever before on government funding.

On 13 July 2001, *Times Higher Education* called the University of Surrey 'the rising star of higher education', going on to say:

> It makes it into the top ten of two league tables of financial strength. Its reserves of more than £100 million are the seventh highest of any university in the United Kingdom [Cambridge was first with £375 million]. And for a university that dates back only to 1966 in its present form, it has built up impressive endowments, its £61 million placing it tenth [again, Cambridge was first, with £661 million]. On endowments Surrey outstrips half of the universities of the research-led Russell Group.

The University had changed greatly during the preceding decade and it now also had to deal with the changes brought in by the Government following the Dearing Report. From 1998/99 tuition fees were paid by students and there was also a remit to increase the number coming to university. The internet, however, also made it much easier for students to find out just what a university's strengths and weaknesses were. Students' Unions had for a long time produced alternative prospectuses, but in the 2000s student experience websites, such as thestudentroom.co.uk and push.co.uk, proliferated, offering insiders' views and allowing comparison of universities in similar fashion to price comparison websites. *Times Higher Education* and the National Student Survey (NSS) both also now produce polls (the latter annually since 2005).

The Stag Hill campus at the beginning of the twenty-first century.

In the light of all this, the University of Surrey, which had always welcomed quite a wide range of students, recognised that it needed to go further in broadening its appeal. In order to establish its future direction, in 2001 Professor Dowling instigated major strategic reviews of the academic strategy and the future shape of the University, as well as its decision-making structure, support services and administrative processes. One result of this was that the University departments were reorganised into seven larger Schools. Another was the creation of a more coherent strategy in health and medical sciences, with much closer ties to the NHS. There was also to be more focus on multidisciplinary research and teaching, and a more proactive approach to developing teaching methods and technologies that would aid effective learning.

Shaping Up for the Twenty-first Century

The next few years saw various initiatives put in train. On the academic front, aiming to make Surrey more attractive and accessible, especially to local students, the University expanded both the mode of course offered, with more part-time possibilities, and the variety of subjects. A Local History degree was established as an option on a part-time BA and BSc degree programme in Combined Studies, with courses held at centres across the county (the courses were discontinued in 2009 following a change in government funding policy which made them uneconomic to run).

Business Management students in the early days. Business Management is now a major area of studies and in 2011 the School of Management becomes the University of Surrey Business School.

More significant in the long run, two new degree programmes were introduced, one in Business Management, now a major area of the University, and the other in Law. Law and Language Studies had been offered at the University for a long time, but the 2000s were to see rapid expansion of Law undergraduate and postgraduate degrees and development of research. Single Honours Law is now one of the biggest courses at Surrey, and there is a well-established placement programme, with students on the Law and International Studies degree spending one term studying at partner universities in Sweden, Finland, Belgium, the Netherlands or Germany, and with work placements in the UK, Belgium or the USA. In recognition of its growth, and as part of the 40th anniversary celebrations of the founding of the University, Law studies became a School of Law in 2007.

Politics has been taught in one form or another for over thirty years at Surrey, originally being studied with languages in the 1970s and 1980s, but in 2004 it became a department in its own right. Over the course of time a Masters programme evolved until it reached its present form in the MA in European Politics, Business and Law, launched in 2000. The Department now focuses on citizenship and civil society, on the role people play in political and policy processes and also on international intervention (see p. 188). Since 2005 the Centre for Research on Nationalism, Ethnicity and Multiculturalism, a joint multidisciplinary research centre with Roehampton, has organised an annual international conference.

Other academic developments at the University in the first half of the 2000s included courses in Computing, developed with input from an industrial advisory board, and in Communication Studies; joint courses, such as the BSc in Financial Mathematics and BSc courses which combine Mathematics with Statistics, Computing, Business Studies, Management or Music; and generic business studies courses for the service sector. Surrey is rated as the top provider for tourism and hospitality in the UK and first for tourism and hospitality in the league tables of *The Times*, *The Independent* and *The Guardian*. In 2001 the Hospitality and Food Management Group was awarded a major government grant to study 'performance and best practice in hospitality'. The same year it began the first degree in e-Tourism. A single School of Engineering was also established at this time, bringing together all studies in the area (though in the 2007/08 restructure, this was divided into two in the new Faculty of Engineering and Physical Sciences), and the School of Biological Sciences was amalgamated with the Department of Chemistry and the Postgraduate Medical School (see below) to form the School of Biomedical and Molecular Sciences under Professor Andy Robertson, with Peter Goldfarb as Director of Research. Its formation not only reflected the University's increasing focus on health science, but repositioned it to direct attention

Professor David Airey receives the prestigious Ulysses award from the United Nations World Tourism Organization for his 'scientific contribution to the theory and practice of tourism policy and destination management', in 2006. The award was made at a ceremony in Madrid.

View across the lake to the Duke of Kent Building.

on what were becoming areas of mounting concern generally, environmental pollution, GM crops and contamination of the food chain.

The 2000s were to see major expansion in health studies. There was an increase in places for nursing students, whose studies would take place in the new Duke of Kent Building, but developments over the next decade were far more wide ranging than this. Launched in mid-1999, the International Centre for Nursing Ethics (ICNE) is a worldwide collaboration of researchers focusing on issues of morality, professional ethics, philosophy of care, cultural and religious values, law and accountability; the Centre publishes its own academic journal. The previous year, 1998, the Centre for Research in Nursing and Midwifery Education had been established to bring an interdisciplinary approach to research in health care education and practice.

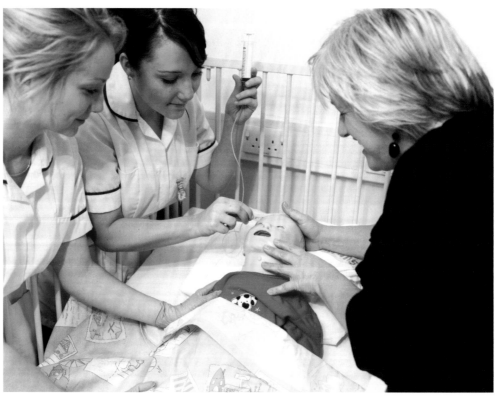

The interdisciplinary Centre for Research in Nursing and Midwifery Education provides a focus for new areas of research.

Early work included an international review of interventions in falls among older people and a study of osteoporosis screening in women.

The largest new development in health in the early part of the new century, however, was the establishment in March 2000 of the Postgraduate Medical School (PGMS) as a centre for health-related research. The University wanted to promote a close association between the School and Royal Surrey County Hospital (RSCH), so that education and research could be linked with clinical practice, and the plan was that in due course the School would move to a new building at Manor Park, close to local health services. Lying alongside Guildford's Nuffield Hospital and St Luke's Cancer Centre, as well as the RSCH, the PGMS was one of the first buildings in the University's new 'health campus'. In May 2004 work began, marked by an unusual ceremony in which Sir William Wells, then Chairman of the University Council, used a 'podger' to tighten the first bolt attaching a 16m-high column of steel to the ground. A year later, the 3500sq m three-storey building (Architects Design Partnership, from a concept by Arup Associates), constructed at a cost of £10 million, opened. Major funding came from the Wolfson Foundation, which gave £500,000 towards the diabetes laboratories, and GUTS (Guildford Undetected Tumour Screening – Colorectal Cancer), which contributed £300,000 towards the endoscopy unit and oncology.

Sir William Wells, Chairman of the Council of the University, carries out the bolt-tightening ceremony on the £10 million Postgraduate Medical School, May 2004.

Joint NHS/University appointments and the establishment of partnerships are key in fostering the exchange of ideas between research and clinical practice. PGMS research areas range from cancer vaccines and viral therapy to diabetes, and it has rapidly acquired an international reputation for its work. There is a training unit to combat bowel cancer, sponsored by GUTS, and the School undertakes bowel cancer screening and some other services for the NHS. The Minimal Access Therapy Training Unit, led by Director Professor Michael Bailey, one of the UK's leading surgeons in keyhole surgery, is an internationally recognised Centre of Excellence for the teaching of laparoscopic surgical techniques. Other key appointments include Margot Umpleby, Professor of Human Metabolism and Head of Diabetes and Metabolic Medicine, whose principal research area is insulin resistance in diabetes, and Professor Hardev Pandha, who became the PGMS's new Head of Oncology.

Another important development was the establishment of the Surrey Sleep Research Centre in 2003, based in the Clinical Research Centre. Bringing together researchers in various disciplines, this recognised the complexity of influences upon sleep, which can include biological mechanisms, psychological aspects and sociological determinants. Around the same time the Centre for Research into the Older Workforce opened. Its focus is legal, policy and health issues related to the over-fifties. With an increasing proportion of older people in the UK, the unit is interested in understanding the attitudes to retirement and work after fifty of older people and employers, and in how the skills of people over fifty can help overcome skills gaps.

Students at the Postgraduate Medical School.

Occasions for Celebration

On 29 May 2002, the University of Surrey and the Borough of Guildford celebrated the University's 35th anniversary. The event was marked with a Service of Thanksgiving and the conferment of degrees on the year's honorary graduates in the cathedral. The High Sheriff of Surrey, actor Penelope Keith, then joined music students from the University and students from the Guildford School of Acting in a celebration in words and music. A procession along the High Street of the high officers of the University and representatives of academic staff, Guildford Borough Councillors and representatives of local schools, colleges, community organisations and churches followed. At the bottom of the High Street, the Chancellor, HRH The Duke of Kent, unveiled *The Surrey Scholar*, a statue commissioned from Allan Sly. This would, said Patrick Dowling, the Vice-Chancellor, stand as a 'permanent reminder of the University in the heart of its home town'. The same day the University launched publication of its second history, *Understanding the Real World: A Visual History of the University of Surrey*, a highly illustrated coffee table book.

The procession makes its way down the High Street for the University's 35th anniversary celebrations.

HRH The Duke of Kent, Vice-Chancellor Professor Patrick Dowling, sculptor Allan Sly FRBS, the High Sheriff of Surrey Penelope Keith and the Mayor of Guildford Councillor Tony Phillips admire *The Surrey Scholar* in Guildford, unveiled for the 35th anniversary celebrations.

Professor Alf Adams was awarded the Queen's Anniversary Prize for Higher and Further Education in 2002. He was presented with the award at Buckingham Palace by HM The Queen and HRH the Duke of Edinburgh in 2003.

There were further causes for celebration. In 2002, the University received The Queen's Anniversary Prize for Higher and Further Education in recognition of its outstanding work over three decades in the fields of ion beam applications and optoelectronic devices, led by Professors Brian Sealy and Alf Adams and their research groups. The Surrey Ion Beam Centre, the only national facility of its kind, is a European Centre of Excellence. First established in 1965, its work has been in the application of ion beams – streams of positive ions that are created by the removal of an electron from an atom to form a plasma, and then accelerated at speeds of up to one-tenth the speed of light (70,000,000mph) and shot at a target – to modify the material, optical or electrical properties or to probe the structure of the target. Applications include SIMOX, an insulating material used in space programmes, analysis of building materials and modification of semiconductor devices and optoelectronic devices – transistors, lasers, microwave sources and detectors of all kinds. Alf Adams commented: 'I am delighted that our research has been recognised with this award. Here at the University of Surrey we invented, explained and helped demonstrate strained quantum well lasers in the 1980s. These devices now generate the signals in every long-haul optical fibre in the world.'

The Ion Beam Centre, a UK national facility supported by the Engineering and Physical Sciences Research Council.

The statue of Alan Turing (1912–54) which stands on the piazza outside the Austin Pearce Building. It was unveiled by HRH The Earl of Wessex on 28 October 2004.

HRH The Earl of Wessex at the Performing Arts Technology Studios.

The following year, SSTL was recipient of the 2003 Tech Track award for the fastest growing technology company. Its clients had included several governments and also NASA. The company, said Patrick Dowling, 'has now built, launched and operated more micro-satellites than any other single organisation in the world'. It was a significant achievement for a company still less than 25 years old. Two years later, SSTL won The Queen's Award for Enterprise in Innovation for its development of micro-propulsion systems on its spacecraft that derive their power from steam rather than highly toxic chemicals. The system had been demonstrated in space on board the UK Disaster Monitoring Constellation satellite which had been able to provide up-to-date imaging to aid agencies during the aftermath of the recent Asian tsunami. HRH The Duke of York came to SSTL to present the award in June 2005.

In October 2004, the University welcomed HRH The Earl of Wessex to unveil a magnificent bronze statue of scientist Alan Turing, the codebreaker and inventor of the machine that became the basis of modern computing. The Earl also visited the Performing Arts Technology Studios, student radio station GU2 and SSTL. Commission of the 8ft 6in statue from John W. Mills marked the fiftieth anniversary of the death of the scientist, who lived in Guildford in his early life. The statue stands on the piazza in front of the Austin Pearce Building, which houses the University's computer labs. The following May, HRH The Duke of Kent opened the new I-Lab, a multidisciplinary research centre for testing user interactions with new technologies.

Left: Professor Sir Martin Sweeting received The Queen's Award for Enterprise in 2005 on behalf of SSTL. Sir Martin pioneered the concept of rapid-response, low-cost and highly capable small satellites utilizing COTS devices to 'change the economics of space'. (SSTL)

Below: Professor Patrick Dowling was awarded the CBE in the New Year Honours List 2001. It was presented to him at Buckingham Palace the following October.

In 2005 Professor Patrick Dowling had been at Surrey for eleven years and he felt it was time to move on. He had done much to transform the University, and in 2001 had been awarded the CBE in the New Year Honours List. After the ceremony at Buckingham Palace, he remarked: 'I am not used to getting letters from 10 Downing Street. It was for helping with relations between universities and industry. In reality that is what the University of Surrey is all about.'

A New Vice-Chancellor and a New Strategy

Professor Christopher Snowden took up his post on 1 July 2005. He had previously been Joint Chief Executive Officer at Filtronic plc, Professor of Microwave Engineering at the University of Leeds and a Visiting Professor in Physics at the University of Durham. The University had made great strides in the opening years of the twenty-first century, but there were certainly challenges ahead. Not the least of these was to deal with recent changes in government policy regarding education, and in particular what Professor Snowden described as 'by far the most contentious issue', the introduction of variable tuition fees in 2006/07.

The University's four vice-chancellors: the bronze of Dr Peter Leggett (Battersea College of Technology 1960–66; University of Surrey 1966–75), Professor Anthony Kelly (1975–94; left), Professor Patrick Dowling (1994–2005, right); and Professor Christopher Snowden (2005–present, centre).

In 2004, the government's White Paper *The Future of Higher Education* had stated, for the first time, a specific target for take-up of university education: it wanted participation of 'towards 50 per cent of those aged 18–30 years by the end of the decade', through in particular wider access and expansion of work-focused foundation degrees. How it arrived at the figure has never been made clear. The Government also planned to reward up to seventy of the best teaching departments by designating them Centres for Excellence and giving them funding of £500,000 a year for five years to spread pedagogical practice – in early 2005 the University was successful in landing a bid to the HEFCE to become a Centre for Excellence in Teaching and Learning. But it was the fees issue that drew most attention. The Higher Education Bill that evolved saw the Government increase tuition fees from a means-tested £1125 up-front payment to a variable top-up fee of up to £3225 that would be set by the institutions themselves. The fees were to be repaid by students after graduation, directly deducted from their pay once their income was above £15,000 per annum. An increased grant now covered both tuition and living expenses – it was anticipated that around 30 per cent of students would be eligible for this. Surrey students were among the 31,000 around the country who staged widespread protests at the proposed increases and there was also industrial action by AUT and NATFHE. To no avail: the Act was passed.

Professor Dowling stated in the 2003/04 *Annual Report* that the fees increase was necessary in order to 'provide much-needed resources for the University to enable it to invest in its future'. A package of scholarships and

Surrey's Big Band achieved the highest standard Gold award at the National Concert Band Festival (NCBF) in Manchester for the third year running in 2005, and was given a special award for this achievement. In 2011, it won a Platinum award at the NCBF in Glasgow.

bursaries was made available to ensure access for poorer students and reward merit. With a view to enhancing the offering to students, key developments were instigated. On the academic front, these included a stand-alone Law School and the new Postgraduate Medical School. There were also plans to develop a campus at Manor Park.

In his final year, 2004/05, Profressor Dowling and the new Senior Deputy Vice-Chancellor Professor John Turner introduced the elements of a new academic strategy – including broadening the University's academic range, widening participation, more focus on teaching and learning, with personal development plans for all students, and further investment in research. However, the strategy did not really bed in effectively, and the new Vice-Chancellor Christopher Snowden's plans for the University were more far-reaching and ambitious – he wanted to make Surrey 'a world-class university for the twenty-first century'. He thus put in hand the creation of a more radical strategy, to be developed by consultation with the University and the management team, and 'built on the principle of involving staff in a very ambitious and dynamic strategy that was easy to understand'.

Professor Stephen Williamson was apponted Deputy Vice-Chancellor for Research as an element of the drive to strengthen research, part of the new corporate strategy.

Surrey Technology Centre provides space for 78 small technology companies and start-ups. About 40 per cent of the tenants of other buildings on the Research Park graduated from this building.

In February 2006 Professor Snowden outlined his thoughts. He felt 'there should be a greater emphasis on the arts, and in particular the performing arts'. He wanted to look at the introduction of an English course and a Performing Arts Centre and also to 'strengthen the Surrey Space Centre'. There would also be a campaign to reduce energy use around the University and property insulation was to be upgraded. 'The key message that I would like to get across,' he said, 'is that the University truly is committed to quality and we are investing in that area as it is so important to us.'

The following year the Schools were restructured into four Faculties to facilitate a more streamlined and student-focused education. This, it was thought, would also reduce costs and lead to greater interdisciplinary cooperation and increased research income. Following a campus-wide job evaluation, and after some negotiation, the new nationally agreed 'pay spine' was brought in. But the most important initiative of 2007 was the launch of Strategy 2007–2017, the corporate strategy for the next ten years. Ambitiously designed to take Surrey to a national and internationally leading position, it aimed to 'significantly advance the University, its staff and students'. It focused on six themes:

- Quality
- International impact
- Distinctiveness
- Collegiality
- Professionalism
- Sustainability

'My goal,' said Professor Snowden, 'is to be amongst the top ten UK universities and in the top 100 universities globally [in ten years' time].' While the University was good at research, he wanted to bring teaching and learning up to the same high standard and to enhance the student experience. There would be a new world-class sports park, construction of more buildings and a general upgrading of accommodation, with reference to sustainable environmentally friendly practices. 'We are also establishing ourselves as a truly international university,' said Professor Snowden. This means, he said, 'becoming global in our thinking', as well as initiatives such as the collaboration with Dongbei University of Finance and Economics (DUFE; p. 212). The University aimed to retain its distinctiveness in its links to the world of work, its enterprise culture and collaboration between pure and applied research. It looked to increase enterprise education and to extend continuing professional development courses and knowledge transfer partnerships.

'We also recognise,' said Professor Snowden, 'that the University has to become more sustainable, both financially and in terms of our environment.' Since the drastic cuts of the 1980s, the University had used Research Park income to subsidise its academic activities, but by 2008 this had started to limit the scope for strategic investment. A key financial goal of Professor Snowden's Strategy was to break even on academic activities by 2012 and use Research Park surpluses to invest in strategic initiatives. This was achieved ahead of schedule in 2011.

Acknowledging that 'simply being good at what we do is not enough to guarantee success, [and that] we also need to be recognised as such', the University also introduced a new logo. It was designed 'to reflect both our strong heritage and our confidence for the future. The stag is an effective representation of the University: bold, independent and ambitious.'

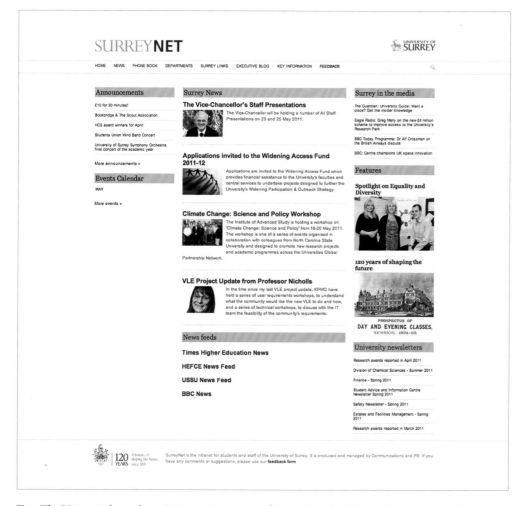

Top: The University's new logo. **Bottom**: Home page of SurreyNet, the University's new intranet hub, which has improved internal communication.

Since 2007, Surrey has introduced a number of changes. The University adopted a Carbon Management Plan with a target to reduce CO_2 emissions by 25 per cent by 2017 (on a 2006/07 baseline) – see Chapter 4 for details of its broader environmental strategy. Internal communication was radically enhanced and improvements were made. There is a new intranet hub, SurreyNet, with not only a bulletin board but also features, news sections and blogs from the senior executives. Professor Snowden, the Vice-Chancellor, holds regular lunches for the different student groups (undergraduate, taught postgraduate, research postgraduate), where issues of concern can be aired. There are Brief Encounters sessions every few months, at which ten-minute presentations are given by staff and students on themes of their choice. The first took place in March 2010, with contributions including caffeine research, the University's Fairtrade Society, Surrey Space Centre and the 'Big Pink Stroll', a fundraiser in aid of Cancer Research UK. Details of the sessions can also be accessed on the web and as podcasts.

One strand of the Strategy is to increase student numbers by over 5,000 over the ten years. In 2006/07, there were 11,595 students at the University. Student applications in 2007 already showed a 40 per cent increase and by 2009/10 the total number of students had reached 14,778. Between 2006/07 and 2009/10 the number of undergraduates rose by 28 per cent to 9,482. In comparison, the increase in enrolments in higher education institutions in the UK as a whole rose from 2,304,705 in 2006/07 to 2,493,420 in 2009/10 (the last figures available), with the number of undergraduates rising in the same period to 1,914,715, a 6.25 per cent increase. Surrey's success in driving

The number of students on campus has grown tremendously in the past five years, and in 2011 stood at 14,947 in total.

up student numbers is thus far above the national average. In 2010/11 total undergraduate numbers at the University stood at 10,534. Vice-Chancellor Professor Snowden is particularly proud that this has not been achieved at the expense of lowering standards; indeed the average tariff points required to undertake a degree at Surrey have improved from 315 in 2005 to 410, with the majority of subjects requiring a minimum AAB.

Widening participation remains part of Surrey's agenda, its importance to students underlined by the fact that it is reported as a priority in the 2010 *National Student Forum Report*. The University first set up a Widening Participation Strategy in 2001 in response to HEFCE funding requirements. This was reviewed in 2004 and 2009, and today outreach is a significant part of University life. The University provides activities for over 34,000 local school and college students each year and every Faculty has a Schools Liaison Officer. The Educational Liaison Centre also runs an on-campus aspiration-raising programme for schools and colleges aimed at students who have the potential to succeed in higher education but are from under-represented groups. It supports students from families with little or no experience of higher education or those needing additional support and guidance. On-campus workshops are offered to a range of age groups. These are very popular and over 2000 young people participate annually. Despite the wave of government and university initiatives, the level of 18–30-year-olds in full-time higher education has, however, remained relatively stable, at just under 40 per cent – perhaps inevitable given that fees are only one deterrent; just as important, if not more so, are social background and the level of education within the family.

The University's outreach activities include on-campus workshops for school children.

Vicki Hansford (centre), Sports Development Officer, who won the mixed coxed fours adaptive rowing in the World Rowing Championships, 2006.

At Surrey, the strengths of the University were increasingly recognised in the late 2000s. In 2008 the University was shortlisted for the *Times Higher Education* University of the Year award (Leicester won). Surrey rose over 100 places in the Shanghai Jiao Tong academic rankings of world universities. And in the 2008 RAE, 88 per cent of University research was rated world class or of international quality (see p. 114 for details). Research funding and grants income reached £25.3 million in 2008/09. Professor Snowden welcomed the encouraging RAE but he was cautious about the future. It heralded, he said, 'a period of austerity in public spending'. Nonetheless, helped by the sale of SSTL to EADS Astrium in December 2008 for £31.3 million – the largest cash sale of a university spin-out company in UK history – the 2008/09 year ended 'very much in line with budget and a breakeven operating result after accounting for our restructuring costs'.

However, as the Government headed towards an election amid the deepest global recession in recent history, a period of astringency crept in everywhere. The University was not the worst hit by any means. Protected to some extent by income from the Research Park and the fact that only 26 per cent of its income derives from core funding (compared with core funding of 30 per cent or more for most universities), while some cost-cutting was required, this was largely achieved through improved efficiency and leaving vacancies unfilled, though there were 49 redundancies (in 2009). Deeper cuts, however, were not to be long in coming. The Browne Review of higher education was instigated by the Labour Government in 2009, but it would be the new Coalition Government, elected in May 2010, that would wield the axe to public funding. No one and nothing could hope to escape its effects.

Academic Developments

Academic changes were led by the restructure into the four new Faculties:

- Faculty of Health and Medical Sciences, with Dean Professor John Hay
- Faculty of Management and Law, with Dean Professor Bob O'Keefe (from July 2010, Professor David Allen)
- Faculty of Engineering and Physical Sciences, with Dean Professor Michael Kearney (from October 2011, Professor Jonathan Seville)
- Faculty of Arts and Human Sciences, with Dean Professor Nick Emler (from July 2010, Professor Phil Powrie)

The four Faculty heads at the time of the restructure in 2007: Professors John Hay (top left), Bob O'Keefe (top right), Michael Kearney (bottom left) and Nick Emler (bottom right).

An important development that preceded the restructure, however, was the foundation of SCEPTrE, the Surrey Centre for Excellence in Professional Training and Development, the result of a £3.4 million government grant following recognition of Surrey's achievement in graduate employability. The only Centre for Excellence in the country not to be attached to a particular discipline, SCEPTrE supports professional training across the University through providing information and resources and fostering exchange of good practice. It helped to transform the quality of teaching and learning during its five years, before HEFCE funding finished in 2010 and the Centre's work came to an end.

There were a number of academic developments in the Faculty of Health and Medical Sciences. Fresh research themes were introduced, including Infection and Immunity, in which the use of systems biology is being applied to understand host/microbe interactions, a new multidisciplinary approach to understanding cellular function. A degree programme in Veterinary Biosciences was introduced in 2009 to meet the shortage of veterinary pathologists and researchers. The Department has close contacts with those working in the field and placements take place at the Veterinary Laboratories Agency and the Institute for Animal Health, both of which also supply some of the teaching resources.

The School of Management (renamed the University of Surrey Business School in 2011) is unique in being the only business school in the world to hold simultaneous accreditation from the Association to Advance Collegiate

One of the MSc International Event Management student teams which organised *Urban Life: Art Interpreted* in 2010.

Schools of Business, the Association of MBAs and the United Nations World Tourism Organization – the first in the UK to receive the latter for both its undergraduate and postgraduate Tourism programmes. It offers a very full programme of courses and has strong links with business. In 2006 the School launched a new Centre for Management Learning and Development and the same year hosted the Leadership Skills Conference. The Centre is concerned with the processes that facilitate learning and development, including action learning, the role that intuition plays in decision making, management and leadership, and transformative learning, such as Neuro-Linguistic Programming (NLP). Significant new courses at the School include the Accounting and Finance degree, offered in conjunction with the Chartered Institute of Management Accountants, the BSc in Financial Services Management, delivered in association with the Institute of Financial Services, and the MBA in Hospitality, all of which were launched in 2007/08.

Founded in 1982 and thus one of the oldest research centres in the University, the Centre for Translation Studies maintains close links with both the Institute of Translation and Interpreting and the Chartered Institute of Linguists. In 2009 the renowned MA in Translation became part of the European Masters in Translation Network launched by the European Commission's Directorate-General for Translation (the EC's in-house translation service) to improve the quality of translation training. It is one of only five university courses in the UK to achieve such distinction.

In 2008 the Department of English opened, with Professor Marion Wynne-Davies at its helm. The focus is on contemporary literature, though the Department also deals with the canon from *Beowulf* onwards. Like Surrey's other degrees, that in English Literature has both an international bias and a placement year, with students working in arts centres, libraries and galleries, and in marketing, teaching and journalism. The creative writing side of the Department is growing, with recent developments including a magazine written by students, *Potlatch*. The Department also has visits and readings from writers, among whom recently have been Emma Darwin and Fiona Sampson, and it conducts workshops in local schools. In 2009, a Theatre Studies programme was inaugurated to explore the ideas and practices in contemporary theatre-making, both nationally and internationally.

The University is also growing its continuing professional development (CPD) courses. These are increasingly being integrated with the standard degrees, with part-timers able to choose particular modules or to

Professor Marion Wynne-Davies, the driving force behind Surrey's new English Literature degree programme, who joined the University in 2007.

Earth Day was staged in cooperation with the Guildford community on 22 April 2010 and showed scientific applications effective for a low carbon lifestyle and ways to reduce carbon in the workplace. Here we see one of South East Physics Network's wave tanks, built to demonstrate to school students how wave power works. The tank here uses the sea snake method: the waves are generated by the student turning a handle, and the waves then bend the different tubes up and down causing the magnets inside them to move inside coils of wire, generating electricity, in this case lighting LEDs.

study for a certain number of hours per week, gradually building up to a qualification. The BSc and MSc in Professional Practice are negotiated awards which offer students from health and social care backgrounds the opportunity to 'shape' awards that fit their careers. 'Their learning is moulded and allows greater opportunity than traditional approaches,' says Melanie Coward, who runs CPD in Health and Social Care.

Health and Electronic Engineering are perhaps the most active CPD areas. The part-time MSc in Applied Toxicology, aimed at in-post scientists, has been running in its present form since 1992 and is now the largest training programme of its type in Europe. It attracts participants from all over the world and contributes towards the requirements for the Register of Toxicologists. Similar part-time MScs are offered in Pharmaceutical Medicine, Nutritional Medicine and Occupational Health and Safety. The MSc in Advanced Gynaecological Endoscopy, delivered by academics and clinicians at the Postgraduate Medical School and run in partnership with the British Society for Gynaecological Endoscopy, is designed to allow students to complete modules alongside their clinical development. It provides gynaecologists with a firm theoretical background in diagnostic and operative gynaecological endoscopy in combination with the development of clinical competence in operative laparoscopy and hysteroscopy.

Electronic Engineering offers a variety of short courses, frequently run in conjunction with industry, ranging from RF (Radio Frequency) Systems and Circuits to Introduction to Satellite Communications. Its MSc in Electronic Engineering is also now available via short courses so that students can study at their own pace and accommodate studying around work commitments. Modules range from Nanotechnology and Spacecraft Systems Design to Image Processing. Students can also undertake projects in industry as part of the course, in the same way as those on the standard MSc. The new Surrey Sports Park (see below, pp. 214–19) also holds CPD courses, the first, for competition managers from around the county, being held in May 2010. The Park also hosts Primary Link Teachers events.

In summer 2010 the University of Surrey welcomed two new Deans, Professor David Allen to the Faculty of Management and Law (FML), in succession to Professor Bob O'Keefe, and Professor Phil Powrie to head the Faculty of Arts and Human Sciences (FAHS) in succession to Professor Nick Emler. New Yorker Professor Allen was previously Professor of Strategic Management at IE Business School in Madrid, ranked third in Europe and sixth in the world, where he had been since 1992; he has also held top management posts in several industries. Plans in his new role include a possible programme on law, business and society, probably an MA.

New Faculty Deans Professor Phil Powrie (left) and Professor David Allen.

There were a number of important developments in FML in 2011. First, Economics was moved from FAHS to FML, which is to be renamed the Faculty of Business, Economics and Law. Hospitality and Tourism is becoming a separate School within the Faculty. This, it is hoped, will give it a higher profile both within the University and, more particularly, outside it. The renamed University of Surrey Business School, with its MBA, will thus also gain wider recognition as a business school. Professor Simon de Lusignan has been appointed the new Chair in Health Care Management.

Professor Phil Powrie, a linguist with interests in film and media, came to Surrey following a successful academic career at the Universities of Newcastle and of Sheffield, where he was Pro-Vice-Chancellor and set up the new Faculty of Arts and Humanities. He wants to build on the strengths of FAHS, in particular 'to look at ways in which departments can work much more closely together' and to expand their internationalism. In 2011 Professor Marie Breen-Smyth was appointed the new Chair in International Intervention in the Department of Politics. Together with Professor Sir Michael Aaronson, she is launching the Centre for International Intervention – cii, lower case to differentiate it from the more conventional association with military force – a multidisciplinary centre concerned with reclaiming the idea of international intervention as a universal human responsibility of those who can offer protection and assistance to vulnerable people on the basis of our common humanity. There is also a new MA in International Intervention.

On 16 June 2011, the £4.5 million Ivy Arts Centre had its grand opening, with a gala show produced and performed by all the arts departments at the University. Housed in a former sports building released after the Surrey Sports Park opened, the Centre operates as performance space for

The Faculty of Arts and Human Sciences promotes the many arts events with posters around the campus.

both those inside the University and for visiting artists. It houses 197 people in the main theatre, with provision for another two dozen people sitting on the first floor balcony. Facilities also include a bar, changing rooms, a green room, three performance dance studios, and costume-making and scenery work-spaces. 'The new Ivy Arts Centre, coupled with the GSA [Guildford School of Acting] opposite it, realises the ambition of creating an arts hub right at the entrance to the campus,' comments Professor Powrie. 'Staff, students and visitors

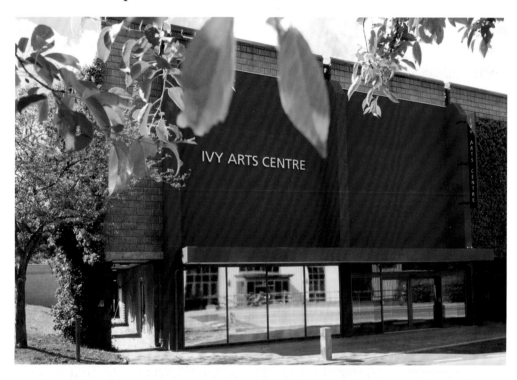

Top: The new Ivy Arts Centre Building, which opened in 2011.
Bottom: The auditorium in the Ivy Arts Centre.

will now enter the University through an arts gateway.' It is also, he says, testament to 'the University of Surrey's commitment to promoting the arts, both as a key academic discipline and as one of the major ways in which we support the creative industries. It also puts another top-class venue on Guildford's cultural map.'

The opening of the Ivy Arts Centre provided an opportunity to refocus Surrey's arts offering and to bring all activities, including the Arts Office, the two Guildford festivals (Music and Books, see p. 205) and the Guildford School of Acting, which came on campus in 2009 (see pp. 198–202), together within FAHS. The objective, says Professor Powrie, is to 'pull together the fine arts and the creative arts into a single and very dynamic arts offering for the University of Surrey and for the Guildford community'. Posters proclaiming the arts 'brand' have appeared across the residences, raising the Faculty's visibility and ensuring students in all disciplines know what is going on. A new website, set up just before Christmas 2010, provides a calendar of events and has resulted in a much higher level of engagement and interest.

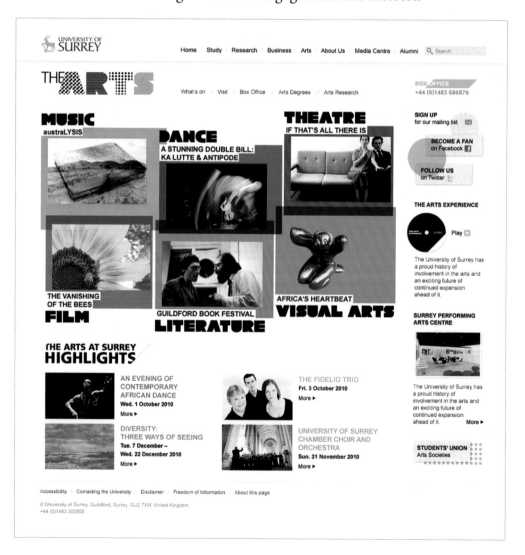

Home page of the new Arts website, launched at the end of 2010, which provides information for students, staff and the local community of arts events at the University of Surrey.

Described recently by an Engineering and Physical Sciences Research Council (EPSRC) spokesman as 'a shooting star among setting suns', the University and its academics have garnered a number of prestigious awards in recent years, a marker of its growing status. It is, of course, impossible to list all awards, but they include the following: Lewis Elton was recipient of the *Times Higher Education* Lifetime Achievement Award in 2005; Professor Airey received the Ulysses award from the United Nations World Tourism Organization in 2006 for his scientific contribution to the theory and practice of tourism policy and destination management; Professor Roland Clift, Centre for Environmental Strategy, was made CBE in 2006 for services to the environment; Dr Malcolm Parry, Director of the Surrey Research Park, was awarded an OBE in 2006; Professor Jim Al-Khalili – well known for his television science series – was awarded the Royal Society's Michael Faraday Prize in 2007 and in the 2008 Queen's Birthday Honours List was made OBE for 'Services to Physics, and in particular for popularising physics and science for the general public through his writing and broadcasting'; Professor Ravi Silva was elected Fellow of the Royal Academy of Engineering in 2008; Professor Sara Arber was elected Fellow of the British Academy in 2008; Professor Sir Martin Sweeting won the Sir Arthur C. Clarke Lifetime Achievement Award in 2008 and the Faraday Medal of the Institution of Engineering and Technology in 2009; Professor Josef Kittler, Head of the Centre for Vision, Speech and Signal Processing, won the Faraday Medal in 2009 for

Left: Professor Roland Clift (left), Centre for Environmental Strategy, was made CBE in 2006 for services to the environment. He is pictured with John Davis (right), the Vice-Chancellor's chauffeur who chauffeured him on the day. (John Davis joined the University in 1968 as Senior Chef. He then became chauffeur and was also mace bearer at the University's graduation ceremonies for 17 years until he retired in 2010.)
Right: Professor Josef Kittler (left), Head of the Centre for Vision, Speech and Signal Processing, won the Faraday Medal in 2009. (Institution of Engineering and Technology)

his work on pattern recognition, image processing and computing; Professor Christopher Snowden was awarded the Distinguished Educator Award from the Institute of Electrical and Electronics Engineers in 2009, the first Briton to be given the prize; Professor Stephen Halloran, Senior Research Fellow and Director of the Bowel Screen Southern programme hub, was made MBE in 2010; and Tim Jackson, Professor of Sustainable Development, was elected to the Academy of Social Sciences in 2010.

The period also saw more general acclaim. In 2006 Professor of Physics Alf Adams and Professor Sir Martin Sweeting, Director of the Surrey Space Centre and CEO of SSTL, were listed by *Eureka UK* among UK academics who had made 100 life-changing developments and inventions. *The Guardian* and *The Independent* also chose them as two of the 'Ten Britons who shaped our world'. And in 2010 Alf Adams' breakthrough in strained quantum well lasers was chosen as one of the Top Ten UK scientific discoveries of all time.

The University has also seen its academics elected to various important external positions. Among these, Professor Sara Faithfull is President of the European Oncology Nursing Society and the Vice-Chancellor, Professor Christopher Snowden, is Vice-President to the Board of Trustees of the Institution of Engineering and Technology, serving as its President in 2009/10, as well as a member of the Engineering and Physical Sciences Research Council and Vice-President of the Royal Academy of Engineering. In 2007, the University of Surrey was elected to chair the Education and Science Council of the United Nations World Tourism Organization, a post it held until 2010.

The plan for Manor Park was that it would eventually provide 4500 student and staff bedrooms, as well as academic and sports facilities.

Manor Park and Campus Developments

By the early years of the new century, following the wave of construction projects in the second half of the 1990s – the Advanced Technology Institute and the School of Management Building opened in 2002 and 2003 respectively – Stag Hill development was nearing completion. International House, primarily as its name suggests a residence for international students, was opened in 2003 at a cost of £8.4 million. Designed by architects Lewis and Hickey to reflect the Advanced Technology Institute Building opposite, its three storeys provide 258 student bedrooms arranged in six-bedroom flats.

The number of students at Surrey was now far in excess of that which had been originally envisaged, however – in 1966, Surrey planned for 3000 students in total – and there remained great pressure on accommodation. By 2000/01, the number of undergraduates stood at 5347, the vast majority of them full-time, and there were a further 3765 postgraduate students. Moreover, government expectations were that, with wider access policies in action, student numbers should rise quite steeply. In fact, by the end of the decade (2009/10), Surrey would have 14,778 students. Tuition facilities needed expansion, and to provide further accommodation the University would need to look beyond the campus at Stag Hill.

International House, right, and, opposite, the Advanced Technology Institute.

Fortunately, those involved in the early plans for the University nearly forty years earlier had been able to acquire a great deal of land. The University's total landholding amounts to 962 acres, with 83 acres at Stag Hill. While the majority of what then remained unbuilt upon was farmland, and some 70 acres was allocated to the Research Park, there was another 186 acres at Manor Farm (including land leased to a hotel). The development of this land at Manor Farm – or as it was to be renamed, Manor Park – would be the key to the University's future. Here, Vice-Chancellor Patrick Dowling felt, the University could 'create a new campus that will meet the University's needs for the twenty-first century … Over the next thirty years or so, we will create a campus that – through the quality of its buildings and landscaping, through its attention to sustainability and environmental issues, and through the facilities it offers for research, teaching and leisure – will rival the best anywhere in the world.'

The University obtained outline planning permission to develop Manor Park for University use that would allow it to construct over 4500 student and staff bedrooms and over 180,000sq m of academic support and sports facilities. In addition the University could expand and develop its sports pitches. Once Guildford Borough Council had given the go-ahead for development and funding had been raised, construction began. The PGMS (see p. 165), opened in 2005, was the second main University academic building on Manor Park to accommodate activities related to medicine – the first being the Clinical Research Centre, opened in 1999 – and was the start of the new wave of quality buildings on the site. By 2011 the University had constructed just over 1800 bedrooms for staff and students, a new sports centre of approximately 13,000sq m and external sports facilities. In 2006 the first phase of the Manor Park residences (Architect, Broadway Mallion) was completed, the second phase following in 2009, for a combined cost of £55 million. The buildings are three or four storeys and grouped to give a 'public' street scene, while also affording some privacy, with semi-enclosed courtyards. The building design uses a limited range of materials, including sustainable cedar cladding

The new Manor Park residences.

An artist's impression of the extended Learning Resource Centre, completed in autumn 2011.

and render, in different proportions in different zones, to create a linked though differentiated effect. A network of footpaths and cycle paths takes students and staff to Stag Hill.

In summer 2011, the last of the current major building projects at Stag Hill came to fruition when the modern Learning Resource Centre became operational. An extension to the east end of the University Library, the £14 million building increases independent study space by 30 per cent. On the ground floor are the campus shop, a bookshop, a concourse and an informal learning zone with café. There is a new Library entrance and mixed study area on the second floor. The third floor accommodates the Department of Languages and Translation Studies.

In addition to major works, the University has been undertaking a programme of refurbishment since the mid-1990s. The cuts in the 1980s and the need to rebuild financially the academic base had resulted in a deterioration of the 1960s building stock. Because all of the buildings were built in such a short period, 80 per cent of the Stag Hill campus buildings were in dire need

Above: Some of the academic blocks, following the extensive refurbishments of 2009/10. Renovation of the older campus buildings has been a major project for the University over the past ten to fifteen years.
Below: The landscaping of the University, here at Stag Hill and at Manor Park, has been much improved over the years, thanks to Nigel Hodge and his team.

of refurbishment and the condition of the buildings was one of the worst in the sector. In the early 1990s Surrey, one of the first universities to do so, conducted an estates appraisal. The lack of investment prior to 1994 in academic and residential buildings was nearly at catastrophic proportions. However, improvements to the fabric of the buildings and upgrading of facilities means the University can now take pride in having one of the best campuses in the sector. The refurbishment has been gradual, measured and coordinated with academic changes and development needs, but in summer 2010 the University put in hand the 'largest redecoration programme that we have ever undertaken' on just under 1000 residential rooms at Cathedral Court, Hazel Farm, Manor Park and University Court. This programme of renovation and refurbishment across the estate included the replacement of all windows, retiling, cavity wall insulation, refitting of kitchens, improved lighting, replacement shower cubicles and vanitory units, renovating and upgrading toilet facilities across the campus, installation of smoke alarms, and new furniture. In 2010, the AD building was the last of the 1960s academic blocks to receive replacement double-glazed window systems and energy efficiency improvements. This marked the end of a 15-year programme that has replaced over 14,000sq m of windows, most of the core ventilation, a large proportion of the electrical distribution plant and all of the electrical infrastructure such as high voltage sub-stations and main intake rooms, across 70,000sq m of non-residential space and over 2000 bedrooms. Although the renovation continues, the only major external work in 2011 was the refenestration of the George Edwards Library to stop ingress of water through the walls and improve its insulation. While such work is far from being the most glamorous of building works, it is essential and makes a real difference to the quality of life for staff and students.

In addition, care of the grounds has continued under the expertise of Nigel Hodge and his team, both at Stag Hill and across on Manor Park, as well as at the Research Park, ensuring that planting and maintenance of the grounds make the campus a pleasant environment to work in and visit. Their most notable achievement in the last five years has been the creation of new sports terraces as part of the overall strategic development plan at Manor Park and at the Surrey Sports Park. This led to head groundsman Iain Main receiving a national award as 'Groundsman of the Year' in 2010, beating premier league football clubs and professional sporting organisations' grounds teams.

In a major achievement for the University, Iain Main was named 'Groundsman of the Year' in 2010 by the Institute of Groundsmanship. He gained commendations from around the globe for the facilities for the Women's Rugby World Cup at the Surrey Sports Park.

The Guildford School of Acting

In 2009, the Guildford School of Acting (GSA) came into the University of Surrey fold, moving its headquarters to a striking building (Architect, Penoyre & Prasadon) at the gateway to the Stag Hill campus in the autumn of that year. The story of the GSA, however, goes back to 1935 when Pauline Grant and Bice Bellairs set up the Grant-Bellairs School of Dance and Drama in London. During the war the School relocated to the comparative safety of Surrey, and in the mid-1960s it was renamed the Guildford School of Acting. It established close ties with Guildford's Yvonne Arnaud Theatre from the start.

GSA's reputation for training multi-skilled performers gained international recognition with the inception of the Musical Theatre course in 1967. It has since gone from strength to strength, establishing a leading reputation under the expert direction of Peter Barlow (GSA Director to 2010) and Gerry Tebbutt (Head of Musical Theatre) – who joined the School in 1994. Graduates have gone on to act in TV soaps and at the RSC, to perform in London's West End and to tour throughout the world. Among the stars are Michael Ball, Bill Nighy and Celia Imrie; recent graduates include Tom Chambers, Daniel Boys and Chloe Hart, who played the lead in *Hairspray*. Today, GSA offers courses ranging from national diplomas to foundation and postgraduate degrees.

GSA expanded gradually over the years, and in 1978 it opened the Bellair's Playhouse in Millmead Terrace, Guildford. By the early twenty-first century the School was spread across seven different teaching locations in the town. Links with Surrey slowly strengthened. GSA classes were taught to General Studies students in the early days at Guildford and in the 1990s degrees at GSA

The new Guildford School of Acting building, which became operational in 2009.

were moderated by the University. The amalgamation of the two can perhaps then be seen as the final step, and it has enabled GSA for the first time to be located on one site, with activities now either in the GSA building itself or in the Ivy Arts Centre across the road.

The new headquarters of the GSA was opened officially by HRH The Duke of Kent in April 2010. (GSA)

Many actors attended the GSA opening. Shown here with Peter Barlow, GSA Director, are, left to right, Brenda Blethyn OBE and Celia Imrie, both of whom were once students at Guildford, and other alumni Helena Blackman, Diana Marchment, Bronagh Waugh and Tom Chambers. (GSA)

Left: Actor Penelope Keith became a Pro-Chancellor of the University in 2009. She is also patron of the University's Annual Fund, which raises money from alumni for student projects.
Right: Brenda Blethyn OBE, GSA-trained and still an active governor, enjoys the performance of the GSA Singers at the official opening. (GSA; photographed by Steve Porter)

The new headquarters was opened officially in April 2010 by HRH The Duke of Kent. There were many high-profile alumni in attendance, including Oscar-nominated actress Brenda Blethyn and actor Penelope Keith CBE, who attended the event in her role as Pro-Chancellor of the University. Brenda Blethyn said, 'I was at the school in the mid-70s. It was a great school then and the new facilities are just wonderful. It teaches a good acting discipline and there is a great camaraderie. The actors here get the very best training.'

The building houses 15 dance and drama studios (two of which can be combined into one larger performance space), ten tutorial/practice rooms, showers and changing rooms, an IT and resource room, and administration offices. There is an open area with reception and café on the ground floor. Peter Barlow, Director of GSA at the time of the move to Stag Hill, said:

> I knew I wanted to create a lively vibrant modern building which had a heart and reflected the nature of the School and the community we try to create at GSA. The architects have done a first-class job of allowing light in and keeping sound out while preserving the warmth we had in our old studios.

From autumn 2011 GSA is mounting many of its productions in the new Ivy Arts Centre, which is also home to the Professional Production Skills students and staff, who are moving from the Millmead site. Productions continue to be staged at other Guildford venues – the Electric Theatre, Mill Studio and the Yvonne Arnaud Theatre – to ensure both GSA's profile within the town and comprehensive venue performance training for the students. Second-year Musical Theatre and Acting students are also selected for the

Top: GSA Performing Arts students practise an ensemble performance. (GSA)
Bottom: The GSA alumni day at its new HQ in September 2010 attracted nearly 200 visitors from all over the world and as far back as the 1940s. (GSA; photographed by Steve Porter)

GSA Singers, a company which performs songs from musical theatre and popular classics for business functions, private parties, weddings and concerts. Recent appearances include the Guildford Music Festival, the Trinity College funding ceremony, the opening of Guildford's new Civic Hall and the 2011 Olivier Awards ceremony at the Drury Lane Theatre, London.

Guildford and the Local Community

The University has continued its involvement with the local community, not only in joint activities with the Borough Council, such as the Book and Music Festivals, and open events on campus, but with volunteer work by students. Ties between town and gown have strengthened over the years, with both perhaps appreciating each other's qualities a little more. Says Guildford MP Anne Milton:

Guildford Cathedral, built shortly before the University, which stands above the campus and has been an important contributor to Surrey life.

> The University has evolved and matured and now rightly deserves the high level of respect and influence it has. Its contribution to Guildford, to research and to the economy cannot be overestimated and I am very proud to be the Member of Parliament representing an academic institution that has contributed so much.

Vice-Chancellor Professor Christopher Snowden has taken steps to ensure that local residents are happy, holding six-monthly meetings with representatives from residents' associations local to the University. The first of these was held in September 2009; for the second, residents were taken on a tour of the new sports facilities. Chaired by the local MP, in order to promote a balanced discussion, the idea of the meetings is to create an ongoing dialogue between the University and residents, so that any suggestions for improvement – from either side – where practical, may be taken up, and likely problems nipped in the bud.

The University offers a range of evening classes to the local community, something it has done for years; classes are also open to staff and students. Today, these are mainly for foreign languages, pottery and drawing. The latter are organised by the Arts Office, which in addition hosts a number of clubs: a Craft Club, a Creative Writers' Group, a Poetry Reading Group and a Photography Society. An informal Book Circle meets around once a month to discuss modern novels or classics. At GSA there is a thriving Saturday School for children and adults, as well as a highly

In the University's early days concerts were held at St John's, Smith Square, London. Here, the University orchestra is being conducted by Professor Sebastian Forbes. (Sebastian Forbes)

subscribed range of Summer Schools and part-time evening courses, all of which are aimed at those considering full-time training. The University hopes to expand its provision of evening classes in due course, particularly in humanities subjects, and several departments are holding active discussions regarding this.

With the cathedral looking onto the Stag Hill campus, one would expect there to be good links between it and the University below, and such is the case. The annual graduation ceremonies have taken place at the cathedral since 1970 by kind permission of the Dean and Chapter. Music has always been important at Surrey and there have been concerts in the cathedral since the University's early days, with the annual concert being a highlight of the academic year. For 15 years from the mid-1970s, concerts were also held at St John's, Smith Square, London. The Dean and Chapter of the cathedral, in

association with the University, began offering choral scholarships in the mid 1970s – today three are offered, for a countertenor, tenor and bass singer each year (subject to a vacancy being available).

The University organises the Guildford International Music Festival and the Guildford Book Festival in collaboration with Guildford Borough Council. Pauline Johnson, in the Department of Music and Sound Recording, is Artistic Director of the Guildford International Music Festival. Established in 1991, initially as a classical chamber music event, that first year the festival included the first solo recital of the young violinist Vanessa Mae; she also made her first ever recording in the Music Department's Performing Arts Technology Studios. Since then the festival has broadened to encompass a wide range of musical genres, as well as dance, digital technology, spoken word and theatre. Held over three weeks in March, it aims to bring international artists to Surrey and to devise events otherwise unlikely to be programmed in the region, and there is a strong contemporary strand. The festival also acts as a showcase for the work of the Music Department, with emphasis on new presentational formats and new works. Using non-traditional concert venues, or using venues in different ways, has therefore become an established feature of the festival.

Over the years, the festival has been host to some rising stars in music, and has also presented many innovative cultural events. Highlights include the first contemporary cultural event in Guildford Cathedral, for jazz saxophonist Courtney Pine and his band, and *The Descent of the Angel*, a gravity-defying vertical dance on the bell-tower of Guildford Cathedral (choreographer and vertical dancer Kate Lawrence from the Dance Department, composer Tim Brookes from the Department of Music and Sound Recording). Events in 2011, the eleventh festival to be held, included Sir Willard White revisiting the repertoire of Paul Robeson, rising star Benjamin Powell, winner of the eighth British Contemporary Piano Competition, the Bollywood Brass Band and renowned guitar player Paco Peña. There were notable performances

Above and opposite: Kate Lawrence from the Dance Department performs *The Descent of the Angel*, Guildford Cathedral, 20 March 2009. The act was also performed on 7 September 2009 as part of the British Science Festival, at the event to switch on the new lighting scheme of the cathedral.

from Surrey's own too: Professor Emeritus Sebastian Forbes conducted the Vox Chamber Choir, new works were performed by Composition students, the GSA Singers performed at Guildford's Continental Café, and Croissant Concerts provided an opportunity to hear some of the University's most talented players.

The annual Guildford Book Festival has been held over ten days in October since 1989. Similar to many such events around the country, it draws in authors and illustrators to talk about and read from their works. The campus has hosted writers from all genres over the years, including Fay Weldon, David Starkey, Sandi Toksvig, Jacqueline Wilson, Ray Mears, Jonathan Coe and Kate Mosse. In 2010, one event featured Tariq Goddard, once a lecturer at the University, speaking about his novel.

A number of other arts events are staged at the University throughout the year. From now on these will be at the Ivy Arts Centre. One is the annual Morag Morris Poetry Lecture, delivered on National Poetry Day in October, and sponsored by one of the University's major donors. Speakers have included Iain Sinclair on John Clare, Peter Porter on W.H. Auden and David Constantine on Thomas Hardy. Amy De'ath became Morag Morris Poet-in-Residence for a semester in February 2011, and this led to a series of workshops and readings.

The GSA Singers have performed at functions both at the University and beyond for many years.

Top: Professor Chris Orr of the Royal College of Art with Arts Administrator Pat Grayburn and Vice-Chancellor Professor Patrick Dowling, left, in the Lewis Elton Gallery. Professor Orr gave the inaugural University Arts Lecture in 2001 in conjunction with an exhibition of his work in the gallery.
Bottom: *All the Gang are Here* by Carol Orwin SWA, a local sculptor, which was installed on the University campus in 2007. Today, sculptures enrich the landscape at Surrey, making it an attractive environment for students, staff and visitors.

The Lewis Elton Gallery, established in 1997, continues to flourish, presenting exhibitions of modern artists which often draw visitors to the campus. The policy is to show the work of artists of international and national repute, local professional artists and student work from affiliated institutions. The University's own collection of art, purchased from its enterprise funds, has grown steadily over the years and today numbers around 500 pieces, which are spread around the campus. Special collections include Eilean Pearcey's drawings of the Indian dancer Uday Shankar (brother of Ravi), now housed in the National Resource Centre for Dance; the paintings of holocaust survivor Arnold Daghani, many of them in unusual media, such as sacking; and portraits of the officers of the University. There are numerous sculptures around the grounds by contemporary artists.

Surrey Science Circus is an annual event which is open to people of all ages. The event features a variety of lectures, exhibits, demonstrations and hands-on activities to inspire and engage visitors in the wonders of science. In 2010 2700 people attended events ranging from disco bikes and custard walking to making nitrogen ice cream and creating a lava lamp.

Another facet of University life is the series of 'Jim meets …' events presented by Professor of Physics, writer and broadcaster Jim Al-Khalili, Professor of Public Engagement in Science. Under an EPSRC Fellowship, Professor

Various activities, including the Light Workshop Drawings shown here, attracted the crowds at Surrey Science Circus 2010.

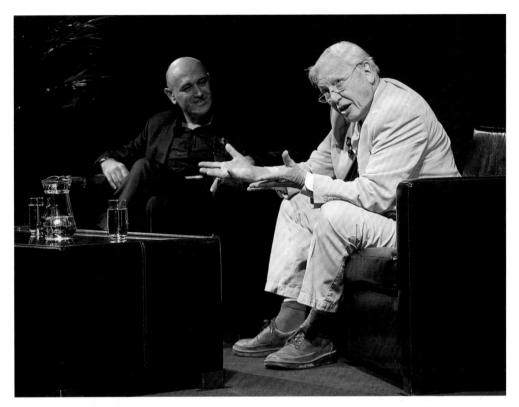

Professor Jim Al-Khalili in conversation with Sir David Attenborough at the University of Surrey, 22 October 2010, part of his series of 'Jim Meets ...' interviews with prominent public figures.

Al-Khalili acts as an ambassador for the University and for Science, and over the past five years he has held a series of, first, public debates and, more recently, conversations with well-known figures. The latter began when he interviewed Professor Lord Robert Winston in September 2009, the year the University hosted the British Science Festival. The festival brought thousands of visitors to the Surrey campus and was hailed by the British Science Association as their most successful for years. The event with Professor Winston was so popular that it led to a series of similar ones, held twice a year. Interviewees to date have included Sir David Attenborough, the Archbishop of Canterbury and Professor Brian Cox. One-off events are also staged, such as a panel discussion on 'The search for the God particle: is science the new religion?'

Robert Winston, Professor of Science and Society at Imperial College, London, joined the University Council in 2008.

International Links

The University's international strategy operates on a number of different fronts, from establishing links and partnerships with academic institutions across the world to providing support services for foreign students at Guildford – the student population is drawn from 140 countries – and devising exchange schemes and placements for Surrey students at foreign universities and international companies. An indication of the importance attached to an internationalist approach is the opening of the Surrey International Study Centre in 2007 and the appointment of Professor Colin Grant as Pro-Vice-Chancellor of International Relations in 2009.

The International Study Centre offers a rigorous foundation year programme for international students wishing to enter specific undergraduate degree programmes at the University. The courses cover not only English language skills – with a programme following the International English Language Testing System (IELTS) (the University is a recognised IELTS testing centre) – but study skills in either Business, Management and Economics or Engineering, Science and Mathematics. The University also runs pre-sessional language classes for foreign students accepted onto degree courses subject to

A visit to Surrey from the Hon. Kapil Sibal, India's Minister of Human Resource Development, and Professor Krishna Ganes, Vice-Chancellor of the Indian Institute of Science Education and Research, Pune. The visit marked a breakthrough in relations with academics at Indian universities and in particular the signing of an agreement between the University of Surrey and IISER Pune.

proficient English. These run for ten weeks before the academic year begins, but can be continued after students have begun their studies. The University's English Language Support Programme gives help with academic writing, grammar and presentation skills to international students who feel they need help with communication in English during their studies.

In the 2000s, the University began to establish the links with foreign academic institutions that have become such an important part of its strategy. The first of these was with the University of Kuopio in Finland. As part of the University Global Partnership Network (UGPN), initiated in 2007 as part of the new Strategy, the University has formed strong associations with a select group of universities: Universidade de São Paulo (Brazil), North Carolina State University (NCSU; USA), Seoul National University (Korea) and Nanjing University (China). These are research-led, but opportunities to study abroad are also being developed, such as the dual Masters programme in Politics with NCSU. The idea of the GPN is, says Colin Grant, to develop 'in-depth, research-led collaboration with a commitment to tangible research outcomes, but also staff and student mobility'.

In 2006, the University of Surrey signed an agreement for collaboration in existing research and in joint teaching ventures with Dongbei University of

His Excellency Dr L.M. Singhvi, Indian High Commissioner, plants the campus Friendship Tree, 21 June 1995. The Friendship Tree celebrates Indo-British friendship and the 125th anniversary of the birth of Mahatma Gandhi. In the foreground, left to right: Mrs Ramaswamy; Hon. Justice K. Ramaswamy; His Excellency Dr L.M. Singhvi, High Commissioner; the Mayor of Guildford, Councillor Mrs Catherine Cobley; the Vice-Chancellor, Professor Patrick Dowling.

Finance and Economics (DUFE) in Dalian, one of the top universities in China. There are now over 1500 students on campus at Surrey International Institute at DUFE (SII, DUFE) studying towards a degree from the University of Surrey. The first Masters students graduated in June 2010 and the first Bachelors students in 2011. Students on the undergraduate and postgraduate programmes, which cover subjects in tourism, management, computing and entrepreneurship, follow similar curricula as in the UK, and are taught by lecturers at Surrey as well as those at DUFE, with periods spent on both campuses. A bilateral scheme, Guildford students can also spend time studying in China. There are similar opportunities for Surrey students to study in the USA, Singapore and Australia.

Professor Snowden sees SII, DUFE as 'the first step in our plans for international expansion'. 'We are aiming,' he says, 'over the next ten years to develop Surrey into an international brand with several institutes around the world.' Associations have been formed in other countries where Surrey's expertise is particularly relevant. One important collaboration is that with four other UK universities to establish a new university in India devoted to the Sciences – the Indian Institute of Science Education and Research (IISER) in Pune. 'Curriculum development is also supported in Iraq, at the University of Kufa,' said Dr Susanne Haywood, Head of International Partnerships in the International Relations Office (to 2011). 'In 2011, Africa will increasingly be on the agenda for globally significant research collaboration on environmental topics and sports medicine.'

In September 2010 the first students at the Hong Kong University School of Professional and Continuing Education joined Surrey programmes in Tourism Management and Hospitality Management. Dr Graham Miller, Director of International Studies, said: 'These new students in Asia are able to undertake exchanges with students in the UK and reflect our desire to create a truly international experience for all our students. The earning opportunities created by these partnerships are tremendously exciting.' By 2012, it is planned that there will be almost as many students studying Hospitality in Hong Kong as there are studying it in Guildford.

The Polish Ambassador, His Excellency Dr Stanislaw Komorowski, visited the University in 2001 to deliver a keynote lecture, 'Poland's Contribution to the Future of Europe'. The Ambassador is shown (left) greeting Rafal Soborski, a Polish scholar (right) in the School of Arts.

Students at both locations have the opportunity to switch campuses for one or more semesters.

Landmark partnerships have also been established with Massachusetts Institute of Technology, California Institute of Technology (Caltech) and the University of California, Los Angeles. One example of these growing links is the Space Technology course lectured by Dr Craig Underwood to Caltech students, appropriately using web technology. There are also strong links between individual Faculties and foreign institutions. In all, the University has multinational partnerships and collaborations with over 50 foreign countries. 'Surrey is actively considering further overseas partnerships based on the SII, DUFE model,' says Professor Grant. 'We are committed to expanding student exchange for academic and professional placements.'

Visits to Guildford from international partners and from dignitaries such as Korean Ambassador Chun Yungwoo, who toured the University in 2009, are relatively frequent and help to reinforce the ties. Deputy Vice-Chancellors Adnei Melges de Andrade and Marco Antonio Zago of the Universidade de São Paulo came to the University in 2010 and there were several delegations from NCSU, led by Vice-Provost Bailian Li, in the late 2000s. Forging of links by individual academics with foreign universities is also encouraged. In November 2009, for instance, Professor Alison Clarke spent two weeks at the School of Law at the University of Xiamen, one of the top ten universities in China, to which she had been invited to present a series of lectures, seminars and discussion sessions on English property law.

Yoon Hiwon, Deputy Vice-Chancellor of Seoul National University and Professor Snowden celebrate the signing of a bilateral global partnership in April 2010.

Professor Alison Clarke of the School of Law with her host, Professor Jiang Yue, outside Xiamen Law School.

Surrey Sports Park

The world-class £36 million Surrey Sports Park (SSP) (Architect, Faulkner Brown) opened in April 2010, and represents the single largest building project the University has undertaken to date. It has been a tremendous boost to student and staff sport, and is also enjoyed by the local community. The impressive facilities include a 50m swimming pool, with adjustable floor levels enabling it to be used for water polo (played in deep water), swimming lessons and other activities. There are three multi-purpose sports halls, with an arena for up to 1000 spectators, six squash courts, including two show courts with seating for 160 spectators, a 12m climbing wall, two activity rooms and a health and fitness suite. The venue also has a 350-seat Starbucks café (apparently, the largest in any UK leisure complex) and its own bar and restaurant, The Bench Bar. Outside are eight floodlit tennis courts, sports pitches, two floodlit all-weather pitches and a 55m sprint track.

The high-quality SSP facilities have attracted league teams to use it for practice, among them the Surrey Storm netball team – the first Netball Super-league game against Glasgow Wildcats attracted over 800 spectators – and Great Britain Women's Basketball Team. SSP is the London and South East Centre for Squash and Racketball and the main training base for Harlequins

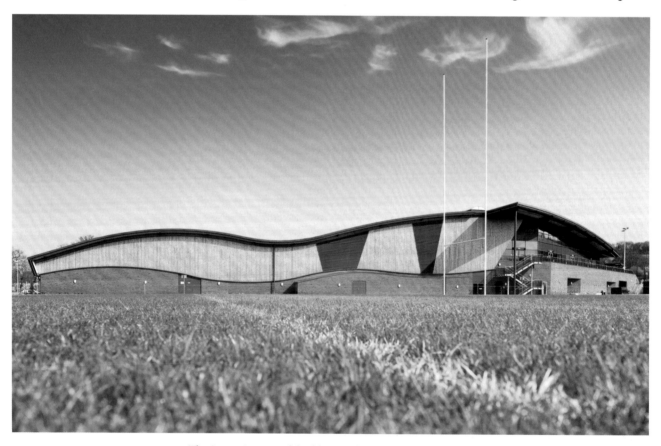

The Surrey Sports Park building, with its unique 'wave' design, by architects Faulkner Brown.

RFU team and local Guildford City Swimming Club. It is also a registered training venue for the 2012 Olympics and Paralympics; Antigua and Barbuda was the first team to sign up, and Nigeria and Singapore have confirmed that

Top: The Sports Park's 50m pool, used by swimmers at all levels from learners to the elite. 'It's a one-stop shop in swimming terms,' said Olympic swimmer Mark Foster. 'Facilities of this standard are absolutely essential to enable people of all levels to reach their full sporting potential.'
Bottom: The Sports Park climbing wall has proved a popular facility for Surrey students.

Surrey Storm's match in the Netball Superleague tournament in 2010 attracted a huge crowd and was televised by Sky Sports.

In October 2010 former West Indian cricketer, Sir Viv Richards OBE, presided over the signing of the Antigua and Barbuda National Olympics Team to use the Sports Park in the run-up to the 2012 Olympics.

Cricketer Alec Stewart (left) and swimmer Mark Foster (right) are two of Surrey Sports Park's network of ambassadors.

they will also use the Park. Players clearly relish what's on offer: 'It's amazing, the facilities are top notch,' says Ugo Monye of Harlequins. 'They give us an adrenalin boost, which is exactly what we need. It's something to look forward to and a massive step up from where we've come from and everything is really exciting.'

Perhaps the biggest event of SSP's first year was the staging of the opening games of the 12-nation Women's Rugby World Cup, held over three weeks in August and September 2010, with teams from New Zealand and the USA holding earlier training camps. In all, 26 matches were held over five days in an arena specially built around the two match pitches. 'It was a great start to the tournament,' said Rob Andrew, Director of Elite Rugby, RFU, 'with great pitches, a sell-out crowd, and a good win for England.' SSP is holding the National Women's Water Polo and England Lacrosse team events in 2011.

While those at the top of their game, such as swimmer Steve Parry (now retired), find SSP 'perfect for elite sports training', former Chief Executive Jason Harborow emphasised the venue as an all-round facility: 'The Sports Park isn't just about top class athletes; this is a facility for the entire local community.' A month after opening, SSP held an Open Day for the public to come and see the facilities, with taster sessions in various sports. There were exhibitions from basketball and football freestylers Tommy Baker and Dan Magness and British Student Squash, as well as a race between Olympic gold medallist Mark Foster and some of Guildford City's finest swimmers. 'The event was a huge success,' said Jason, '[it] attracted approximately 3500 people throughout the day, there was a masters record broken by Mark Foster and a world record broken by Dan Magness.' Currently around 2000 local people a day visit SSP, and there has been a tremendous increase in use of the facilities by schools and schoolchildren through the Park's outreach scheme, with 300 children on the learn-to-swim programme each week and others taking part in group fitness classes. There were also summer camps for juniors in 2010 and 3000 youngsters took part in the P&G Surrey Youth Games.

While the University had extensive sports opportunities at its old site at Stag Hill, there are now more classes than ever. Campusdance provides around twenty classes a week across all styles, from salsa and African to ballet, street dance and tap, and there are a host of fitness classes. There are currently 3400 student members, and increasing. Many, like Physics student Jonathan Lintott, acquire new skills:

> I have been able to train in sports I wouldn't otherwise have seen myself being given the chance to do outside Surrey. Having trained in mountaineering, I am now qualified as a climbing instructor, and can now train others to practise mountaineering safely and competently.

The High Performance Athlete Support Scheme (HPASS) awards bursaries to top sports performers who wish to combine their academic interests with sport. The University is also part of a government initiative, the Talented Athlete Scholarship Scheme (TASS).

The new sports facility is not just about achieving success in the sports arena, however. The University holds to the view that achievement in one

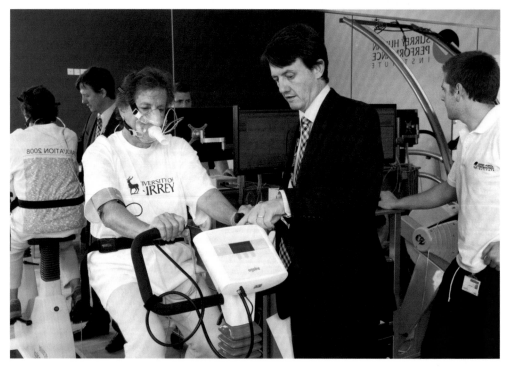

Surrey Human Performance Institute provides a range of individually personalised fitness and medical assessments to enable everyone – from elite Olympic athletes to the general public – to learn more about their health status, manage weight loss and optimise fitness and performance.

sphere can help lift progress elsewhere, improving participants' 'game', their mindset and their physical condition. Thus, sport becomes the foundation for a 'high performance' culture across the University and beyond. Sport is also integrated into the University's core teaching and research, with burgeoning studies in areas associated with sport, public health and improving human performance, though there are no academic courses on sport itself. The Human Performance Institute at Surrey Sports Park works with the University's Clinical Research Centre alongside a developing number of partners in health services and elite sports to deliver exercise, health and wellbeing testing for clinical and elite performance populations.

Student Life

Student life has been enhanced considerably in recent years with new academic and sports blocks opening, and increased, more modern and upgraded living accommodation. A new Student Registry Centre was opened in 2006 and there have been improvements in student support services such as the laundry and restaurants. With the expansion in arts subjects and the addition of GSA, the student population is more diverse then ever before. Students seem to welcome the mix, and the opportunity this gives them not only to rub shoulders with those studying completely different subjects but people from distant parts of the globe. 'The University's wonderful free language programme has enabled me to learn Chinese, something I have always wanted to do … [and] I can practise with my Chinese flatmates,' says Joanna Kosmicka,

A typical student room today. This one is in Stag Hill Court.

Nutrition and Dietetics student. 'I adore Surrey for its truly vibrant and international environment, with plenty of events every week and chances to meet people from all over the world.' Around 20 per cent of the University's students are from non-EU countries.

Benefitting from all the new facilities, the student experience is possibly better now than at any time previously. In the Student Experience Survey produced by *Times Higher Education* in 2011, Surrey came 43rd equal, its highest scores awarded for having a 'Good' environment around the campus, 'Good' industry connections and a 'Good' library and library opening hours. Home students also marked Surrey as the 'Best in the UK' in terms of 'Overall Satisfaction for the Arrival Experience' in the i-Graduate survey of universities. All new students are given a two-day orientation programme at the beginning of the academic year, part of Welcome Week, an initiative introduced in 2008 as part of a drive to improve the experience at Surrey for Freshers. The 2010 Week was voted the 'most successful ever'. The University has also introduced Court Life Mentoring at the residences. Teams of mentors are allocated to each court, and their job is to try to help with the myriad problems of communal living by 'signposting' students to finding their own

Students take a break from studies. For many, the social side of university life is as important as the academic side.

solutions. The mentors also organise social events so that students in the individual courts can get to know one another.

'At Surrey, the social side is as good as the academic side,' says Politics student Rowan Cole. 'The Students' Union is one of the largest in terms of the number of societies it runs and the active participation of its students. There's a big sense of community. People like to get involved.' The Students' Union (SU) regularly holds seminars and workshops to develop students' personal skills across a wide range of areas including time management, interpersonal communication and teamworking in order to enhance their employability. It also coordinates many volunteering activities as well as social and fundraising events. Apart from RAG week, this includes overseeing an expanding number of clubs and societies. At present there are 84 societies, from various national ones, such as the Brunei Society and the Iranian Society – whose activities include Persian Dance Classes, gala performances and food exhibitions – to the 40-odd-strong Gospel Choir, the Gliding Club and the Surrey Space Society. Given the strength of the latter area of studies at Surrey, it is no surprise to

Above and below: RAG week is an important event in the University calendar.

Large numbers of international students now come to the University, and there are many clubs to cater for them. Here, we see celebrations for Chinese New Year in 2011.

Above and opposite: Music students are able to use Faculty facilities outside teaching hours and take full advantage of this.

find that it is one of the most populous societies; in 2009 it hosted the UK Students for the Exploration and Development of Space annual conference, an event attended by 200 enthusiasts from all over Britain. Guilfest independent music festival, held annually in Stoke Park, which presents major bands such as, in 2008, Motorhead, Brian Wilson of The Beach Boys, and The Happy Mondays, also draws the student crowds.

Faculties also hold their own events and the departments of the Faculty of Arts and Human Sciences (FAHS) provide their students with extra-curricular resources. 'The Department of Music and Sound Recording is well kitted out with lots of large practice spaces and three excellent recording studios,' said Sam Eads (Music, 2006–10). 'I love all the extra-curricular activities you can do within the Department such as the Chamber Choir, Composer-Choreographer weekends and recording in the Department's studios.' The School of Law holds an annual mooting competition, which in 2009/10 held its final in Guildford's Guildhall before a bench of judges which included Judge Critchlow from Guildford Crown Court, Rosalind Malcolm, Professor of Law at Surrey, and Phillip Blatchly, a barrister from Guildford Chambers. Some events have an international flavour: students usually celebrate Chinese New Year, and in 2010 the Surrey Tourism Events Society, which was launched at the 2009 Freshers' Fair, and the Food and Wine Society (one of the older societies, having been founded over 25 years ago) joined forces to take a cohort of students through the Champagne region of France and to Paris.

The new facilities at the Surrey Sports Park have been welcomed all round. There are 36 University clubs for sports, ranging from American football and archery to volleyball and water polo, and including some of the more unlikely suspects such as ultimate frisbee, mountaineering and cheerleading. 'It has boosted Surrey sport

massively and is a fantastic addition to the overall Surrey experience,' says student Ellen Robinson. While some students are happy simply to participate, others are more competitive. In 2003, for instance, the University sailing team was successful in the British Universities Sailing Association championships, with two of its four Laser II dinghies finishing in the top ten.

Students also have their own small media empire, with a newspaper, a radio station and a television station. The first student periodical, *Battersea Polytechnic*, began in 1907 with the encouragement of the Prinicipal, Dr Rawson. This later became *Polygon*. The first University publication, *barefacts*, began in 1968, with the aim of keeping the two sites at Battersea and Guildford up to date with each other's activities. In November 2008, it was relaunched with a new design as *The Stag*. Creative Writing students often take a hand in its production. Although its standard has inevitably gone up and down over the years, it has received some high commendation. In 2003, *barefacts* won the award for Best Student Campaign in the National Student Journalism Awards. This was for the newspaper's 'Lights, Camera, Action' campaign advocating better lighting and safety on routes to and from campus, which resulted in installation of CCTV, the painting of the Tesco underpasses and cutting back of foliage. Launched in 2002 after a series of attacks in or near the underpasses on campus, the campaign gained widespread support, including that of Guildford MP Sue Doughty.

Winning finalists in the School of Law's mooting competition 2009/10, Mr William Chalmers and Miss Naushin Shariff.

Students taking part in Guildford Sport Relief Mile on campus in 2010.

There has been a radio station at the University of Surrey since the 1970s, but the name GU2 came with a rebranding in 2000. The station, a mix of music, comedy and chat, quickly established a high reputation, and was crowned UK Student Radio Station of the Year in November 2002. One of the presenters also picked up an individual bronze award. Station manager at the time Gaz Davies said: 'This really is a fantastic achievement. To be nominated for "best student radio station" after our first year of full-time broadcasting shows the level of commitment and dedication on behalf of all the station members.' On 8 February 2009 the University of Surrey television station released its first TV production, a news programme, since when *M.A.D. News* has been produced on a regular basis.

Fundraising and volunteering are a major part of the University experience. In 2006, the Students' Union (SU) refocused, giving greater emphasis to both student welfare and what Andy Blair, then SU Deputy Director, described as 'social enterprise … helping students develop their skills and networks in a way that benefits both them and the community'. The 'V Project', for instance, is a volunteering scheme that enables students to take part in local community schemes. Students also take part in mentoring schemes such as Schools Without Walls. In 2009/10, 97 Surrey students tutored and mentored in local schools and colleges, 26 supported a playground activities scheme and 38 helped with a reading mentors scheme. There are also many money-raising events for charities: the Trampoline Club did a sponsored bounce on

9 November 2008 and in over 2030 moves raised £350 for the Breast Cancer Campaign, for instance; and over 1200 students participated in Guildford Sport Relief Mile in 2010, raising nearly £44,000.

Academic departments are also active on the volunteer front. Mishal Dattani (2004–09), for instance, was a volunteer for the National Centre for Domestic Violence's office in Guildford through his studies at the School of Law. Around 25 students are recruited for this each year, each putting in a half-day whenever time allows. 'Being at Surrey,' he said, 'allowed me to be exposed to things that I don't think I would have experienced elsewhere. My volunteering gave me the opportunity to understand the process of family law and it was tremendously useful to know how it operated.' He also valued the fact that volunteering enabled him to 'make a difference' and it helped him to obtain a job when he left.

Left: Mishal Dattani, who studied in the School of Law, found his volunteer work at the National Centre for Domestic Violence's office in Guildford both enjoyable and invaluable work experience.
Below: Cherie Booth QC opens the Surrey Law Centre, 12 July 2010. The Surrey Law Centre is one of the most important initiatives and collaborations of the School of Law in recent years.

Surrey students at the Surrey Law Centre.

In a recent development, which Professor Rosalind Malcolm regards as 'one of the most important developments to take place since I established the Law School', students from the School of Law have begun helping at the Surrey Law Centre, Guildford's new walk-in centre just off the High Street, as the result of a collaboration between the two. Four placements are given to law students – there is also a volunteer scheme – to work with solicitors helping disadvantaged young people who cannot afford to pay for legal advice. The first collaboration of its kind in the UK, the scheme was launched by Cherie Booth QC on 12 July 2010 with a public lecture at the University. The Centre helped 2600 people in 2010 and provides 'a vital service for the community', according to Manager Laura Melbourne. Professor Rosalind Malcolm comments: 'Surrey Law students can now work for extended periods of time at the Law Centre, gaining experience in handling client enquiries, interviewing clients and giving advice.' She is now exploring running a clinical legal education programme with Surrey Law Centre as the next development in the collaboration.

Today, the challenges of finding work following their degrees may be harder than for many years, yet today's generation of Surrey students undoubtedly feels that the University does its best to equip them to do so and that it also provides them with the facilities and opportunities to experience many things that would otherwise be beyond them. The future fees increases will place greater demands on both students and their lecturers. For many, however, their university days will probably still be remembered as one of the most formative times of their lives.

Chapter 6

Conclusion: Looking to the Future

'Surrey has come far since our beginnings at Battersea,' says Vice-Chancellor Professor Christopher Snowden. Though it shares many of the Polytechnic Institute's original attributes and ethos, the University today is a very different place and with some very different attitudes. Higher education has been transformed from the preserve of a narrow elite (only 6 per cent in 1962) to having participation of nearly 40 per cent of all young people. The polyglot mix of students who swarm around the campus are very different from the earnest young men and women who studied when Battersea Polytechnic Institute opened its doors. The University today is in all senses modern. Its research and its teaching incorporate very much twenty-first century approaches and investigate the issues of twenty-first century life.

In February 2009, the campus experienced its worst weather for 18 years, with snow up to 50cm deep in places. There were further heavy snowfalls in early 2010, as shown here, and in the lead-up to Christmas that year.

The University of Surrey is now almost halfway through Strategy 2007–2017, which aims to position it as a leading national and international institution. Considerable progress, says Professor Snowden, has been made towards this goal. Surrey is not yet in the top 10 UK and top 100 world universities, but in 2009/10 it entered *The Guardian* top 20 for the first time (it is in the top 500 of the Academic Ranking of World Universities) and the ambition remains. The University has seen, he says:

> a 25 per cent rise in entrance standards, over 75 per cent increase in applications and 30 per cent increase in research bids that have been won by Surrey over the past four years. There have been major strides in building our international position, with the new Surrey International Institute at Dalian in China and the founding of the University Global Partnership Network, with growing relationships in the USA, China, South Korea and Brazil. Surrey has retained its pre-eminent position as the UK university with the highest graduate employment.

This has put the University in a good position not only to withstand the buffeting from the proposed cuts in government funding, but to continue to strengthen its offering. Professor Snowden is determined that the University should be sustainable economically. The academic base – that is, the net tuition cost: tuition fees received less the cost of providing education – used to lose money, he says, whereas now it breaks even, thus allowing the receipts of the Research Park and spin-out company income to be used for strategic growth.

There is no doubt, however, about the challenges ahead. Not the least of these are the effects of the new Coalition Government's fiscal policy on education introduced in 2011. When the Government was elected in May 2010, in order to bring down the economic deficit it set about the most savage cuts in the public sector budget since the Second World War. No part of British life or the British economy could hope to remain immune. Playing havoc with national budgets, the cuts have led to a great withdrawing of funds from higher education. At Surrey this amounts to over 60 per cent from the teaching block grant and 70 per cent from the capital teaching grant over the next four years. The new policy will also see increased tuition fees introduced, from 2012, at a level that a dozen years earlier would have seemed inconceivable. And there are secondary effects too, such as the cutting of budgets to the grant-giving research councils, the result of which will be felt far down the line.

The Vice-Chancellor, Professor Christopher Snowden, 2011.

229

Shortly after the Government was elected in 2010, it announced a wide-scale reform of higher education and student finance. The Comprehensive Spending Review in October 2010 revealed a plan to cut funding of higher education by 40 per cent by 2014/15 with, as Professor Snowden notes, an 'unprecedented 63 per cent squeeze to its teaching grants, removing all funding for teaching arts, humanities and social sciences'. For 2011/12, the cut in capital funding of education is 58.1 per cent, while cuts in teaching and research amount to 6.5 per cent (teaching by 8.2 per cent and research by 2.8 per cent) – the cut in the latter for Surrey is 1.8 per cent. Humanities subjects suffer most, while science and technology subjects, seen to produce tangible, direct economic results, are being favoured. Indeed, this had been signalled seven years earlier in the government's White Paper of 2003 which gave short shrift to the arts and humanities, which received barely a mention. On top of this the Government is introducing stringent controls on visas for international students, which is a threat to all UK universities, especially Surrey with its strong international student community. The number of foreign students at British universities has doubled in ten years, and at Surrey they represent nearly 20 per cent of the student body – in 2009/10 tuition fees from non-EU students brought in £25.9 million. There is also a cap on UK and European student numbers, with fines for institutions if they exceed it. A fund for 20,000 extra university places has been scrapped.

In November 2010, following publication of the Browne Report, *Securing a Sustainable Future for Higher Education*, the Government announced that from 2012 the cap on tuition fees was being revised. In order to plug the gap left by the decrease in core funding, universities would be able to charge between £6000 and £9000, the higher level subject to the institution meeting various conditions regarding wider access and outreach that had to be agreed with the Office for Fair Access. The income level at which graduates will

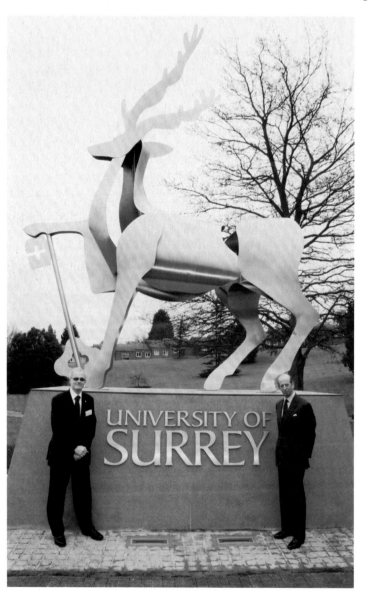

Allan Sly FRBS's *The Surrey Stag*, a stylised interpretation of the University's crest. Professor Snowden commented: 'Our heritage is linked closely to the stag which now appears as our visual identity.'

have to start paying off their fee loans is being raised to £21,000 (from £15,000) and the loans will now be subject to tapering interest dependent on income – it is claimed that only around 40 per cent of graduates will pay the whole loan off (the fee loans have a limited indemnity and will be written off after thirty years), and 20 per cent will pay less than currently. A new National Scholarships Programme for poorer students is being introduced and maintenance grants are being raised to £3250, an increase of 12 per cent.

The tuition fee increase was passed by Parliament shortly afterwards, and in effect sees the transformation of universities into something approaching commercial enterprises, in a competitive environment where only the most 'successful' will flourish – predicated on consumer choice driving out the less fit. The reduction in grant and introduction of fees is the most radical change to higher education in a generation. For one thing, as Vice-Chancellor Professor Christopher Snowden told *Surrey Life*, 'the pendulum swing from the Government to the student as the main funder of teaching in higher education has begun'. The universities themselves, not the Government, are expected to shoulder any shortfall in funding. Government funding has nearly halved in the past twenty years, he points out, dropping from £9000 per year, per UK/European student in 1990, to £5100 today – public funding of higher education is 0.7 per cent (2007), below both the OECD average and the USA, which both stand at 1 per cent. Total spending on higher education as a proportion of GDP is also low, at 1.3 per cent (it was 1 per cent in 2000), compared with other countries: the OECD average is 1.5 per cent and in the USA the figure is 3.1 per cent – though two-thirds of its funds come from the private sector, and its fees are higher.

The reforms also call into question the nature of what a university education should provide – is it the training of the mind across a range of disciplines and the fostering of intellectual enquiry, or is it training for employment and the creation of a stream of money-generating research

Thinking of my Future by Zimbabwean sculptor Christopher Chipfuya, Art Conservator at the National Gallery of Harare. The sculpture was given to the University in memory of Sir David and Lady Orr by their daughters and was unveiled by Baroness Bottomley of Nettlestone, Pro-Chancellor, on 28 February 2010.

231

and knowledge transfer? A century ago, teaching of humanities dominated in the traditional universities, and even in the 1930s over half of students were studying in arts faculties, but in the past three decades these areas have lost out so that today, according to Cambridge's Professor Stefan Collini, only some 18 per cent of undergraduates study pure 'humanities' subjects. As the Browne Report makes only too clear, in future the focus will be on science and technology, whose study can be seen to lead to direct economic benefit, and, increasingly, on research, rather than humanities where the impact is less tangible. While emphasising 'student choice', the Browne Report also underlines the fact that the 'benefits' from studying are largely to be judged by the higher earnings that will ensue, rather than by any larger, more liberal, measure. While Surrey has always taught arts subjects at some level, its original remit was to teach technology and, to a lesser degree, science subjects. In the past decade, going against the grain, the University has extended its offering with a new English Literature degree among others. In the light of the cuts, some universities will be trimming arts subjects but, as Professor Snowden told *Times Higher Education* in November 2010, Surrey will not:

> The reason most students go to a residential university is that they're looking for an experience – and that is a lot more than simply gaining the qualification. … If you talk to science and engineering students, they are really happy to be here with students studying, for example, dance or music or English. They see this as the richness of experience they come to university for.

The Government's reforms and the raising of the tuition fee in particular provoked widespread and vehment protests. Surrey students joined the 52,000 marching under the banner 'Fund our Future: Stop Education Cuts' to Conservative Party headquarters at Millbank on 10 November 2010. There were further demonstrations in January 2011 and the Students' Union mounted a National Campaign Against Cuts and Fees. In March 2011 over a quarter of a million marched through London to Whitehall in protest against the cuts in public funding. Yet while students hit the streets, and those in academic life were uneasy, there was no avoiding the fact that higher education would have to shoulder some of the impact from the Government's swingeing cuts in public sector budgets. 'Higher education was always going to have its funding cut by the Government in the current round of cuts,' explains Professor Nigel Seaton, Senior Deputy Vice-Chancellor:

> We will still be affected by this, but the new deal on fees greatly reduces the impact. We will be able to maintain, and indeed improve, the experience of our students, and continue to do high-quality research for the benefit of the economy and for society more generally.

The Browne Report stipulated that only in 'exceptional cases', such as the most costly courses, would the universities charge the full £9000, and the Government assumed that many would not, but that the average would be a mid-range £7500. But the problem is, Professor Snowden explains, that, with the steep reduction in core funding, £7500 merely allows the universities to break even, allowing no funds towards the bursaries for poorer students – necessary to meet the Government's wider access ambitions – or for capital funding for facilities and equipment such as computers and whiteboards. The reality is that in order to accommodate the steep cuts in funding, and also to offer – and to be seen as offering – quality, over two thirds, including Surrey – and also Oxford, Cambridge, Manchester, Essex, Imperial College London, Exeter and Durham – have announced their intention to charge the full £9000. All universities will charge above £6000.

'Our priority is to safeguard the quality of the student experience,' said Professor Snowden, announcing the rise. Although the University receives only around 26 per cent of its income from core funding, the steep cuts as well as the impact of changes in immigration policy, 'uncertainty over the future allocation of student places and concern over the exact level of the HEFCE funding for STEM [Science, Technology, Engineering, Mathematics] subjects has added additional risk to the teaching income for UK universities,' he said. Committed to ensuring that 'anyone capable of meeting the academic standards in its offers should be able to come and study', the University offers bursaries to students from families with incomes below £35,000, and an indication of its success in attracting low-income students is that in 2010 the University spent £1 million more than budgeted on this. From 2012, a new package of bursaries and fee waivers is being made available to encourage applications from families with lower incomes. Malcolm Hunt, Students' Union President in 2011, proclaimed the result 'disappointing', though:

> it has not come as a great shock. It is now the responsibility of the Students'
> Union and the University to work together in order to ensure that Surrey
> offers an ever improving quality of education and student experience while
> remaining accessible to students from a range of different backgrounds.

One result of the widescale reforms is that, as Professor Seaton puts it, 'this puts our students even more in the driving seat' – not only because of higher fees, but because the mechanism of payment means that funding to a large degree follows the students. Universities and other higher education institutions will have to make more of an effort to listen to students and to promote their institutions' strengths:

> This [the changes] will lead to high expectations and an even greater focus
> on the student experience. Fortunately, Surrey's pre-eminent position for
> graduate employment will be a major factor in attracting students to Surrey – we will need to ensure that we can preserve this lead as competition
> for students increases in the new funding environment.

Although the Executive expresses caution and concern about the future, the University is nonetheless in relatively good shape. Overall, the University achieved a consolidated surplus of £4 million in 2009/10 and income grew by 8.7 per cent on the previous year. It is now near to achieving its goal of breaking even in its core activities, with a deficit of £0.6 million in 2009/10, an improvement of £1 million on 2008/09. The Research Park is very successful, feeding the Foundation Fund for research and capital projects with around £9.5 million per year from rents. Research income has shot up, with a 40 per cent increase, says Professor Snowden, in the past two years – 'this year,' he says, 'it will be close to £30 million, which is pretty substantial' – and the University is now ranked 15th in the volume of EPSRC grants. Its last RAE saw 88 per cent of research rated world class or of international quality and the reformed Research Excellence Framework (REF), due in 2014 – which will not only count the best research of each academic during the period, but acknowledge up to 25 per cent of an academic's effort on the 'wider impact of research', that is the commercialisation of the research and public engagement (the transmission of the research to the public) – should see further improvement. There are eleven associated institutions, as well as strategic partnerships with leading universities such as California Institute of Technology and Massachusetts Institute of Technology. Total student numbers stand at 14,947, an increase of 40 per cent in the past five years. The University is energetically addressing the student experience and, while there is no room for complacency, student satisfaction is certainly and signficantly increasing.

Indeed, the last few years under Strategy 2007–17 have seen some major improvements to the student experience. In 2011, the Learning Resource

The most recent Surrey graduates throw their mortarboards in the air outside Guildford Cathedral after the graduation ceremony, April 2011.

Centre and the Ivy Arts Centre opened, and academic departments such as Management and Law have been strengthened with additional academic posts. Schemes such as the Global Graduate Award, which enables undergraduates to study foreign languages for two terms, are also popular – over 1000 students per year take up the opportunity, and three times that number are involved in short language courses. It is a significant investment of the University, at around £800,000 per annum, but represents an important strand of the desire to enable students to operate effectively internationally.

There are plans, too, for the future. Following a review of the Strategy in 2011, there has been some fine tuning of it, but these are tweaks, and the overall aims remain the same. 'It has stood the test of time well, and still is a very good match to the University's ethos and goals,' says Professor Snowden.

> We have retained the six imperatives of *quality, international impact, sustainability, distinctiveness, collegiality* and *professionalism* which we believe are essential to achieve our vision and confirm the core values of the University. Our focus on delivering the best possible experience for our students remains a fundamental goal and the desire to help prepare our graduates for life and employment is reflected in our commitment to the professional training year and determination to continue to aim for the highest quality of teaching, learning and scholarship. Our commitment to achieving world-class research activities has been demonstrated with the recent recruitment of new Chair holders from throughout the globe who have internationally leading research reputations.

Professor Snowden is conscious that over the past decade the focus in universities generally on research – one result of the RAE determining funds – has perhaps been a little at the expense of teaching. The University has been addressing this for the past five years, investing heavily in the student experience and giving greater attention to the quality of teaching. Surrey is also tackling the drop-out of students, and the number of students who leave without a qualification or do not finish their courses has already improved considerably. Widening participation, too, remains, Professor Snowden says, 'fundamentally important to the University'. Surrey has a 'very cosmopolitan mix, with members from over 130 countries, drawn from all backgrounds in society and an unusually high number of mature students', but he would like to see more students from under-represented sectors, as well as from beyond the south-east. This will not, however, be at the expense of quality: if anything, grades required will go up not down. University applications for 2011 are higher than ever before, and at Surrey they have risen by 80 per cent over the past five years.

There are also new building projects in the pipeline. Planning consent has been granted for the University to build a £6 million reception centre and residence building, with restaurants and a bar, at Manor Park Student Village. The

2430sq m three-storey building, designed by Scott Brownrigg, will act as the landmark gateway to Surrey's Manor Park residences. The University is also planning a £7 million Surrey Multi-faith Centre (fundraising is continuing), with a synagogue, Muslim prayer hall, gurdwara and chapel under one roof. The design is based on a flower, 'where roots and stem are communal areas, and the petals spaces for worship and contemplation', said Anglican Chaplain Revd Canon Jonathan Frost (now Bishop of Southampton; his successor is Revd Andrew Bishop who comes to the University and the cathedral from a parish role in Basingstoke). For some years, the University has had a Festival of Faiths, as well as holding fortnightly dialogues between students of different faiths, beliefs and cultures, but this is a much bolder initiative and it will be the first building of its kind in the UK. Currently the different faith communities find their facilities, not only for worship, but for pastoral care, stretched and this imaginative answer to the problem, the result of cross-faith discussion, will serve six major faiths under one roof: Islam, Buddhism, Christianity, Sikhism, Judaism and Hinduism. 'Our vision is to establish a centre in which ... understanding will be deepened, differences explored and friendships formed across barriers of religion, history and culture', Professor Snowden explains. The Centre will also be open to the local community.

Artist's impression of the Multi-faith Centre, designed by BCH, London, for which fundraising is continuing.

Since 1891, the institution has been transformed from Polytechnic Institute to College to University. Conceived as a 'noble Institution, where the Priceless Treasures of Art, Science, and Literature shall be within reach of all', it may have been recast as what Professor Snowden describes as a 'research-led institution pursuing learning, scholarship and research with the aim of advancing and disseminating knowledge', but though it is larger, stronger and research plays a much bigger role, the educational vision has in many ways changed remarkably little over the years and it is recognisably the same institution. The 120th anniversary celebrations will, in tune with the austerity of the times, be low-key, but there will be a lasting legacy in the wayfinding project which will see pathways, lecture halls and buildings named after those who have been significant in the University's history. A graduation ceremony will also be held for Battersea alumni.

Today, the University of Surrey faces a future as challenging as at any time in its history. The Comprehensive Spending Review and the proposals in the Browne Report on higher education funding and student finance will lead to a period of unprecedented change in the UK higher education sector over the next five to ten years. 'However, through the diversity of its activities and its many and varied core strengths,' says Professor Snowden, 'the University of Surrey is in a much better financial position than many institutions to meet these challenges in pursuit of its long-term goals – although the scale of what the sector will face should not be underestimated.' The economy of higher education has been fractured and it will need time to rebuild. Politically and economically, nation-states are subject to global changes as never before, while society's demands are increasingly complex and as demanding as they have ever been. Yet this presents universities such as Surrey not only with daunting problems, but with opportunities to make a real difference. 'We believe,' says Professor Snowden, 'that in times of economic strife universities such as Surrey play a crucial role in developing the future members of our global society who will steer not only this country but other nations to future success.'

In 2011, the University celebrates the 120th anniversary of its foundation at Battersea.

237

Appendix

Honorary Graduates

Doctor of the University

22 October 1966
Sir John Adams, CMG FRS
Austen Harry Albu
Sir Leon Bagrit
Sir Alec Issigonis, CBE FRS
The Rt Hon. The Earl of Munster, KBE
Dame Sybil Thorndike, DBE

6 January 1968
Julian Bream, OBE
Professor Joseph Cathala, Officer
    Legion d'Honneur
Sidney Frank Rich, OBE
Dr Ralph Winton West, CBE (posthumous)

2 December 1968
Professor Carl Hirsh
Sir William Houghton
Dr Francis Edgar Jones, MBE FRS
The Rt Hon. the Lord Nugent of Guildford
Lady Ruth Nugent
Professor Sir Alfred Grenville Pugsley,
    CBE FRS

3 December 1969
Sir Harold Montague Finniston,
    FREng FRS
Professor Sir Michael James Lighthill, FRS
Dr Arthur Douglas Merriman, GC OBE
Dr Edward John Victor Pasmore, CBE
Dr Beatrice Shilling, OBE

5 December 1970
Professor Etienne Paul Grandjean
Professor Sir George Porter, FRS
The Rt Revd George Edmund Reindorp
Sir Ernest George Woodroofe

4 December 1971
Professor Stephane du Chateau
Sir Edward Fennessy, CBE
Sir Laurens van der Post, CBE

1 December 1972
Professor Dennis Gabor, CBE FRS
Philip Victor Marchant
Dr Charles Garrett Williams

1 December 1973
Yehudi Menuhin
Dr Rendel Sebastian Pease

Lord Robens of Woldingham, the University of Surrey's first Chancellor, chats to actor Dame Sybil Thorndike, who received an Honorary Doctorate at the first Honorary Degree ceremony held at the Civic Hall in Guildford, 22 October 1966. (Central Press Photos Ltd)

Distinguished scientist Sir Leon Bagrit is presented with his Honorary Doctorate, at the first Honorary Degree ceremony, Civic Hall, Guildford, 22 October 1966, by Professor F.M. Arscot. Seated in the front row, from left: the Pro-Chancellor, Sir George Edwards; the Vice-Chancellor, Dr Peter Leggett; and the Chancellor, Lord Robens. (*Surrey Advertiser*)

Ceremony for the conferment of an Honorary Fellowship, Honorary Degrees and Diplomas, 4 December 1971. Left to right: Sir Edward Fennessy, Professor Stephane du Chateau, Dr Peter Leggett, Lord Robens, Sir Laurens van der Post, Charles Wallace Tonkin. The latter, 'Tonks' as he was always known, was Pro-Vice-Chancellor during the years leading up to and during the move to Guildford and managed Battersea during building operations.

30 December 1974
Professor Sir Hermann Bondi,
    KCB FRS
Philip Sydney Henman
John William Penycate

27 August 1975
Sir Alfred Charles Bernard Lovell,
    OBE FRS
Sir Frederick Lincoln Ralphs
Lady Jackson, DBE (Barbara Ward)

29 November 1975
Sir Charles Forte
The Rt Hon. Lord Gardiner of Kittisford
Dr Douglas Malcolm Aufrere
    (Peter) Leggett
Sir Ronald Wallace Wates
The Rt Hon. Viscount Watkinson
    of Woking
Lt-Col. Herbert James Wells, CBE MC

4 December 1976
Sir Kenneth George Corfield
Professor Thorold Dickinson, CBE
Dr Joseph Needham

26 January 1977
The Rt Hon. Lord Robens of
    Woldingham, PC

3 December 1977
Sir Frederick Charles Frank, FRS
Elisabeth Frink, CBE
Sir Claus Adolf Moser, Comdr de l'Ordre
    Nat. du Mérite (Fr.)

1 December 1978
Professor Ralf Gustav Dahrendorf
Sir Ralph Freeman, CBE
Professor William Valentine Mayneord,
    CBE FRS

30 November 1979
Sir Henry Frederick Ross Catherwood
Professor Otto Gustaf Edholm
Sir George Robert Edwards, OM CBE
    FREng FRS
Professor Reginald Victor Jones,
    CB CBE FRS
Sir Shridath Surendranath Ramphal,
    CMG

28 November 1980
Dr Duncan Sheppey Davies
Dr Eric Duckworth
Vernon Handley
Sir Francis Avery Jones, CBE

4 December 1981
Dr Jack Birks, CBE
Sir Ernest Thomas Harrison, OBE
Dr Richard Hoggart

3 December 1982
John Eveleigh Bolton, CBE
Professor Sir David Gwynne Evans,
    CBE FRS
John Royden Maddox
Sir David Alexander Orr, MC

2 December 1983
Sir Arnold Stanley Vincent Burgen, FRS
Viscount Etienne Davignon
Sir Ieuan Maddock, CB OBE FRS FREng
Sir Georg Solti, KBE

7 December 1984
Professor Rosalinde Hurley
Robert Malpas, CBE FREng
Thomas Irvine Smith, OBE
Sir John Vane, FRS

6 December 1985
Dr ir Hendrikus Ludovicus Beckers
Dennis Joseph Enright
Sir John Harvey-Jones, MBE
Samuel Curtis Johnson

12 December 1986
Sir Anthony Alfred Caro, OM CBE
Dr Ronald Frederick Coleman
Dr Desmond George King-Hele
Professor Sir William Macdonald Paton,
    CBE FRS

11 December 1987
Bernard Albert Eastwell, OBE
Dr Kevin William Keohane, CBE
Sir John Emms Read
Henri Charles Vidal

9 December 1988
Professor Ke Jun (Tsun Ko)
Sir Richard Anthony Meyjes
Brian Frederick Street
Sir Francis Leonard Tombs

Sir Alec Issigonis (1906–88), the designer of the Morris Mini-Minor, with one of the cars at the Fighting Vehicles Research and Development Establishment, Chertsey, Surrey. (Photo by Derek Berwin/Getty Images)

HRH The Duke of Kent confers the award of Doctor of the University upon Sir George Edwards at Guildford Cathedral, 1979.

8 December 1989
Sir Geoffrey Allen
The Rt Hon. Lord Cockfield of Dover
Sir Charles Hugh Reece

6 July 1990
The Rt Hon. Lord Wolfson of Marylebone

20 July 1990
John Stuart Bevan
The Revd Dr Donald English

7 December 1990
Sir Walter Bodmer, FRS
Baroness Cumberlege of Newick, CBE
Sir Denis Rooke, CBE FRS FREng
Professor Jon Stallworthy

19 July 1991
Professor Paul Joseph Black, OBE
Dr Gerhard Weiler

29 November 1991
Professor George Alfred Hugh Elton, CB
Sir Charles Bernard Groves, CBE
Dr Carole Jordan, FRS
The Lord Rayner of Crowborough
The Rt Revd and Rt Hon. The Lord Runcie
   of Cuddesdon
Leonard John Weaver, CBE

17 July 1992
Academician Igor Semyonovich Kon

24 July 1992
The Very Revd Desmond Anthony Beirne

Top: Sir Georg Solti (1912–97) was awarded an
Honorary Doctorate in 1983. Here he conducts the
Chicago Symphony Orchestra, to which he was
appointed conductor in 1969. (Photo by *Evening
Standard*/Getty Images)

Centre: A group of past and present Honorary
Doctors of the University assembled with the
Chancellor and Vice-Chancellor in front of the
altar in Guildford Cathedral. This marked the
25th anniversary of the University and followed the
degree ceremony on the same day, 29 November
1991.

Bottom: Mary McAleese, President of the Republic of
Ireland, was made an Honorary Doctor at Guildford
Cathedral on 3 December 1999. Shown with her is
the Vice-Chancellor, Professor Patrick Dowling.

31 July 1992
Richard John William Aston
Professor Robert Anthony Bernard Leaper, CBE

4 December 1992
Professor Sushantha Kumar Bhattacharyya
His Eminence Cardinal (George) Basil Hume
Leonard John Kail
Professor Claude Levy-Leboyer
Professor Howard Joseph Newby
Professor Alexander Michael Ross
Professor William Duncan Paterson Stewart

30 July 1993
Professor David Burman Edgar
Professor Alexander Shurbanov

3 December 1993
Dame Elizabeth Esteve-Coll
Zena Oxlade, CBE
Professor Kenneth Packer, FRS
Sir Austin William Pearce, CBE FREng
Professor Roger Penrose, FRS
Dr Heinz Riesenhuber

8 July 1994
Dr Peter Brinson
Geoffrey Lomer, CBE FREng
Chikahisa Nagai
Professor Yasuharu Suematsu

22 July 1994
Professor Peter Clifford McIntosh

29 July 1994
Professor Henry Chadwick

9 December 1994
Peter Bonfield, CBE FREng
Bryan Hildrew, CBE FREng
Dr Zenon Jagodzinski
Professor Anthony Kelly, CBE FREng FRS
Dr Alan Rudge, CBE FREng FRS
Charles Sandbank, FREng

27 July 1995
Baroness Perry of Southwark

1 December 1995
The Rt Revd Michael Adie, CBE
Dr Cham Tao Soon
Professor Rita R. Colwell
Baroness Caroline Cox of Queensbury
Sir Diarmuid Downs, CBE FREng FRS

1 July 1996
Dame Judith Olivia Dench, OBE

19 July 1996
The Rt Hon. Baron Nolan of Brasted

25 July 1996
Monica Mason

20 December 1996
Professor Patrick Boulter, FRCSE FRS
Professor Sir David Davies, CBE FREng FRS

12 June 1997
Professor Ernst-Ulrick Schlünder

13 June 1997
Sir Rocco Forte

30 June 1997
David Terence Miller
Nicholas Andrew Serota

23 July 1997
Rt Revd John Jukes, OFM.Conv.
Sir Trevor McDonald, OBE

24 July 1997
Marilyn Speers Butler
Iona Margaret Balfour Opie

5 December 1997
Evelyn Elizabeth Ann Glennie

12 December 1997
Ivor Forbes Guest
Nabil Mohammed Shaban
Sir John Meurig Thomas, ScD FRS

19 June 1998
Sir Richard Eustace Thornton, OBE

3 July 1998
Sir Richard Charles Hastings Eyre, CBE

22 July 1998
Professor Hendrick Cornelis Gerard Kemper

24 July 1998
Revd Dr Kenneth Gerald Greet

4 December 1998
Dr Paul Bélanger
Peter Kenneth Blair, OBE FREng
Dr Sam Ramsamy

17 June 1999
Siobhan Davies, MBE

18 June 1999
Professor Akito Arima
General Sir Rupert Anthony Smith, KCB
　DSO OBE QGM

22 July 1999
Professor John Race Godfrey Tomlinson,
　CBE

3 December 1999
Professor Stephen Campbell Holt, OBE
Mary Patricia McAleese
Sir Richard Sykes, DSc FRS
Dr John Michael Taylor, OBE FRS

10 December 1999
Margaret Mary Douglas, CBE

3 July 2000
Patrick Caulfield

14 July 2000
Tanni Grey-Thompson, OBE

21 July 2000
Michael David Wheeler

1 December 2000
Ron Dennis

14 June 2001
Sir Eric Ash, CBE FREng FRS

2 July 2001
Professor Anthony Douglas Cragg
Jocelyn Herbert

27 July 2001
Dr Michael Marland, CBE

30 November 2001
Sir John Parker, FREng FRINA FIMarE
Dr Andrew G. Rickman, OBE

13 June 2002
Dr Robert Hawley, CBE
Dr Alan Hayes, CBE

17 July 2002
John Stephen Morrill

25 July 2002
Professor John Sutherland

26 July 2002
Brian William Alderson

6 December 2002
Penelope Keith, OBE
H.E. Cardinal Cormac Murphy O'Connor,
    STL PhL
Peter Saraga

19 June 2003
The Hon. Judge David Edward, CMG
    QC FRSE

20 June 2003
Professor Michael Baker, TD FRSE
Mary Baker, MBE
Professor Otto Pick, CMG

30 June 2003
Lord Puttnam of Queensgate, CBE

16 July 2003
Gerald O'Collins, SJ

24 July 2003
Philip Pullman

25 July 2003
Steven Pinker

2 April 2004
Sir David Martin Brown, FREng
Professor Roger Howard Clarke
Lennart Meri
Her Majesty Queen Noor of Jordan

17 June 2004
Sir Daniel Norton Idris Pearce, CBE TD DL
Derek John Thomas, CBE DL

28 June 2004
Terry Gilliam

22 July 2004
Sir David Attenborough

Above: Jonny Wilkinson of England prepares to kick at goal during the Investec Challenge Series match between England and New Zealand at Twickenham on 21 November 2009. He was awarded an Honorary Doctorate that year. (Photo by David Rogers/Getty Images)

Opposite top: British sculptor Sir Anthony Alfred Caro, OM CBE was made a Doctor of the University on 12 December 1986. Here he poses for photographers during the inauguration of his exhibition at the La Pedrera building, Barcelona, 2002. (© Julian Martin/epa/Corbis)

Opposite bottom: Beatles producer George Martin (centre) with David Pickett (right), Lecturer in Recording Techniques and Head of Tonmeister™ Studies, and students at the University of Surrey (*c.* 1980) in the old studio in the Hall Undercroft before the Performing Arts Technology Studios were built. (Dr David Pickett)

8 April 2005
Professor Michael Gibbons, MBE
Dr Ernest Littauer
Professor David Wood

17 June 2005
Sir Harold Kroto
Alec James Stewart, OBE

28 June 2005
Richard Bayliss Hudson

21 July 2005
Nancy Lane, OBE

22 July 2005
Paula Rego

16 June 2006
Professor Patrick Dowling, CBE
Janet Gaymer, CBE
Professor Jerrold Marsden

30 March 2007
Claire Rayner, OBE
Sir David Varney

21 June 2007
Thomas Joseph Black
Peter Molyneux, OBE

22 June 2007
The Rt Hon. The Lord Browne of Madingley
James Douglas Moir Robertson, CBE
Lord Sainsbury of Turville

4 April 2008
drs Jan (Mac) Derwig, RA
Neil James Kipling

17 June 2008
Professor Richard F. Casten

18 June 2008
Professor Jean Hooper, CBE

19 June 2008
Arie de Geus
Sir George Martin, CBE
Sir Ray Tindle

20 June 2008
James (Jimmy) Patrick Page, OBE

2 April 2009
Professor Peter Bunyan
Martin Earwicker

3 April 2009
Jonny Wilkinson, OBE

24 June 2009
Noel Fitzpatrick
Vicki Hansford

26 June 2009
Elon Musk

7 September 2009
The Lord May of Oxford

15 April 2010
Judge Linda Dobbs
Adrian White

15 July 2010
Peter Hutley
David Sheard

16 July 2010
His Honour Judge John Bull QC, DL

12 April 2011
Professor Andrew Hamilton

12 July 2011
Lady Diana Kerr

13 July 2011
Roger Black

14 July 2011
Sir Michael Aaronson
John Williams

15 July 2011
Professor John Sexton
Dr Graham Spittle

Master of the University

2 December 1968
Harold Arrowsmith

11 July 1980
Grenville Bertram Brook

17 July 1981
Hubert Beresford Walker

4 December 1981
Walter Ronald Hayward

16 July 1982
Maurice Kerridge

15 July 1983
Brigadier Keith Hudson, CBE

13 July 1984
Bertram Eric Twyford
Herbert Culverhouse Weller

12 July 1985
Winifred Logan

11 July 1986
John Anthony Charles Humphries, OBE
Marga Elizabeth Schmitz

10 July 1987
Harry Walter Grafton
Eilean Pearcey

8 July 1988
Eric Russell Chamberlin
Iraj Mottahedin

7 July 1989
Ronald Francis Eatwell
The Revd Anthony Landsell Lovegrove

6 July 1990
Morag Morris

5 July 1991
Bill Bellerby, MBE
Doreen Bellerby, MBE
Dr Halla Beloff
Martin Hughes
Mary Lloyd-Jones

Bill Bellerby (right),
Alderman, Former Mayor
of Guildford and Honorary
Freeman of the Borough,
receiving an Honorary
Masters Degree on 5 July 1991.
Shown with him are, left,
the Chancellor, HRH
The Duke of Kent and,
presenting the award,
Dr Joe Bullock, former
Lecturer in Chemistry.

17 July 1992
Barry Michael Rose
Helen Patricia Sharman, OBE
Babette Esther Stern

31 July 1992
Calton Hearn Younger

9 July 1993
Naim Ibrahim Attallah
Gerald Fleming

30 July 1993
Canon Gerald Greenwood

8 July 1994
Gordon Clifford Hartman

7 July 1995
Patricia Maureen Grayburn
Shobana Jeyasingh, MBE
Leonard James Schwarz

21 July 1995
Thomas Andrew Bligh

27 July 1995
Jan Beaney (Mrs Udall)

14 June 1996
Brian Francis Conroy, MBE

19 July 1996
Antony Reginald Kenney, LVO

26 July 1996
Anthony Nicolson

25 July 1997
Howard A. Berry

23 July 1998
Gulam Khaderboy Noon, MBE

24 July 1998
Geoffrey Stuart Duncan

17 June 1999
Barry Andrew Stone

3 July 2000
Robert Malcolm Pride

14 July 2000
Ann Marion Thomson

15 June 2001
William Mark Seeman
The Very Revd Alexander Gillan
    Wedderspoon

18 July 2001
William K. Spofford

29 May 2002
Dr Arthur Richard Chandler
David Watts

13 June 2002
Bryan Robert David Yendole, CBE

26 July 2002
Lorna Mary Nancy Vlasto

21 July 2004
Robert John King

17 June 2005
Anne Christine Roberts

19 July 2006
William Barry Keates, CBE

22 June 2007
Peter William Beardsley

3 April 2009
James Strawson

Master of Music

17 July 1976
Professor James Blades, OBE

Master of Science

2 December 1968
Clifford Courtney Aynge Gibbs

12 July 1975
Kenneth John Joyner
Ronald Frederick Nunn

17 July 1976
Douglas Boraston Peplow

15 July 1977
Alan Fryson Mitchell
Johannes Jacobus Zonsveld

14 July 1978
Frederick Henry Norman Hambrook
Eric Thornton

1 December 1978
John William Wakely

13 July 1979
Hector Aitken Wainwright

Bachelor of the University

5 July 1991
William Wilfred Richard Groves
Frank Keitch
Allan Wipper Wells, MBE

9 July 1993
Joy Gallop
John Stevens, BEM

14 June 1996
Edwin Charles Valler, MBE

12 June 1997
Warwick John Brench

19 June 1998
Kenneth John George

23 July 1999
Frank Charles Pope

9 December 2000
Jean Marie McGinley
Eileen Walker

17 June 2004
John Glynwyn Davies

17 June 2005
Tony Watling

16 June 2006
Gill Irene Gibbs

Fellow of the University

4 December 1971
Charles Wallace Tonkin

30 November 1974
Arthur Ernest Johnston, CBE

Bibliography

The principal published sources for this book were the various publications issued by the University over the years: *SurreyMatters; Surrey Life; Surrey Graduate* (now called *Forever Surrey*), the alumni association's magazine; the *Annual Report* (previously *Annual Review*); *barefacts* and its successor *The Stag*, the Students' Union newspaper; one-off publications such as *Breakthrough* and the 2010 booklet *Art and Architecture*; and articles and information on the University website, including its intranet SurreyNet. Figures for student numbers come from 'Numbers by Study Method', provided by the Registry of the University: these figures are of actual heads, not full-time equivalents, as is sometimes the practice in university statistics.

The preceding histories of the University were enormously helpful for the early material, especially that written by Christopher Pick:

H. Arrowsmith, *Pioneering in Education for the Technologies: The Story of Battersea College of Technology 1891–1962* (University of Surrey Press, 1966)

Roy Douglas, *Surrey: The Rise of a Modern University from the Foundation of Battersea in 1891 to the Silver Jubilee of the University of Surrey 1991* (University of Surrey Press, 1991)

Christopher Pick, *Understanding the Real World: A Visual History of the University of Surrey* (University of Surrey Press, 2002)

Other publications that proved useful were:

Books

Russell Chamberlain, *Survival: The Rise, Fall and Rise of the Guildford Institute of the University of Surrey* (Piton, 1995)

Brian Edwards, *University Architecture* (Spon Press, 2000)

Sir James Mountford, *British Universities* (Oxford University Press, 1966)

Articles

Rebecca Attwood, 'It's all about them', *Times Higher Education*, 14 January 2010, **http://www.timeshighereducation.co.uk/Journals/THE/THE/14_January_2010/ attachments/032-040_THE_JAN1410_Layout%20lo.pdf**, accessed 23 February 2011.

Rebecca Attwood, 'We can work it out', *Times Higher Education*, 2 September 2010, http://www.timeshighereducation.co.uk/story.asp?sectioncode=26&storycode=4 13277, accessed 15 March 2011.

Simon Baker, 'We don't need a government push, just rational regulation, says v-c', *Times Higher Education*, 18 November 2010, http://www.timeshighereducation. co.uk/story.asp?storyCode=414286&sectioncode=26, accessed 4 December 2010.

David Barnes, 'Ready for the storm?', *Times Higher Education*, 18 March 2010, http://www.timeshighereducation.co.uk/story.asp?storycode=410843, accessed 4 February 2011.

Paul Bolton, *Education: Historical Statistics*, House of Commons Library, 2007, SN/SG/4252, http://www.parliament.uk/briefingpapers/commons/lib/research/ briefings/snsg-04252.pdf, accessed 13 February 2011.

Lord Browne et al, *Securing a Sustainable Future for Higher Education: An Independent Review of Higher Education Funding and Student Finance*, 12 October 2010, http://www.bis.gov.uk/assets/biscore/corporate/docs/s/10-1208-securing-sustain- able-higher-education-browne-report.pdf, accessed 13 February 2011.

Stefan Collini, 'HiEdBiz', *London Review of Books*, Vol. 25, No. 21, 6 November 2003, pp. 3–9, http://www.lrb.co.uk/v25/n21/stefan-collini/hiedbiz, accessed 30 January 2011.

Stefan Collini, 'Browne's Gamble', *London Review of Books*, Vol. 32, No. 21, 4 November 2010, pp. 23–5, http://www.lrb.co.uk/v32/n21/stefan-collini/ brownes-gamble, accessed 13 February 2011.

Jo Confino, 'Sustainability depends on breaking free of our consumerist fixation', *The Guardian*, 2 December 2010, http://www.guardian.co.uk/sustainable-business/ consumerism-sustainability-short-termism, accessed 17 February 2011.

Max Davidson, 'Has university taught us anything?', *The Telegraph*, 15 July 2009, http://www.telegraph.co.uk/education/universityeducation/5826704/Has- university-taught-us-anything.html, accessed 13 February 2011.

Education at a Glance 2010: OECD Indicators, OECD, 2010, www.oecd.org/edu/eag2010, accessed 28 March 2011.

Alison Goddard and Claire Sanders, 'Analysis: Which university has the deepest pock- ets?', *Times Higher Education*, 13 July 2001, http://www.timeshighereducation.co. uk/story.asp?storyCode=163860&sectioncode=26, accessed 23 February 2011.

Higher Education Statistics Agency, *Higher Education Student Enrolments and Qualifications Obtained at Higher Education Institutions in the United Kingdom for the Academic Year 2009/10*, Tables 5a and 6a, http://www.hesa.ac.uk, accessed 15 January 2011.

Stephen Machin and Anna Vignoles, *Education Policy in the UK*, Centre for the Eco- nomics of Education, 2006, pp. 20–22, http://cee.lse.ac.uk/cee%20dps/ceedp57.pdf, accessed 13 February 2011.

National Student Forum Annual Report 2010, http://www.bis.gov.uk/assets/biscore/ corporate/docs/n/10-p83-national-student-forum-annual-report-2010.pdf, accessed 17 March 2011.

NUS Student Experience Report, 2008, http://www.nus.org.uk/PageFiles/4017/ NUS_StudentExperienceReport.pdf, accessed 23 February 2011.

Participation Rates in Higher Education: Academic Years 2006/2007 – 2008/2009, Department for Business, Innovation and Skills, 31 March 2010, **http://stats.bis.gov.uk/he/Participation_Rates_in_HE_2008-09.pdf**, accessed 20 March 2011.

Ian Poole, 'Future satellite technology – an interview with Sir Martin Sweeting', *Radio-Electronics.com*, February 2010, **http://www.radio-electronics.com/analysis/satellite/2010-02/future-satellite-technology-sir-martin-sweeting.php**, accessed 5 February 2011.

'Tertiary education graduation rates', *Education: Key Tables from OECD Fact Book*, No. 1, OECD, 2010, **http://www.oecd-ilibrary.org/education/tertiary-education-graduation-rates_20755120-table1**, accessed 9 February 2011.

Stephen Tetlow, 'For economic inspiration, look to space', *BBC News Business*, 31 Janaury 2011, **http://www.bbc.co.uk/news/business-12311286?print-true**, accessed 4 February 2011.

Trends in Young Participation in Higher Education: Core Results for England, Issues Paper 2010/03, HEFCE, 2002, **http://www.hefce.ac.uk/pubs/hefce/2010/10_03/**, accessed 16 February 2011.

UK Science Parks Association, 'Surrey Research Park's SSTL prepares to send the first mobile phone satellite into space', 31 January 2011, **http://www.ukspa.org.uk/news/tenant_news/content/3213/surrey-sstlmobilesatellite**, accessed 4 February 2011.

University and College Union, *Universities at Risk: The Impact of Cuts in Higher Education Spending on Local Economies*, December 2010, **http://www.ucu.org.uk/media/pdf/t/a/ucu_universitiesatrisk_dec10.pdf**, accessed 4 February 2011.

Ellie Zolfagharifard, 'Sir Martin Sweeting, chairman of Surrey Satellite Technology', *The Engineer*, 1 November 2010, **http://www.theengineer.co.uk/in-depth/interviews/sir-martin-sweeting-chairman-of-surrey-satellite-technology/1005753.article**, accessed 4 February 2011.

Websites

Academic Ranking of World Universities:
   http://www.arwu.org

Higher Education Statistics Agency:
   http://www.hesa.ac.uk

Office for National Statistics:
   http://www.statistics.gov.uk

Unistats: information from the Student Satisfaction Survey
   http://unistats.direct.gov.uk/

Universities and Colleges Admissions Service (UCAS):
   http://www.ucas.ac.uk

Acknowledgements

A book of this kind cannot be written without the extensive cooperation of others. First, I would like to thank those at Strathmore Publishing, Nicholas Jones and Elspeth McPherson, who commissioned me to write the book and supported me in its research and writing throughout, as well as Talitha Minchin, who designed it. Researching the history of the University and its associated enterprises, the Surrey Research Park, Surrey Satellite Technology Ltd and the Surrey Sports Park, gave me an opportunity to see how such an institution has grown and developed from the end of the nineteenth century to the early twenty-first century. It has been a fascinating journey.

The first half of this book depends to a large extent on the previously written histories of the University by H. Arrowsmith, Roy Douglas and Christopher Pick, and to them I give my thanks. In the time allowed for this new book to be written, I could not have done it without treading in their footsteps and the first three chapters of the book rely on Christopher's work in particular.

At the University a huge thank you must be extended to Maureen Shettle, University Archivist, who not only helped with the written sources, but also gathered most of the older pictures and arranged for their scanning. James Strawson, ex-University Secretary, highlighted for me the chief events of the past decade, and also helped with contacts at the University. Sam Jones, James Newby and Madeleine McGowan bore patiently with my many queries and were instrumental in gathering pictures and in the organisation of the project. Anthea Banks, Beth Herbert, Emily Sims and Emma Gray helped me navigate my way in researching the work of the four Faculties.

Many at the University made time in their busy schedules to talk to me about research and events within their Faculties and/or to provide me with information, as well as checking parts of the text. In this respect, thanks must be given to the following: Professor Alf Adams, Professor David Airey, Professor Jim Al-Khalili, Jo Baker, Professor Marie Breen-Smyth, Dan Brown (Surrey Sports Park), Dr Dunstan Brown, Professor Karen Bryan, Derry Caleb, Graham Carruthers, Professor John Chew, Professor John Chilton, Professor Marios Chryssanthopoulos, Professor Greville Corbett, Melanie Coward, Mario Creatura, Mishal Dattani, Professor Terry Desombre, Dr Sherril Dodds, Dr Fiona Doloughan, Professor Steve Downes, Professor John Eade, Professor Emeritus Sebastian Forbes, Dr John Forrest CBE, Dr Anna Franklin,

Professor Emeritus Bill Gelletly, Chris Gethin, Madeleine Gibb (Guildford School of Acting), Professor Mark Gillan, Professor Peter Goldfarb, Professor Colin Grant, Pat Grayburn, Hilary Harris, Professor John Hay, Professor Tim Jackson, Caroline Johnson, Pauline Johnson, Aqila Kaleem, Professor Michael Kearney, Dr Ailsa Kolsaker, Peter La, Professor Susan Lanham-New, Professor Matthew Leach, Beryl Makinson (Surrey Research Park), Professor Rosalind Malcolm, Peter Marshall, Susan Martin, Sharon Maxwell, Dr Graham Miller, Joanna Moore, Professor Benedict Murdin, Audrey Nice (Surrey Satellite Technology Ltd), Dr Malcolm Parry (Surrey Research Park), Professor Phil Powrie, Rob Purcell, Dr Monique Raats, Professor Graham Reed, Harri ap Rees, Helen Roberts, Professor Alan Robins, Keith Robson, Professor Margaret Rogers, Professor Adel Sharif, Hilary Sherlock, Tim Sinnamon, Professor Christopher Snowden, Alison Stevens, Roger Stickland, Brian Stratford, Dr Karen Swales, Professor Sir Martin Sweeting, Professor Rahim Tafazolli, Steve Tyler, Hilary Underwood. Outside the University, I would like to thank Anne Milton MP, who also provided information.

On the picture side, I would like to thank the following at the University, who put a great deal of effort into tracking down the pictures and supplying them in what was a very short time period: Amintha Buckland, Sam Jones, Madeleine McGowan, Maureen Shettle, Paul Stead, Heather Styche-Patel and others in the Marketing and PR and Communications Departments. Copy pictures of material in Westminster-Kingsway College Archive were made by Suzanne Bosman. Dr Ernest Littauer, Professor John Chilton, Allan Wells, Matthew Arcus and Sue Pounder (for Charles Arcus), and Glenda Patterson (for Thomas A. Wilkie) helped with sourcing pictures and providing information. Except where otherwise credited, all pictures are from the University's collection and from the Media Centre; the University of Surrey photography by Paul Stead.

Index

Page numbers in *italic* indicate illustrations